A Praeger World Affairs Special

SOUTH AFRICA: CRISIS FOR THE WEST

SOUTH AFRICA:
CRISIS FOR THE WEST

Colin and Margaret Legum

FREDERICK A. PRAEGER, *Publishers*

New York · Washington · London

FREDERICK A. PRAEGER, *Publishers*
111 Fourth Ave., New York 3, N.Y., U.S.A.
77–79 Charlotte Street, London, W.1, England

Published in the United States of America in 1964
by Frederick A. Praeger, Inc., Publishers

Library of Congress Catalog Card Number: 64–22216

Printed in the United States of America

Contents

South Africa: Crisis for the West

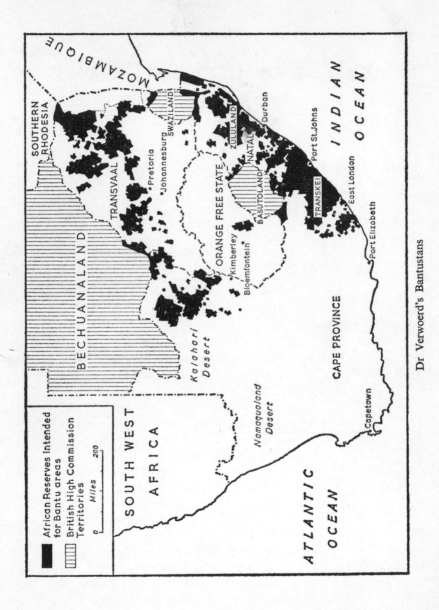

Dr Verwoerd's Bantustans

Legend:

- African Reserves Intended for Bantu areas
- British High Commission Territories

Miles 0 200

SOUTHERN RHODESIA

MOZAMBIQUE

BECHUANALAND

TRANSVAAL

SWAZILAND

ZULULAND

NATAL

Durban

Port St.Johns

INDIAN OCEAN

East London

TRANSKEI

Port Elizabeth

ORANGE FREE STATE

BASUTOLAND

Pretoria

Johannesburg

Kimberley

Bloemfontein

Kalahari Desert

CAPE PROVINCE

SOUTH WEST AFRICA

Namaqualand Desert

Capetown

ATLANTIC OCEAN

INTRODUCTION

1: THE CRISIS

> If ever there was a community which was called upon
> by the world situation to be cautious, fair and human,
> to think on fundamental lines, it is South Africa. . . .
> We do not want this little experiment [of white civilisa-
> tion] in South Africa to fail because of our short-
> sightedness. This little community deserves something
> better than to be wiped out in the march of world
> events. That is possible if the Europeans do not rise
> to the mission that is theirs on the Dark Continent.
> *General J. C. Smuts, July 13, 1949*

It is the argument of this book that the racial crisis in the
Republic of South Africa cannot be resolved without international intervention. It is no longer a question of whether
such intervention will take place, or even whether it should.
It is already happening.

Intervention cannot be halted, it can only mount. The
only relevant question is what form it takes. The wrong kind
can cast deep shadows over the Republic, over Africa and
over the world. The right kind can prevent what in any event
is likely to be an unhappy situation from becoming a tragedy:
possibly one of the worst in this already violent century.

We do not pretend that it is an easy matter for the West
to do what we will propose. But whether the West intervenes
now or later, it is not going to be able to keep out.

For these reasons we argue that there ought to be no
further postponement of a decision to embark on effective
intervention by the international community. Already the
chances of success are less good than they were three years
ago. In another three years it might well be too late to avoid
the kind of tragedy most to be feared: a race war which will
turn South Africa, for a time at least, into a country fit for

neither whites nor blacks to live in. That kind of tragedy must cut deep into the bonds which unite the world community.

External intervention began in 1946 when the United Nations refused to treat the country's race policies as a domestic matter. The International Court of Justice has already given an opinion that South Africa is in default of its international obligations over its administration of the Mandated territory of South West Africa; and the General Assembly has repeatedly—now almost unanimously—condemned South Africa's racial policies. So the international community is already involved.

It is profitless to limit the argument to whether the UN was right or wrong in reaching these decisions. The matter has been decided on the broad issues, with only two of the UN members—South Africa and Portugal—dissenting. Nor is the UN likely to reverse these decisions. For the UN, therefore, the die is cast. Future debates are likely to revolve only around the question of how it can make its decisions effective.

But while the UN debates its tactics, the thirty-five independent African states can be more direct. Decisions taken at the Addis Ababa summit conference in May 1963 committed the Organisation of African Unity to direct involvement in the 'liberation struggle' to overthrow 'white supremacy' in South Africa, as well as in the Portuguese territories and in Southern Rhodesia. Again, whether their decision is right or wrong is, for the moment, irrelevant. The fact is that they are involved, and there is not the remotest chance that they will pull back. Their intervention, moreover, has the approval of the Asian and Arab world, of the Soviet bloc and of China. Only the Western world remains hesitant and ambivalent over the consequences of intervention. Therefore this book is directed primarily at Western opinion and leadership.

What should the West do? There are three ways of looking at the South African problem. It can be seen as a moral problem; or as one ultimately affecting national interests —Western relations with Africa and with the coloured world, trade and influence; or as a possible threat to world peace into which the major powers will inevitably be drawn. From whichever of these ways the West chooses to look at South

Africa, our argument remains the same: that even if the West wishes to remain aloof it cannot succeed indefinitely.

Since there is clearly no likelihood of Western nations' supporting forces which seek to maintain a regime committed to defending *white supremacy* in Africa, the quicker the West makes up its mind, the better its chances of protecting its own proper interests. Thus, even at the narrowest and most selfish level, it would be folly to try and maintain the present equivocal policies.

How much time do we have to make up our mind? Almost none. Through three sessions of the Security Council in 1963 the West dragged its feet reluctantly from one defensive gambit to another, each time moving closer towards the Africans' immediate demand for an arms embargo against South Africa. The situation will be even more difficult at future meetings of the United Nations, when the demands for action will be much stronger. Early in 1965 the International Court at The Hague will probably rule on South West Africa. If it decides against South Africa, the United Nations will be faced with the necessity of deciding what action it must take to compel South Africa to comply with the Court's decision. What could the United Nations do if, as seems likely, South Africa remains in flagrant dereliction of its obligation over the Mandate? Could it accept that there is nothing it can do to ensure that its decisions are obeyed in a matter which touches directly on the principle of 'international accountability'? Or will it go forward with a policy demanding compliance with its decisions? If it chooses the latter course—which is the more likely alternative—what steps would the West be prepared to support? Answers to these questions cannot be given off the cuff. \The complexity of the situation needs to be looked at with a greater sense of urgency and realism than has so far been suggested by Western delegations at the United Nations.

But there are other problems than those posed for the West by the United Nations. The most compelling is the situation inside South Africa, which is moving almost irresistibly towards violence. In the long run violence in South Africa can mean only race war.\ Although it is obviously impossible to predict the speed with which political events are likely to move, it is possible to describe with some confidence the pattern and the tempo of the 'liberation struggle' in southern Africa. The pattern is what might be called the 'Ben Bella strategy' (which has a validity and dynamic force of its own regardless of whether Mr Ben Bella survives as the leader of Algeria).

Early in 1963 Mr Ben Bella outlined in private discussions with South African leaders his ideas on how southern Africa should be 'liberated'. His plan is based on the straightforward military notion of knocking off the weakest enemy and moving step by step towards the strongest. Thus the first target becomes Angola, already under heavy pressure from the liberation forces based on the Congo Republic. Two results might be expected to follow the defeat of Salazar's forces in Angola. First, the other major Portuguese colony, Mozambique, would be unable to hold out for long against a concerted liberation war waged from Tanganyika. Second, the frontiers of independent Black Africa would, for the first time, border the northernmost frontier of Dr Verwoerd's Republic—at the Cunene River which divides Angola from South West Africa. Northern Rhodesia and Nyasaland become independent in 1964. At this point Southern Rhodesia would be held in a nutcracker. If 'white Southern Rhodesia' should try and hold out, it could be squeezed from the north, west and east. On present showing, South Africa would not move to protect Southern Rhodesia, for the best of military and international reasons. And even if the Republic were unexpectedly to move forward, the only result would be to speed up the whole process.

The establishment of a representative government in Southern Rhodesia would push the frontiers of Black Africa up against the Limpopo in the north, and the Lebombo mountains in the east. At this point, the 'liberation movement' inside South Africa would have the chance for the first time of establishing friendly bases all along the frontiers of the Republic. These independent neighbour states might then be expected to play a similar role for the liberation movement in South Africa as that played by Morocco and Tunisia for the FLN in Algeria.

But there the analogy with Algeria ends. If it ever reaches this point—and in the absence of decisive UN intervention it almost certainly will—South Africa is likely to begin its military struggle with an OAS type of government in power: there will be no metropolitan power and no General de Gaulle to curb or weaken 'the generals' or the *colon* extremists.

How long will it take to reach this point? Here one can only guess: perhaps two or three years before the collapse of Angola; another year for Mozambique and Southern Rhodesia —if they have survived that long. Thus one would fix the crisis point at between 1966–68. But, by then, the pattern of violence inside South Africa will have passed the point at which one can hope for any reasonable settlement between the races.

Basic to our argument is the recognition that the power structure inside the Republic rules out any hope of inter-racial agreement without intervention. Left to themselves, the whites in South Africa are incapable of making the minimum concessions acceptable to the African majority; and the Africans will settle for nothing less than a fully representative government. This is the crux of the argument for a *deus ex machina* to compel a settlement. Even then, the most that can be hoped for in South Africa is a settlement of some kind which will avert an upheaval destructive of all the racial communities. Even now, there can be no hope of achieving a 'solution', if by this one means a result completely satisfactory to all communities.

The argument for effective international intervention is based upon concern for the future of our white compatriots as much as for our non-white compatriots. The real enemy is 'white supremacy' which threatens the security of the whites while humiliating the rest. The whites in South Africa find themselves today in a trap into which they were led by three centuries of mistaken policies.

2: ORIGINS OF THE CRISIS

> The race problem is so tremendous that unfortunately
> many people still cannot form a realisation of it. . . . It
> is impossible to remove the results of the mistakes of
> the past three hundred years in a few years.
>
> DIE TRANSVALER, *October 23, 1961*

Contrary to common belief, the South African crisis does not
originate in the election of the Afrikaner Nationalist government in 1948. The apartheid regime has sharpened the conflict, hardened feelings on both sides of the colour line, and
made a non-violent situation violent. But far from producing
the crisis, the apartheid government is itself one of its products.
It represents the response of Afrikanerdom to the first serious
black challenge to the traditional system of white supremacy
since the crushing of Zulu power in 1838.

The first exclusively Afrikaner government came to power
sixteen years ago on an appeal resting almost entirely on its
promise to strengthen and safeguard 'white supremacy', or
baasskap. From the earliest beginnings of European settlement in the Cape of Good Hope in 1652, white supremacy has
been the essential reality of the struggle for power in South
Africa. Each government has rested its appeal upon it: each
has reflected the existence of two exclusive but mutually
dependent societies, divided from each other entirely by
colour, with power and privilege firmly held in white hands.
The notions of racial exclusivity and mutual dependence, combined with white political domination and economic privilege,
convey the essential elements of South African politics through
the centuries. The only important difference between the
various governments was the emphasis each gave to coercive
or co-operative methods in maintaining the *status quo* in these
respects. But even governments which preferred a persuasive
approach did not shirk the use of coercion whenever black
rebellion flickered.

South Africa's is not a class but a caste system in which
all the whites are Brahmins and all the rest Untouchables:
what Lancelot Hogben once called a pigmentocracy. It is
distinguished from other political systems which rest on minor-

ity rule by the *total* and *permanent* ban it places on those who are not white from rising above their dependency status, no matter what their gifts or qualifications; while assuring to the most imbecilic or degenerate of whites an automatic place in the Valhalla of white privilege. This is not a rough judgement. It is a precise description of the system which prevails in South Africa.

White South Africans are themselves as much the victims of their history as are the Africans. The social traditions and political structures of a caste society produced under frontier conditions were frozen and entrenched into the constitution of the Union of South Africa when Britain granted independence in 1910. Since then, not surprisingly, no political party proposing a dilution of white privilege has had any hope of election to office by the white electorate. The alternative was too easy and too attractive. By maintaining exclusive political power, the whites have been able largely to shape events. If physically threatened, they could take physical measures to protect themselves; if greater security or privilege seemed desirable, this, too, could be arranged. But today this is no longer so. With the gathering of nationalist momentum in post-war Africa, and new international perspectives gaining ground among the former colonial powers, the pendulum has begun to swing. Now Africans in South Africa can see some hope for their future, while the whites can see only uncertainty. Although the whites still hold power, their position is no longer even tacitly conceded as of right: their mastery is now under challenge.

No physical barriers are capable any longer of keeping the two societies apart. This is the nub of the present crisis. To expect white South Africans to accept this reality is to expect them to deny feelings and rationalisations which have been imbibed for generations with their mothers' milk. The idea of two societies in South Africa is as old as the history of white settlement.

Mixing between whites and blacks was condemned as a 'disgrace to the Netherlands and other Christian nations'[1] within sixteen years of the arrival of the first settlers. By 1685 there was an official ban against intermarriage between *burghers* and freed slave women. And within a single generation a society had been founded on the notion that all the masters were white and all the servants black. In those early days there arose the current view that manual labour is 'kaffir work'. An eighteenth-century Dutch governor, General Janssens, said of the settlers: 'They describe themselves as humans and Christians, and the Kaffirs and Hottentots as heathens; and by believing in this they permit themselves everything.'[1] Another contemporary wrote: 'The common Europeans have become gentlemen, and they desire to be well attended upon.'[2] At the end of the eighteenth century a percipient young Dutch seaman said of the settler: 'From his youth onwards, accustomed to call for slaves, he believes that he is elevated above all, and may only be obeyed.'[3]

Having exchanged their underprivileged lives in Europe for the uncertainties of seventeenth-century Africa, the early immigrants deliberately set themselves up as a new aristocracy: a 'white aristocracy' in a black continent. When the frontiersmen felt this 'way of life' threatened by the policies of the British overlord, who had established himself in South Africa early in the nineteenth century, the Great Trek of the Boers* took place into the interior. The 1837 Manifesto of the outstanding Trekkers' leader, Piet Retief, outlined the basis of their race policy. It was to 'adopt such regulations as will maintain the proper relationships between master and servant'. This regulation became a cornerstone in the constitutions of the Transvaal and Orange Free State Republics. To leave no doubt about the nature of their Republics, the Boers insisted that 'all citizens should be exclusively white'. In this way the white aristocracy which had grown up in the Cape Colony was transplanted to the interior. 'All masters, all farmers, all Gentlemen,' a minister of the Dutch Reformed Church wrote of the Boers in the Transvaal in 1858.[4]

Although the white aristocracy was conceived, established and maintained by the Boers, it was readily accepted by the successive waves of French Huguenot, German and British immigrants. This society, born out of the conditions of a frontier society, persists still in modern South Africa. The white aristocracy is the South African 'way of life'. The bitter quarrels between Boer and Briton never prevented their com-

* Literally, farmers.

ing together whenever either was attacked by the Bantu tribes. This white solidarity in the face of black challenge is another consistent feature of South African history. It is called 'drawing *laager*',* from the original method of defence adopted by the frontiersmen. The wars between Boer and Briton never touched seriously on their relationships with the Africans— a point made by a Boer delegation to Joseph Chamberlain in 1903, after the end of the South African war (1899–1901): 'It is necessary to make it plain to the Natives that the war altered the relations between the two white races, but not between the white and coloured populations of the country.'[1]

There have always been rebels against the political beliefs of the white aristocracy. The latterday Christian opponents of 'white supremacy' like the Reverend Michael Scott, Father Trevor Huddleston, Bishop Reeves, Dr Joost de Blank, Professor B. B. Keet, Dr Geyer and the Reverend Beyers Naudé had their precursors in the early missionaries like Dr van der Kemp, the Reverend John Philips and Bishop Colenso of Zululand. The 'Cape Liberals' were the equivalent political force which warned of the danger of perpetrating two exclusive, racial societies.

Unfortunately, these early liberals had little influence with the British Liberal administration which in 1906 succeeded the Conservative administration which had waged the South African war. As an act of atonement and generosity, the British Liberals restored independence to the Boer Republics on condition that they accepted unification with Natal and the Cape Province. The conditions for unification were settled at a National Convention (1908–1909) which was attended exclusively by whites. Africans were denied any voice in deciding the terms of the Act of Union by which modern South Africa achieved its independence. Chief Albert Lutuli was to comment on this Act fifty years later: 'This was the big divide, the great segregation Act. *Inter alia*, it debarred non-whites from parliament. It denied those of the Orange Free State, Transvaal and nearly all in Natal franchise rights. Only in the Cape Province did a limited number of non-whites have the

---

* The *laager* is a ring of waggons, their wheels bound together by thick thorn-branches, within which the frontiersmen gathered their families. This served as a fortress from within which they could concentrate their fire on the unmounted *impis* before these could come within assegai-throwing range.

vote. The South Africa Act set the pattern for subsequent discriminatory and unjust laws that have tormented non-whites since, and have made them political and social outcasts in their fatherland.'[1]

But at the National Convention in 1908 there were strong warnings against the folly of ignoring the African majority. One of the Cape Liberal leaders, Mr J. W. Sauer,* warned the Convention:

> In no circumstances whatever can permanent peace ever be founded on injustice. . . . We have proved the principle [of granting the franchise to Natives in the Cape] correct . . . for we have tried it and found it to work. . . . If we are to be a contented country the interests of all must be represented in the parliament of the country, and there must be political equality. . . . The great principle of justice itself is at stake in this discussion; and there must be a just native policy or the white man will go under in South Africa. Justice cannot be tampered with, with impunity; justice for the natives would secure the position of the white man in South Africa for all time. . . . We cannot govern the natives fairly unless they are represented by their own elected representatives.

But the voice of Sauer inside the Convention and of his supporters outside, like W. P. Schreiner and Olive Schreiner, represented a tiny minority. The temper of the dominant majority was shown in the first South African parliament three years after independence during a debate on the notorious Land Act of 1913. This permanently prohibits Africans from buying or even renting land outside of their own scheduled areas, and confines their property rights to an area about one eighth of the surface of South Africa. The proposal was strongly attacked by the former Cape Premier, Mr John X. Merriman. In another of the many warnings that were ignored at that crucial period, he was reported in *Hansard*:

> Let them think what the industry of the natives had done for us. Who had built our railways, who had dug our mines, and developed this country as far as it was developed? Who had been the actual manual worker; who

* Ironically enough, his son, Mr Paul Sauer, is a senior member of Dr Verwoerd's Cabinet and was the chairman of the National Party's commission which conceived the policy of apartheid in 1947.

had done that? The Native: the coloured races of this country. We must never forget that we owed them a debt in that respect—a debt not often acknowledged by what we did for them. Proceeding, he said that they ought to think what they owed to the docility of the native, and the wonderfully easy way in which they had been governed when treated properly. He also paid a tribute to the honesty of the natives.[1]

In reply to this speech Mr J. G. Keyter spoke for the majority of MPs. 'His experience was that the native should be treated firmly, kept in his place and treated honestly. . . . They should tell him, as the Orange Free State told him, that it was a white man's country, that he was not going to be allowed to buy land there or to hire land there, and that if he wanted to be there he must be in service.'[2]

Thus South Africa was launched into its modern age committed to the racial and political policies formulated by the Cape frontiersmen and the Boer Republics. By 1910 the expansion of white settlement had already greatly weakened tribal society. The tribes who resisted were crushed; the others were allowed to live within areas agreed by treaty. The result was to deprive the pastoralists of most of their land. Today, seven eighths of all the land is owned by whites. Africans are not allowed to own land except in the twenty-six separate reserves, measuring about 35 million acres.

But the white aristocracy needed its black servants. 'Always', Paul Kruger reminisced, 'the new immigrants' first concern was to get coloured labour.'[3] The new mines of Kimberley and the Witwatersrand needed quantities of labour. Thus a deliberate policy was established to compel Africans to enter the economy of white society. Special taxes on huts and on all Africans over eighteen forced the young men to enter the 'cash economy'. In the towns the Africans were segregated socially and residentially. To regulate the flow of labour and to control the Africans in the white areas, successive governments have upheld and encouraged the policy of migratory labour. Even when this policy began to fail in the industrial areas, it was rigidly enforced for the mining industry—as it still is today.

The land policy—reinforced by social, economic and

fiscal pressures—forced Africans in increasing numbers into the white areas. Their presence was essential to white industry. When the Zulus failed to offer their labour in sufficient numbers for the new sugar plantations in Natal, the government imported indentured labour from India in 1870. This policy produced what is now called 'the Indian problem'. In 1913, the mining interests persuaded the government to import Chinese labour; but a 'Chinese problem' was averted by a successful parliamentary protest in Britain as well as in South Africa. The pattern is unmistakable: whatever the results, the aim was, and is, to provide the white master with enough servants: black, brown, and even yellow.

Industrialisation, especially during the second world war, attracted a flood of Africans to the towns. Expanding agriculture had a similar effect on the countryside. The direct result was to make the 'white areas' increasingly black. Yet neither the onset of industrialisation nor the rise of an urban working-class weakened the political structure of the white aristocracy; ideas about a 'class struggle' or a supra-racial proletariat never became popular although they had their adherents. The white workers—struggling against exploitation of cheap labour—defended themselves by adopting a 'civilised labour policy', where 'civilised' means whites. Attempts by socialists in the Labour Party and the trade union movement to make a reality of the notion of 'equal pay for equal work' failed for lack of support.

As the white aristocracy grew richer through the expansion of industry and agriculture, new opportunities were created, willy-nilly, for non-whites. They became a substantial urban proletariat, forming their own trade unions or joining those of the whites where they were allowed to do so. They began to produce a substantial middle class, thanks largely to a mission-inspired education system which, until recently, put South Africa educationally ahead of most other countries in the continent. These developments did not pass unnoticed: the Afrikaner nationalists gave increasing emphasis in election campaigns to the *swart gevaar*—the Black Danger. Matters came to a head during the second world war. It was then that the African emerged from the shadows to take his place at the centre of South Africa's political preoccupations.

He was to be seen everywhere: an indispensable force in industry and a growing force in the trade unions; an influential factor in Church life; a significant figure in urban society; a rising factor in the economy's purchasing-power; and, above all, an increasingly insistent voice in demanding the right to participate freely in the social, economic and political life of the nation. His leaders drew inspiration from the promises of the 'new world' that was to follow the ending of the war, and placed their faith in the promises of the Atlantic Charter.

Thus—detribalised, urbanised, missionised, industrialised, modernised and, above all, educated—the African loomed ominously large on the near horizon of the white aristocracy. By 1945 it was clear to everybody that South Africa had to make a fresh choice: either to go forward towards a fully integrated society, or to retreat to the policies of the Boer Republics and the *status quo* entrenched in the Act of Union. General Smuts' United Party government was indecisive; the Afrikaner nationalists were fiercely single-minded. In 1947 they produced their policy of apartheid, and in the 1948 elections Smuts was narrowly defeated. The white electorate chose to mount the ramparts in defence of white supremacy. It was this decision which brought the long-simmering crisis to its present climacteric.

Part One
Power in Society

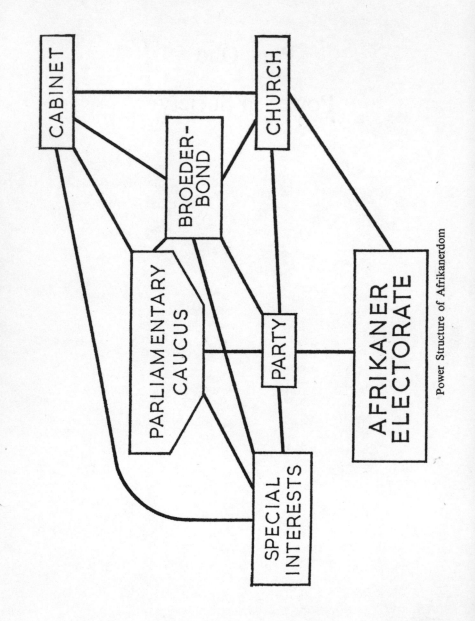

Power Structure of Afrikanerdom

I

AFRIKANERDOM

Today South Africa belongs to us once more. For the
first time since Union, South Africa is our own. May
God grant that it will always remain so.
Dr D. F. Malan, May 1948

For a nation with its back to the wall, there is nothing
for it but to fight or vanish.
Dr H. F. Verwoerd, November 1962

*   *   *

1: ITS POWER STRUCTURE

Afrikanerdom is the systematic expression of an exclusively
Afrikaans-speaking political, cultural and social movement,
committed to preserving its uniqueness by establishing its hege-
mony over the whole country. It is Afrikaner nationalism's
most militant reaction to the 'alien domination of the English',
and an expression of its fear of eventual black domination.
Afrikanerdom has become a force for counter-domination: it
seeks to maintain 1,800,000 Afrikaners in a superior position
to 1,200,000 English-speaking South Africans, and in supremacy over 13,000,000 non-whites.

Since Afrikanerdom achieved power in 1948, three questions have presented themselves. Can it maintain its power?
What concessions is it likely to make to try and retain power?
What is the likelihood of its being willing, or able, to undertake fundamental changes in the present society, in response to
internal and external pressures? The answers must be found
in the power structure of Afrikanerdom.

To judge by outward appearances, power would appear
to lie with the National Party, or even with Dr Verwoerd alone
as 'the strong man' of his government. But this impression is
misleading. Verwoerd could be defeated overnight if he pursued policies not acceptable to certain groups within the power

structure, or if he were to refuse to adopt policies demanded by its more influential pressure groups. Dr Malan was forced to retire against his own wishes when he refused to accept the need for a new version of apartheid demanded by the Broederbond, largely under the influence of Verwoerd.

At a different level, the government could fall if it displeased comparatively small but nevertheless important sections of the white electorate. Under the present political system, the contest for power lies chiefly in trying to woo two groups of voters: the Afrikaners in the rural areas, and the Afrikaner workers in the town. To retain power, Afrikanerdom needs to win the lion's share of these voters who today form the backbone of its strength. On the other hand, the United Party needs to win only a substantial minority of these voters (between one quarter and one third) to get sufficient additional strength to return to government. *The crucial fact about South African politics is that no government can win or hold power, under the present dispensation, unless its policies appeal to that section of the white community which stands to lose most if the automatic privileges, which today go with a white skin, are given up.*

Thus the power of Afrikanerdom is diffused and remotely operated. Ultimately it is dependent on the goodwill of, perhaps, forty per cent of the white electorate. But even though the leaders of Afrikanerdom cannot lose sight of this fact, they are engaged also in dealing with wider forces in society which threaten to undermine, not only the government, but the entire social system. Their problem is to reconcile the narrower, essentially selfish, interests of the white electorate with the wider national and international interests which they know they dare not ignore. These two conflicting pressures have produced a deep cleavage between the Afrikaner leadership and its electorate.

Afrikanerdom owed its success in 1948 to its ability to unite the great majority of Afrikaners despite their diversities and the conflicting pressure groups within their society. It is a brittle unity. In the past, it has been assured largely by the threat of 'alien' domination: in recent times, by fear of an African revolt and threats of external pressure. Unity is maintained through a complex structure of organised pressure groups. These are: the Broederbond; the Party; the Church; the Culture front; the intellectuals; and a number of special interests. While in broad agreement over basic objectives, the interests of these groups are not always identical, and their views about correct tactics sometimes diverge. This makes for rivalry and a continuous interplay of ideas.

Afrikanerdom's political power has been considerably reinforced by the authority of office. It now exercises control not only socially through its cultural, religious and economic organs, but also bureaucratically. It is assured of the loyalty of the civil service, the powerful state-owned corporations, the army and the police: each is strongly manned by its supporters, and leadership is in the hands of men picked for their proven loyalty.

A meaningful discussion about the power structure of Afrikanerdom must start with the Afrikaner component of the white electorate on which everything turns. (See diagram, p. 16.)

THE ELECTORATE

> A social economic order that mainly consists of a governing white people and a more numerous voteless black proletariat has become in our time an anachronism. It is a basically precarious and explosive dispensation and the forces of current history will clearly not tolerate it any longer.
>
> DIE BURGER, *March 1961*

On that chilly, surprising day in May 1948 when General Smuts went down to defeat and Dr Malan's exclusively Afrikaner government came to power, the white liftman greeted us jubilantly with the remark: *Van vandag af is 'n kaffer weer 'n kaffer* (from today a kaffir is once again a kaffir). This remark summed up that bitter election campaign. It expressed the deepest reaction of the Afrikaner electorate.

The liftman, 'Oom'* Koos Coetzee, was a man in his early sixties. He had arrived in Johannesburg twenty years earlier when the depression drove thousands of marginal farmers from the land. Untrained, he was lucky to get work in traditionally a category reserved for whites. His wages ensured him a living standard not much higher than

* Uncle: a familiar term for an older man.

that of an African in the upper-income group. 'Oom' Koos
formed part of the broad human wedge between the white and
the black societies. His home was in that part of Johannesburg where white and black suburbs jostled each other un-
easily. Living at the bottom of white society, his preoccupation was with the education of his children and with the fear
that he himself would soon be 'no better off than a kaffir'.
There were many Africans in the building who worked as
white-collar workers. They were usually smartly dressed and
habitually spoke English. Although they were not allowed to
ride in his lift, they affected to look down on him. His own
sense of dignity was no match for their 'cheekiness'.

'Oom' Koos saw salvation in the victory of a government
which would 'keep the kaffir in his place': that place being
somewhere a good deal below his own. He was, after all, part
of the 'white aristocracy'. What this meant for him was that
his children had every opportunity to move up the social and
economic ladder, and that there would be people whose social
status would always be lower than his own. 'Oom' Koos was
an extremely nice man—quiet, courteous, sympathetic and
essentially decent—except when it came to 'kaffirs'. He was
very angry one day when two African lawyers (Mr Oliver
Tambo and Mr Nelson Mandela) asked him to direct them to
the offices of a Building Society. He agreed they had been
perfectly courteous, but what had upset him was that these two
geleerde (educated) *kaffers* had business relations with his
employers. Somehow, this had put them in a class above himself. But Dr Malan's government would know how to make
them 'kaffirs' again.

Koos Coetzee was by no means an extreme case. His
anxieties, ambitions and attitudes are typical of those Afrikaners who form the broad base of the pyramid of the white
aristocracy. In the rural areas they are, for the most part, the
owners of small farms, or the managers and foremen on the
large farms. In the towns they are the small traders, the artisans, the semi-skilled workers, the policemen, the clerks and
the civil servants. In the cities they are the miners, the skilled
workers, the railwaymen, the shop assistants and clerks, and
the transport workers. In the context of white society, they
are the underprivileged group; but in the context of the wider

South African community, they are specially privileged. Their social position is automatically assured. The 'civilised labour policy' and the Job Reservation Act ensures them preference in employment, and guarantees them the available skilled jobs in industry as well as the better-paid jobs in commerce, industry and the civil service. They are favoured by sub-economic housing schemes, and, if they are farmers, by an elaborate system of subsidies. Their children are assured free education and a comparatively high standard of schooling. They are beneficiaries of welfare legislation and social provisions which do not apply to the non-whites. There are plans now for a national health service for whites.

This group has two over-riding interests: that the Afrikaner should not be beneath 'the English', and that the white man should be above the black man. Of these two interests, the second is the more important. If the leadership of Afrikanerdom adopted policies which seemed to threaten this primary interest, this group would withdraw its support, even if it meant ending the rule of Afrikanerdom. 'Oom' Koos had himself voted for Smuts in previous elections. His loyalty to Afrikanerdom is not beyond question: what seems to be beyond question is his loyalty to the idea of *baasskap*. In the past the Afrikaner vote was always divided between competing parties: the fact that it was united in 1948 gave Afrikanerdom its first real victory.

The Verwoerd regime cannot ignore the wishes of this politically decisive element in the white electorate. In 1948 they voted for the government on the straight issue of *baasskap*—the white man as the boss. It was Afrikanerdom's most popular slogan. Apartheid was presented as a means to maintain *baasskap*. Twelve years later when *baasskap* was officially repudiated as an instrument of policy, the government was faced with the immeasurably difficult problem of re-educating its supporters to believe that to go on talking about *baasskap* would bring about those very dangers it was supposed to be able to avert in 1948.

THE BROEDERBOND

The Broederbond has become a cancerous growth in the living body of South Africa. It is an arrogant, self-chosen elite, operating by stealth and intrigue, its early cultural aspirations swamped by neo-fascist ideas on race and culture. By refusing to face the facts of the twentieth century, it is driving the country to its destruction. It is an evil that must be rooted out before it is too late.

RAND DAILY MAIL, *November 22, 1963*

The Broederbond is a secret society, narrowly exclusive, modelled on Masonic lines—but deeply hateful of Masonry. It forms an influential caucus within Afrikanerdom. What is known of 'the Bond of Brothers' comes mainly from the comparatively small number of *broeders* who have broken with it. Even with their help it is difficult to determine the Broederbond's real power and influence. It is almost certainly the most powerful single organisation within Afrikanerdom, though by no means all-powerful. The average Afrikaner voters know and care little about the Broederbond; it impinges not at all on their daily lives, working as it does through other groups. For the most part, Afrikaners seem to accept the Broederbond as a movement mysteriously working in their interests. The rebels against the Broederbond have come from its own top leaders, or from other elite groups of Afrikaners.

Its members include most of the members of the cabinet (the Prime Minister has admitted to being a member for twenty-five years); important office-holders in the National Party and the Dutch Reformed Church; leading figures at the universities, and senior officials in the civil service, especially in the education departments. Its total membership is kept deliberately small; the latest estimate gives it about 3,800 members. But there is at least one *broeder* in almost every town, in every branch of public life, in most large educational institutions and church communities, in municipal and provincial councils, and in every cultural organisation. In this way the Broederbond's tentacles reach all over the Republic.

There have been several attempts to destroy it. The most serious was made by one of the greatest Afrikaner leaders, General J. B. M. Hertzog—the 'father' of the Afrikaner

National Party—when he was Prime Minister in 1935. Twelve
years later they destroyed him utterly. The hatchet-man in
the operation against Hertzog was the present President of the
Republic, Mr C. R. Swart. A second attempt to break it was
made during the second world war by influential members of
General Smuts' Government. Smuts read through the dossier
on the Broederbond prepared by this group and, his thoughts
on the war, wrote on it: 'Put it away for ten years.' By then
Smuts had been defeated. A third attempt to destroy the
Broederbond is presently being waged by several former
broeders who have become thoroughly alarmed by its methods.
They are led by the Reverend Beyers Naudé, formerly a minister of the Dutch Reformed Church and editor of one of its
important publications. He resigned his ministry to become
Director of the new ecumenical Christian Institute. Supporting him are Professor Geyer—formerly professor of theology
at Pretoria University—and Professor B. B. Keet, former professor of theology at the Dutch Reformed Church Seminary
at Stellenbosch.

The *Afrikaner Broederbond* was formed on May 24,
1918—under the name of *Jong Suid-Afrika* (Young South
Africa)—with fourteen members. By 1935 the number had
grown to 2,528. Its founders claimed they built it 'on the
Rock of Jesus', and that it was 'accountable only to God'. Its
original purpose was to assume trusteeship over the cultural
needs of Afrikanerdom; and it explicitly disavowed participation in politics. This object soon changed. In 1934 its then
chairman, Professor J. C. van Rooy of the Potchefstroom University, and its secretary, Mr I. M. Lombaard, announced in a
secret circular: 'Let us bear in mind the fact that the main
purpose is for Afrikanerdom to reach its ultimate goal of
dominance in South Africa. Brothers, our solution for South
Africa's troubles is that the Afrikaner-Broederbond must rule
South Africa.'

Its method of work was described at a secret meeting in
Bloemfontein on December 13, 1943, by one of the leading
broeders, Dr H. F. Verwoerd: 'The Afrikaner-Broederbond
must gain control of everything it can lay its hand on in every
walk of life in South Africa. Members must help each other
to gain promotion in the Civil Service or any other field of

activity in which they work, with a view to working themselves up into important administrative positions.'* Dr Verwoerd was at that time the editor of *Die Transvaler*. His subsequent rise to power was considerably helped by the Broederbond.

The society is built on a small hand-picked membership: to qualify a member must be over twenty-five, Afrikaans-speaking and a Protestant; and must have some influence in his branch of society. Candidature must be sponsored by two *broeders*; sponsored candidates are kept in ignorance of their nomination, but are carefully watched for several years before being voted upon by the whole body of *broeders*. Three negative votes are enough for disbarment. Only after the candidate has been approved is he told of his suitability for membership and invited to join.

The initiation is elaborately ritualised. A former member has described what happens:

> In complete darkness a corpse-like body lies on a bier, wrapped in a black winding sheet on which is embroidered in letters of blood: VERRAAD (Treason). A bloody dagger is thrust to the hilt in the body of the 'corpse'. A torch throws brief flashes of light on the scene, while the chaplain intones:
>
>> 'He who betrays the Bond will be destroyed by the Bond. The Bond never forgives and never forgets. Its vengeance is swift and sure. Never yet has a traitor escaped his just punishment.'

There is much psalm singing and bible kissing throughout its ritual; but in the eyes of the esoteric fraternity, the Great Architect of the Universe has hitherto designed only one model: the *Ware Afrikaner* ('true Afrikaner'). The members use secret signs of recognition, handgrips and special passwords. The mystic symbol is *Die Lig van Majuba*—'The Light of Majuba'.† The members speak at their confidential get-together *onder Die Vierkleur*: the *Vierkleur* is the four-coloured flag of the old Transvaal Republic. Members who have qualified for the second degree of initiation are told that 'under the protection of

---

* This statement made in secrecy came into the hands of Smuts' advisers.

† At Majuba Hill in 1877 the Transvaal Republicans defeated the British forces in what they regard as 'the first war of independence'.

the *Vierkleur* of the Transvaal, Afrikanerdom will always triumph'. The third degree pays homage to an image of *Geliefde Suid-Afrika* (Beloved South Africa).[1]

The Broederbond is organised in five sections. At the head stands 'the Trinity'—the Supreme Chief and two assessors. These are nominated by the Executive Council, comprising 'Twelve Apostles'. The Apostles and the 'disciples' (drawn from the cells in the organisation) form the General Council. The local branch, or cell, consists of from five to ten members; and each division consists of forty members. Finally, there is a Vigilance Committee: the spying network which operates throughout the organisation.

After 1933 the Broederbond became keenly interested in the Nazi Party. Several of its leading members spent time in Germany studying Nazi methods. Two of these are Dr N. J. Diederichs, the movement's financial expert, now the Minister for Economic Development; and Dr Hans van Rensburg, who later led the Broederbond-inspired organisation, the *Ossewabrandwag* (Ox-Waggon Sentinels), the leading subversive organisation during the second world war. For a time, too, the Broederbond experimented with a Nazi student from Germany, Herr Gerlach, as a youth organiser; but he was a failure.

The Broederbond formed several organisations to enable it to concentrate Afrikaner power. They created *Volkskas*, a bank to mobilise Afrikaner finance previously diverted into 'alien banks'. From a small start with a capital of £700 it has become one of the largest financial institutions in the country. The Broeders saw to it that not only private investors but public authorities transferred their accounts to *Volkskas*. But their most ambitious financial institution was the *Reddingsdaadbond*, an organisation originally intended to provide economic support to 'save the poor whites among the *volk*'. The movement now controls a chain of enterprises ranging from funeral undertakings, retail businesses, factories and hospitals to a cold storage company. From birth to death the Afrikaner can be catered for by 'the institutions of the faithful'. The profits belong to the shareholders and directors of these companies. One of the important achievements of the *Reddingsdaadbond* is that it has enabled hundreds of young

Afrikaners to achieve positions of wealth and influence in commerce, industry and mining.

The Broederbond also formed a youth movement, 'the *Voortrekkers*', to rival the Boy Scouts; and a students' movement, the *Afrikaner Studentebond*, to oppose the National Union of South African Students. Recently it launched a militant youth body, the *Ruiterjag*: its former head is now the chairman of the S.A. Broadcasting Corporation. Cultural activities are directed through the *Federasie van Afrikaanse Kultuurvereenigings* (FAK)—the Federation of Afrikaans Culture Associations. This is the instrument through which the Broederbond speaks to the public. FAK, in turn, operates through a network of subsidiary cultural and educational institutions which touch on every aspect of the Afrikaners' life. So successful was the Broederbond that even before the National Party came to power its members controlled three of the four provincial Education Departments and a number of departments of the central Civil Service. Its secret circulars show how its members, having secured positions of influence, ensure that only *broeders* or those considered trustworthy by the organisation are promoted. It circulates to its cells lists of major vacancies occurring in the Civil Service and the provincial and municipal administrations, inviting names for suitable candidates. The same system is used in ensuring professional or business appointments where a *broeder* is in a position of influence.

A marked feature of its work is in the schools. It initiated and won a campaign to convert the country's bilingual schools into unilingual ones, and to compel students to accept home language education: too many Afrikaner children, it was felt, were being educated in English. It spearheaded the campaign for 'Christian National Education', one of its dearest causes. It promoted the successful campaign to end the system of 'Open Universities': the English-speaking universities which had been open to non-white students. Today, the Broederbond exercises control over Afrikaans-speaking teachers' and parents' organisations, which control all appointments, as well as over all the institutions of Afrikaans education.

This extensive network enables the Broederbond to operate an effective pressure group inside the National Party, the government and parliament. Not all Nationalist members of parliament are admitted to the Broederbond; but none can survive its active antagonism. The Broederbond is thorough, relentless and ruthless. Any prominent Afrikaner who falls foul of it is branded a traitor, publicly pilloried in the Afrikaans press, and virtually isolated within the Afrikaner community. But as in all esoteric political organisations, quarrels and divisions regularly occur. So far, the Broederbond has survived five known internal crises. The fact that it has survived is perhaps more important than the crises themselves. However, these divisions show that the Broederbond is subject to the same pressure of ideas as any other South African group: it is not impermeable. Though it has managed in the past to contain these internal tensions, there is no certainty that it will not break up under greater stresses.

The two issues which most seriously tested the Broederbond in the past were the 'unity of the white races' and the correct interpretation of apartheid. The latter question will be discussed later. Dr Malan quarrelled with the Broederbond in the 1920s because he insisted that a 'united Afrikanerdom' should allow for political co-operation between Afrikaans and English-speaking South Africans; whereas the Bond insisted on Afrikaner exclusivity. Later, Dr Malan made his peace with the Broederbond—at least for a time—and they supported him for the Premiership.

However, the opposition to white unity has changed; Dr Verwoerd is now its most ardent advocate. Of course conditions have changed too; 'white unity' today automatically means Afrikaner domination over the English, which was not so when first Hertzog and later Malan favoured it. Therefore this aim is no longer felt to be a threat to the ideals of Afrikanerdom: on the contrary, it is thought necessary to preserve white rule. In a circular issued on August 1, 1962, the *Broederbond* told its members:

> The main task remains the separate existence of the Afrikaner nation, with its own language and culture. . . . We must do everything in our power to persuade English-speaking people to co-operate with us on the basis of the principles of the National Party. . . . We should

constantly be on guard that this does not result in the Afrikaner becoming more Anglicised as the English-speaking person is Afrikanerised. . . . It is not they who must assimilate us in their circles, but we who must assimilate them in our circles.

In 1935 when General Hertzog launched his famous onslaught on the *Broederbond* he said: 'When will this mad, fatal idea cease to exist, with some people thinking that they are the chosen gods to rule over others? The English-speaking people tried it and did not manage it over the Afrikaans-speaking. The Afrikaans-speaking also tried it, and did not succeed over the English-speaking people. Neither the one nor the other will ever succeed in dominating the other.'[1]

But General Hertzog was wrong. Politically, the Afrikaner-Broederbond has succeeded.

THE DUTCH REFORMED CHURCH

The Dutch Reformed Church has in the past made it clear by its policy and its statements from the Synod that it can approve of the policy of separate development provided it is applied in a fair and honourable way without encroaching on or violating the dignity of human beings.

Declaration by DRC *leaders, April, 1960*

We of the Dutch Reformed Churches are standing quite alone in our interpretation of the Scriptures on the question of apartheid. We are not only standing against the convictions of other churches in South Africa, but we differ from the Reformed Churches of the world. All the Dutch Reformed Churches in this country stand for apartheid in the churches and in politics . . . I think the Dutch Reformed Church leaders are very honest in their standpoint. But you can be very honest and yet be very wrong in your thinking.

Professor B. B. Keet, former professor of Reformed Dogmatics and Christian Ethics at Stellenbosch University, 1963

The Dutch Reformed Church* is the rock on which

---

* The entity usually described as the Dutch Reformed Church (DRC) comprises the following communions: the five federated *Nederduitse Gereformeers Kerke,* the *Nederduits de Hervormde Kerk,* and the *Gereformeerde Kerk.*

Afrikanerdom has been built. *Die Boer met sy Bybel en sy Roer* (the Boer with his Bible and his Rifle) is the Afrikaner's symbol of his own role in history. The Church itself towers at the centre of every village and town in the country. Even those Afrikaners who no longer attend church regularly—and their numbers are growing—remain nevertheless strongly under its influence, and especially its social pressures.

It would be hard to say whether most Afrikaners regard politics as the stuff of religion, or religion as the stuff of politics: the point is they are thought to belong together. Within itself the Church has had to face all the problems of a multi-racial society: its dilemma has been to reconcile the teachings of a universal religion with an exclusive nationalism.

For almost two centuries, between 1652 and 1829, the Church recognised no colour bar: whites, coloureds and blacks worshipped together. But with the abolition of slavery and the increase in black converts, this practice was challenged in 1829. It took twenty-eight years to reach a compromise. This frankly acknowledged that, because 'of the weakness of some' white Christians, it might be necessary to allow whites and blacks to worship in separate places. Nevertheless, it affirmed that it was 'desirable and scriptural' that non-whites should be absorbed into existing communities. But this compromise proved unacceptable in practice. When the DRC Mission Church was established in 1881 racial separation at worship was adopted 'not as a matter of principle but as one of practice'.[1]

In 1962 the DRC white membership stood at 691,214, and its adherents numbered 1,145,747. Its non-white membership had grown to 230,772 (an increase of 7,000 in one year), and its adherents to 650,000. A high proportion of its non-white members are Coloureds. African membership is confined largely to the rural communities. Its vigorous mission activity, on which over £1 million is spent annually, extends beyond the frontiers of the Republic; until recently it was active in Nigeria. When readers of the DRC organ, *Die Kerkbode*, wrote recently to complain about its introducing pictures of non-whites, the journal vigorously defended itself: 'Considering that the population of South Africa is predominantly non-white, the day may come when the majority of the members of our Church will be coloured. That will be a happy day, and will crown the missionary work for which we are sacrificing so much today.'[1]

The Church sees itself as the 'defender of Western Christendom' implanted by divine guidance in southern Africa to give battle to the enemies of Christ and the *'volk'*. In 1963 *Die Kerkblad* published a list of these enemies: communism; Islam; 'the fraud of Roman Catholicism'; the 'sickly sentimentalism and sensationalism of Methodism'; 'the liberalism which is like a cancerous growth in the Western world'; materialism; 'education without dogma'; modernism; and the 'false unifying of Churches at the expense of truth'.[2]

It is quite wrong to suppose that the DRC is controlled by the politicians: it jealously guards its autonomy and seeks itself to influence politicians and policies. This is done through religious, cultural and social organisations; through the policy decisions of its Synods; through the active partici-pation in public life by *predikants*; through the control of educational institutions (schools, teachers' training colleges and the theology departments of universities); through its influential religious publications; and, most effectively, through systematic *huisbesoek* (house-visits): no party canvasser is more diligent at door-knocking than the *predikant*. Finally the Sunday sermon is perhaps the most directly influential mass education medium in Afrikanerdom.

The National Party naturally looks to the Church to mobilise support behind apartheid: the DRC responds by providing scriptural justification for its policy. This has resulted not only in the Church's isolation within the world movement of Protestants, but in producing an active dissident group among its own members. The doyen of this group is the venerated septuagenarian, Professor B. B. Keet—the only surviving member of the quintet who translated the Bible into Afrikaans. He has repudiated not only apartheid for the Church and the State, but the whole concept of racial dis-crimination. A second professor of theology, Dr A. L. Geyer of Pretoria, was found guilty of heresy by an ecclesi-astical court on the complaints of his own students; but he was subsequently cleared by the courts of the land.

A third professor, Dr Ben Marais, who teaches history

of Christianity at Pretoria University, played a leading part in
the preparation of the warning published under the title
Delayed Action, in which eleven DRC ministers called on white
South Africa to abandon its present habits of thought and
racial policy before it was too late. This manifesto created
a furore in Church circles. At public meetings there were
demands for the authors of *Delayed Action* to be drummed
out of the Church. But though they were repudiated and
condemned, this extreme action was not taken. Notwithstanding this fierce Calvinist reaction to dissent, several other
attempts have been made to rally the DRC behind the ideas of
a modern Christianity.

The latest move has come from an outstanding minister
and a member of the Broederbond, the Reverend L. F. Beyers
Naudé, who left his pulpit in 1963 to become a director of a
multi-racial Christian Institute. Beyers Naudé belongs to a
family of *predikants*; he has himself been a minister for
twenty-three years, and was a staunch believer in the mission
of Afrikanerdom. His life was changed by the shootings at
Sharpeville in 1960. 'The tense months that followed Sharpeville brought long and earnest discussions among churchmen',
he explained. 'It was then that the full implications of
traditional race policies were borne in on me. The more I
had to do with the missionaries and the non-white ministers of
the Church the more I realised the urgent need for better
understanding.' Preaching his last sermon to his community,
many of whom were in tears, he said it was a strange phenomenon that Christian men accepted the word of God in theory—
but made it powerless in practice. 'Like the false prophets in
Jeremiah's time, they gave the nation the false assurance that
no disaster could touch them as long as the Temple was in
their midst. They called "peace, peace" when Jeremiah
warned it was no true peace. Are there not also national
traditions which cannot stand up to the honest test of Scrip-
ture, but which we place alongside, or above, the Word?'[1]

The fate of the Reverend Beyers Naudé and his family
as a result of his action is the fate of every dissenter of
prominence in the Church: social ostracism, reinforced by
public attack. As he sadly admitted: 'The Afrikaner who
deviates is apt to be labelled a traitor, to be accused of falling

for the "bribes of the English", a sell-out of his people, and a political renegade."[1] It takes a brave man to denounce the teachings of Afrikanerdom.

It is over-optimistic to interpret the rebellion of this brave few as the beginning of a new chapter in the life of the Church. It shows that consciences are deeply troubled, and that there are individual Afrikaner leaders who are capable of breaking with the past. But it also shows the great power of the Church to overcome these challenges without too much difficulty.

But however intolerant to its own nonconformists, the Church has not remained untouched by the country's crisis. There has been a remarkable transformation in the teachings of the sermons on Sundays. It is commonplace today for the minister to upbraid the community for their treatment of non-whites, and to stress the importance of looking upon Africans and Coloureds as people entitled to decent treatment and human rights. This new policy rests on the growing awareness that for apartheid or any other policy to succeed, the goodwill and co-operation of non-whites are needed. But the Church has never publicly criticised any of the government's actions over apartheid.

There are now three voices contesting for influence in the Church. The smallest is that of the dissenters. A second speaks for those who desire to keep the Church as a crusading instrument for Afrikanerdom; and the third represents those who wish to see it act as a conciliator in the racial conflict. The extremism of Afrikanerdom's crusaders is shown by this sermon preached by the Reverend G. J. J. Boshoff on the day after the attempt on Dr Verwoerd's life in June, 1960. One might ignore this sermon if it had not been published extensively in the Afrikaans press.

> The wounding of Dr Verwoerd on the eve of our Day of Humiliation has made big tears fall on our altar. Nobody will tell the Afrikaner what he is to say at the altar ... The Afrikaner's altar is his biggest weapon, his nuclear bomb, his firing squad. For three centuries the history of the Afrikaner people has been one long *via dolorosa*. There is nothing that the enemy fears so much as an Afrikaner who prays. The black giant of Africa

is eating bread for which he has not sweated, he wants
to wear clothes that do not fit him, he wants to pay with
what he does not yet have, distribute what he does not
yet possess, wants to talk about things he does not yet
understand, wants to be where he still is not. By contrast, the white giant is entirely ignored. The real giant
of Africa, the white man—and his name is Afrikaner—
does not come into the picture at all. Our nation was
born small, but it has grown to giant proportions. The
real difference between the white giant and the black
giant is—knowledge on the one side, ignorance on the
other. The black giant has so far lost nothing except
his balance. Now he is asking for what he does not yet
own, and what he has not yet lost. He is asking for the
cancellation of the Ten Commandments, our spiritual
contract with God.... We must unite in the face of the
common danger. The black masses of Africa do not
seek the white man's friendship but his destruction....
For every white man in South Africa the hour of eleven
has struck. The Afrikaner people is no longer fighting
isolated enemies like the Dingaans, Colleys and Milners
—the whole world is arrayed against him. The emergency of 1960 is a repetition of the plight of our nation
when in 1838 the Voortrekkers faced the black savage.[1]

This is the fierce sickness of the spirit of Afrikanerdom:
it gushes forth at times of greatest anxiety. But it is by no
means the dominant element in Afrikanerdom. A more
rational view is presented by Professor J. H. Coetzee, of
Potchefstroom:

What is involved is the problem of coexistence in Africa,
today and tomorrow and in the distant future.... Those
who do not want to live with the others must find refuge
elsewhere. It sounds cruel and hard, but how else?...
The white man does not want to leave Africa: his
material and spiritual interests are here; he cannot leave
Africa so easily; it is his only fatherland; he may not
leave Africa; his task and vocation bind him here. How,
under the changed circumstances not to surrender his
interests, to keep a place in his fatherland and to fulfill his
vocation?... The white man still has a place and a
task in Africa. He will have to carry on that task in the
near future by a revaluation of his means and position.[2]

In its revaluation of South Africa's needs the Church has gone further than the Party in the direction of partition. In April 1961, the Transvaal Synod of the DRC (one of the most influential of the Synods) declared that the salvation of white and non-white lay in 'eventual total territorial separation' with full development opportunities for everyone, each in his own domain. As time was running short, the Synod urged the government to speed up the process of separation 'with all its might; and it called on Church members 'gladly to make the sacrifices demanded by separation to assure all races a secure future'. The difficulty the Church faces is that its members show little sign of making any sacrifices, gladly or otherwise.

THE INTELLECTUALS

The fate of South Africa could be decided in this decade.
Dr A. L. Geyer, Chairman of SABRA

The cloistered intellectual is a rarity among Afrikaners. The intellectuals' traditional role is as 'men of action'. They inspired Afrikaner nationalism; they fostered the idea of Afrikanerdom; they fought to establish its power. On all these issues they began as tiny minority elements, well ahead of their times. Their capacity for effective action is undeniable. They have grown accustomed to political leadership, and in recent years they have even taken the leadership in finance, mining and industry.

This versatile breed of intellectuals has until quite recently considered it important to complete at least part of its studies abroad. It is misleading to think of them as people without knowledge or experience of the outside world. If they act in ways that perplex Europeans and Americans, it is because they see South African problems in terms of their own exclusive nationalism. By no means all Afrikaner intellectuals adopt this ethnocentric view: a number of the best Afrikaner brains strongly oppose Afrikanerdom and are often the toughest and most courageous opponents of racial thinking. But they cease to play an effective part in Afrikaner society.

Amongst the Afrikaners, the intellectual has always been accorded the same role as the *melamed* of Jewish society or the *mallam* of the Muslim world. He is looked up to for guidance and support. He has the prestige of learning, and is the example held up to ambitious young Afrikaners. He provides a reassuring ego-identification against the ordinary Afrikaner's feelings of inferiority in relation to the English. At the same time he is often suspected of not being sufficiently practical in political affairs.

There are four university centres of influence. Stellenbosch, Potchefstroom, Bloemfontein and Pretoria. The traditions of these four are by no means identical: for example there is a long history of friction between the two most important—Stellenbosch and Potchefstroom. The latter still dwells in the conservative traditions of Calvin's Geneva. Until recently it held a dominant position: two of the Trinity in Die Broederbond came from Potchefstroom, including its former Chief Leader, Professor J. C. van Rooy. But the ideological influence of Stellenbosch rose with the star of its prize product, Dr Verwoerd. Stellenbosch has always been the cradle of the National Party. It is also the unruly nursery of apartheid, noisy with the arguments that have not ceased since the concept of apartheid entered the minds of the Stellenbosch professors in the middle 1940s. Their plunge into the policy of 'Separate Development' marks a turning-point in the ideas of Afrikaner intellectuals. It also marks the point at which the intellectuals took another of their famous leaps far ahead of the thinking of ordinary Afrikaners.

It had happened before, when the Society of True Afrikaners was formed by eight young Paarl teachers, writers and ministers in 1875. Their purpose then was to establish the right of Afrikaans, still in its formative period, to be the language of the Afrikaners, instead of Dutch. The general reaction at that time was: 'What! Do these little schoolteachers and Valley wine farmers want to make a civilised language for us out of a Hotnot tongue?'[1] Their second leap ahead of contemporary parochial ideas was taken between 1877 and 1881 when small groups of intellectuals in the Cape, the Orange Free State and the Transvaal began to preach the need for a wider unity than that offered by the political loyalties to the two Boer Republics and the Cape Colony. This was the beginning of Afrikaner nationalism. A third was their decision in 1934 to change the *Broederbond* from a cultural movement into a political society, dedicated to the idea of achieving Afrikaner domination over 'the English' at a time when all the great Afrikaner leaders (including most of the Boer generals) were working towards 'national unity of the two white communities'. Each of these movements was denounced and bitterly opposed by the dominant political leadership of the time. Yet each time these small elites emerged as the dominant influence.

The leap into the realm of apartheid belongs to the same genre as these three political acts. For the intellectuals apartheid represents a mid-twentieth-century response to the challenge of colour. It is based on the realisation that whites cannot indefinitely dominate non-whites; that *baasskap* is doomed. But their ideas emerged into the political arena in 1947 when the dominant political thinking was still concerned with the maintenance of *baasskap*. The intellectuals understood that 'the kaffir' would never again be 'a kaffir'; that henceforth he would insist on achieving his independence in precisely the same way as the Afrikaner nationalists had insisted on theirs. But how to put this across? Two tasks faced the intellectuals : to make *apartheid* meaningful and effective, and to change the Afrikaner's basic attitude to 'the Bantu'. The popularising of the term Bantu (which means, literally, *the People*) was their contribution to getting away from the current use of 'kaffirs', 'natives, and 'black men'. They rejected 'African' as being associated with liberal ideas; besides it has no Afrikaans equivalent—other than Afrikaner, which would be unthinkable.

Both these tasks have so far defeated them. They have never fully agreed among themselves about the proper methods for achieving apartheid, although they are agreed about the ultimate objective to establish separate national states through Separate Development. Nor have they yet succeeded in getting official support for their view that apartheid can work only if it has the willing co-operation of 'the Bantu', and that this depends not only on their being treated with dignity and respect, but on their being brought into full consultation.

The organisation created by the intellectuals to develop these ideas about apartheid and to educate white opinion is the South African Bureau of Racial Affairs (SABRA). It is based on Stellenbosch. SABRA draws together the intellectuals in the universities and schools, the Broederbond, the Church and, to a much lesser extent, the National Party. Since 1947, when the first Apartheid Commission reported its findings to the National Party, the intellectuals have become increasingly influential within the Party; but they have also grown increasingly impatient with the politicians for not facing honestly up to the sacrifices that effective Separate Development would require from the whites. Some of them have publicly criticised the government's willingness to apply with vigour only those aspects that demand sacrifices from the voteless nonwhites. One important change is their awareness of how little time remains to evolve and implement a lasting solution to the racial problem. In 1956 SABRA's vice-president, Professor N. J. Olivier, said: 'We do not have unlimited time. Those who think we can wait fifty or a hundred years for a solution are living in a dream world ... I wonder if we have even one generation to find a solution.' In 1960, the chairman of SABRA, Dr A. L. Geyer, set an even shorter limit. 'The fate of South Africa could be decided in this decade.'

SABRA has twice come into conflict with the government. The first time was over the emasculation of the Tomlinson Commission's report for the development of the reserves.* The second time was in 1959 when they proposed to call representative African leaders into consultation with themselves: the government stamped hard on this proposal.

The main division in the ranks of the intellectuals is over the meaning of 'territorial separation'. An influential but growing minority is convinced that the only hope of success lies in complete partition, with the whites settling for a much smaller part of the country than they now occupy. But whatever their disagreements, the intellectuals are convinced that political expediency is robbing the country of even that little time which they believe still remains, if its racial problems are to be tackled with sufficient courage and toughness to ward off catastrophe. The restless intellectuals cause the Party and the government more anxiety than does the political opposition.

* See page 51.

In addition to the rebels in the Church, a small but highly influential group of intellectuals has found conditions intolerable inside the laager and have left it despite the cold isolation which they know to be the penalty for rebellion. In every case the rebels have adopted a more liberal attitude on race questions. One group, led by the late Senator H. A. Fagan and Mr Japie Basson, MP, attempted to form their own party, the National Union, but soon abandoned it in favour of the United Party. The majority has gone even further to the left. Professor P. V. Pistorius, who joined the Progressive Party, sounded a grim warning in his significantly titled book *No Further Trek*: 'We have become so accustomed to group values and group traditions that a complete revaluation of values will be necessary. What we call tradition will have to be examined mercilessly and critically, and the criterion will have to be the interests of the whole. That whole will have to be South Africa and humanity as such. . . . It will be a hard and grievous task. It will be a bitter and inevitable price to pay for survival. At the present moment it seems unthinkable that we all will be prepared to pay that price. In that case we will inevitably perish.'[1]

A rebellion among Potchefstroom University professors was led by two of the Broederbond's most stalwart members: Professor L. J. du Plessis, a former member of its Trinity, and Professor J. H. Coetzee, one of the founders of the *Ossewabrandwag* and an executive member of SABRA. With the present Minister of Justice, Mr J. B. Vorster, he was one of those imprisoned during the second world war by the Smuts Government because of their activities in the *Stormjaers*, the militant wing of the *Ossewabrandwag*. Among Coetzee's reasons for resigning was, he said, the disregard of the Verwoerd Government for the feelings of non-whites in their application of apartheid. Though he remains a believer in segregation, he insisted that the terms must be settled with the co-operation of African leaders. 'By this I do not mean the co-operation of chiefs and tribal Bantu. I mean the co-operation of the African National Congress leaders—men like Lutuli for whom I have the deepest respect, and Champion and Professor Z. K. Matthews.'[2]

THE PARTY AND ITS PRESS

> Only the National Party had a colour policy which
> assured the white man that he would retain his full
> control over national affairs. Only the National Party
> was heading for racial peace and the eventual absence
> of racial discrimination, because only when the races
> were separated and lived as neighbours could
> discrimination vanish.
>
> *Dr Verwoerd, 1961 Election Address*

> I see the National Party today, not as an Afrikaans or
> English or Afrikaans-English party in the future, what-
> ever it may have been in the past. I see it as a party
> which stands for the preservation of the white man, of
> white government in South Africa.
>
> *Dr Verwoerd, August 19, 1961*

Afrikanerdom maintains political control through the
Herenigde Nasionale Party, the Reunited National Party,
formed in 1940 on the 'reuniting' of General Hertzog and Dr
D. F. Malan in their common opposition to South Africa's
entry into the war. Its two immediate predecessors were the
Afrikaner Party and the *Gesuiwerde Nasionale Party* (the
'Purified' National Party). The 'purification' of the latter had
occurred when General Hertzog took the original *Nasionale
Party* (formed in 1914) into coalition with General Smuts'
South African Party to form the United Party in 1933. A
hard core of Afrikaners had resisted this coalition. Led, at
first, by Mr J. G. Strijdom and later by Dr D. F. Malan, the
'purified' nationalists started life with less than a dozen MPs.
They had only one seat in the whole of the Transvaal, none at
first in Natal, half a dozen in the Orange Free State, and a few
in the rural areas of the Cape Province. By 1943 it had
43 seats in a parliament of 151 members, and by 1948 the
number had grown to 79, including its allies.

The Party holds all the seats in the Orange Free State
which provides the bulk of the most intransigent MPs. The
Cape Province, on the other hand, provides the Party with
its 'liberal' wing, except for a minority which supported Mr
Eric Louw until his recent resignation as Foreign Minister.
The Transvaal returns a mixed bunch of MPs, ranging from
die-hards to moderates. Natal is the only province in which

the Party is still in a minority. It controls all the seats in South West Africa. As a rule the provinces tend to vote as a bloc on questions of leadership, although the Cape Province caucus divided its allegiance between its own leader, Dr T. E. Dönges, and the Transvaal leader, Dr Verwoerd, when the latter was elected Prime Minister in 1958. The Orange Free State caucus, having voted for its own leader, Mr C. R. Swart (now President of the Republic) in the first ballot, swung behind Dr Verwoerd in the second.

The Party has an active mass membership, but is ruled by an elite. Although it is nationally controlled through a Federal Committee, each province remains strongly autonomous. Party policy is theoretically made by the provincial congresses, but these operate mainly as sounding-boards for the leaders. The resolutions passed at these conferences are invariably more extreme than those adopted by the government. There has been a growing tendency in recent years for Party leaders to speak against the more outrageous resolutions and to lecture the rank-and-file on the need to face up to modern realities. The provincial executives and the parliamentary caucus exercise a much more direct influence on the government's policies than do the rank and file. Although individuals frequently criticise government policy, they have a strongly conformist tradition. The power structure within the Party makes it comparatively easy for the policy-makers to control it by ensuring that their nominees are elected to the provincial executives and the Federal Council. It is here that the Broederbond plays an especially important part.

The Party's parliamentary representatives are largely made up of lawyers and successful farmers. But the lawyer MPs do not—as one might have supposed—represent the SABRA type of intellectual; they are usually 'practical politicians', much more concerned with what goes on in the *platteland* than on the campus. There is little that distinguishes them from the farmers in parliament. The handful of intellectuals actively identified with SABRA policy play a comparatively minor role in parliament. This swamping of the intellectuals by the 'practical politicians' is, of course, explained by the kind of electorate on whom they must depend. Dr Verwoerd is the outstanding exception. But even he has to walk warily to avoid offending the rank and file more than he judges wise. Even so, as will be made clear, his policies have opened up a seemingly unbridgeable gap between the present government's leadership and its supporters.

The Party relies heavily on its press. The Afrikaner is a great believer in the written word; and because the popular press is overwhelmingly English and anti-government, the Party press plays an unusually important role. Party papers make few concessions to popular tastes: they are in the strictest sense political papers of the kind one finds in Holland and Scandinavia. But these papers are not owned by the Party as such. Their boards are controlled by different groups of political interests within Afrikanerdom: e.g., *Die Transvaler* by Dr Verwoerd; *Die Burger* by Dr T. E. Dönges, the Minister of Finance, and likeminded Cape nationalists who are not particularly well-disposed to Dr Verwoerd. Each paper circulates in its own region: *Die Burger* in western and northern Cape Province; *Die Oosterlig* in the eastern Cape; *Die Transvaler* and *Die Vaderland* in the Transvaal; *Die Volksblad* in the Orange Free State; and *Die Nataller* in Natal. The exception is *Dagbreek*, a Sunday paper under the vigorous editorship of Mr Willem van Heerden, which has a national circulation. No newspaper in the English language supports the National Party.

FINANCIAL AND SPECIAL INTEREST GROUPS

> It seems strange that we can erect a factory on a partnership basis (with the Malay government) in Kuala Lumpur, but may not do so in Umtata in the Transkei.
> *Dr Anton Rupert, Chairman of the Rembrandt Tobacco Corporation, 1961*

Up to 1940, the Afrikaner's position in finance, industry and commerce was almost entirely that of an employee. His stronghold was the land: but even there the tendency was for a comparatively small number, perhaps 50,000, to develop large farm holdings, while the others remained smallholders or gave up farming and gradually drifted to the towns. With boom conditions during and after the war, the big farmers rapidly accumulated great wealth. The true rural aristocrats are the Cape wine farmers and fruit growers. Latterly they have been joined by the wool growers, the wheat and maize farmers, the Transvaal fruit growers, and the Natal sugar-planters (few of whom, until quite recently, were Afrikaners). Their entry into the business world was through producers' co-operatives which became important accumulators of capital. They built their own creameries, canning factories and distilleries; and arranged for their own marketing. Their surplus capital went into insurance companies, building societies and the Broederbond-inspired *Reddingsdaad* business concerns.

Thus, for the first time, a substantial number of Afrikaners became capital producers. As a predominantly rural movement, the National Party had always been the champion of the farmers against the towns; and on its victory in 1948 it naturally became a Farmers' government responsive to the pressures of the various farming interests, each of which was intensively organised.

The Afrikaners achieved a second breakthrough into the business world through their intellectuals. They work in the huge government-controlled industries like steel, electricity, oil-from-coal, fertilisers and transport. By the end of the second world war, the heads of all these state enterprises were Afrikaners. A typical example is Dr Harry van Eck, chairman of the Industrial Development Corporation. His flair for industry has made the IDC one of the most successful state ventures in the country. Its purpose is to encourage development in fields where private enterprise has not ventured: examples are *Foscor*, the £40 million fertiliser industry, and the textile factories in the so-called 'Border Industries' near the reserves.

By 1951 the Afrikaners had ceased to be a predominantly rural people. They became the dominant white employee element in seven fields of activity: agriculture and fishing; mining; building and construction; railways; road transport; civil and provincial services and municipalities; and education. But they were still a minority in manufacturing industry, commerce and finance, medcal services and private legal practice.

In 1938–9 Afrikaners owned only 3,170 firms with a combined turnover of £61 million. Ten years later they owned 13,047 firms with a turnover of £322.5 million. They controlled eleven giant financial concerns: *Volkskas* (£100 million), *Sanlam* (£90 million), Rembrandt Tobacco Corporation (£42.5 million), Trustbank (£41.5 million), *Saambou* (£32.5 million), *Santam* (£12.5 million), *Sentrale Finansieringkorporasie* (£10 million), *Bonuskor* (£8 million), African Homes Trust (£8 million), *Federale Volksbeleggings* (£7.3 million) *Federale Mynbou* (£4 million). Their economic power was further strengthened through government control of ten public utilities and financial and industrial corporations: the Land Bank; Klipfontein Organic Products; Electricity Supply Commission; Industrial Development Corporation; Iron and Steel Corporation; *Sasol* (oil from coal); *Saiccor*; *Foscor*; and the Fisheries Development Corporation. Afrikanerdom's successful breakthrough into the business world is best illustrated by the rise of two of South Africa's newest tycoons: both Stellenbosch intellectuals.

Mr William Bedford Coetzer, B.COMM., a director of fifty major companies, was one of the young Afrikaners who responded to the Broederbond's appeal to capture 'the citadel of finance now in alien hands'. In 1941 he joined one of its sponsored organisations, *Federale Volksbeleggings*, formed only a year before with a capital of £20,000 to develop fishing, coal mining and industry. By 1948 it had amassed capital and reserves of more than £1 million. Next it formed the Trust Bank and, in 1953, the *Federale Mynbou*, with Coetzer at its head. It branched out from coal mining to gold, chrome, asbestos, soda ash, salt and other mining investment. But Coetzer was strongly aware of the company's lack of 'know-how' in mining. 'Here is where we learn from the English', he told his colleagues, and went to seek the advice of the late Sir Ernest Oppenheimer. He found the Diamond King friendly but cautious. But in 1963 Sir Ernest's heir, Mr Harry Oppenheimer, led the English-speaking world of mining finance into partnership with the new Afrikaner class of financiers. Main Street Investments was formed with Coetzer as chairman and Oppenheimer on the Board. This partnership between Oppenheimer—long regarded by Afrikanerdom as the embodiment of alien financial control—and

Coetzer, brought this comment from the Johannesburg *Financial Mail*: 'Mr Oppenheimer saw the advantages of a voluntary link with Afrikaner capital and Afrikaner leadership, although some say he left its implications a little late. . . . Well-entrenched "English" finance appreciates Mr Coetzer's approach and quick appreciation of the interdependence of foreign and local capital, imported and locally trained skills, of South Africa's natural resources and imported plant and know-how.'![1]

The story of Dr Anton Rupert is even more spectacular: in fifteen years he has succeeded in making himself the Czar of the world's cigarette market. In 1948, at the age of thirty-two, he gave up his teaching post at Stellenbosch to found the Rembrandt Tobacco Corporation. Today, more than one out of every fifty cigarettes smoked in the world bears the trade mark of his group. He controls twenty-five factories in fifteen countries, and markets his products in 160 countries. His group's consolidated assets stand at over £35 million; the parent company's investments are over £5½ million. As a result of the thrustful policy of this former Stellenbosch don, his group can claim credit for introducing the world's first King Size cigarette (Rothman's), the first King Size filter cigarette, the first Menthol filter cigarette, the first King Size cigarette with a 'multi-filter', the first superporous cigarette paper, called 'multi-vent', and the first 'ultra-modern gold band filter'.

Perhaps the most striking feature of this Afrikaner nationalist is his success in forging links with the Afro-Asian world at a time of growing hostility to South African products. At the 1963 annual general meeting of his shareholders in Stellenbosch, Dr Rupert boasted that 'during the past year we were singularly honoured by having the new Group factory at Petaling Jaya in Malaya formally opened by the Tunku Abdul Rahman, the Prime Minister of the Malaysian Federation, and the factory in Kingston, Jamaica, opened by the Rt. Hon. Sir Alexander Bustamante, Prime Minister of Jamaica. In April this year the factory in Lusaka was officially opened by Dr Kenneth Kaunda, Prime Minister Designate of Northern Rhodesia when that country shortly obtains its independence.'[2] His overseas policy is to have local directors on all his boards:

Africans in Rhodesia, Jamaicans in the West Indies, Malays in Malaysia and Fijians in the West Indies.

What changes in Afrikanerdom's attitude might one expect these Afrikaner financiers and industrialists to produce? In 1961 Dr Rupert pleaded for the replacement of apartheid by what he termed 'co-existence'. He believes 'the problem of underdeveloped Africa is more one of collapse than of revolution; when the educated African leader realises that South Africa is a bridgehead to industrial civilisation, we shall become better friends still.' He offers a recipe for partnership in making available a competent body of experts to every emerging state in Africa; in building up industries and commerce on a basis of partnership with them; in persuading the West to allow the products of young countries into their markets; and in helping to foster education to create an educated middle class. 'Whatever we can still save will only be done by true partnership. For democracy first needs a responsible "Body Economic" before a responsible "Body Politic".'[1] He is a man of optimism and confidence. In 1964 he became the first large South African industrialist voluntarily to fix a minimum wage of £1 a day for all his employees. When, in 1960, the African National Congress tried to call a strike in favour of 'a pound a day minimum wage', the government and the press unanimously condemned the demand as 'hysterical nonsense'.

The organ of Afrikaner big business, *Volkshandel*, recently commented that world opinion could not be despised. Its recipe for meeting overseas hostility was recognition in the Republic that Western leaders believed in the dogma of equality. The government, it suggested, should in future differentiate as little as possible on the grounds of colour but 'rather on the basis of the level of civilisation'. It acknowledged that black nationalism could not be stopped in the Republic; the whites would therefore have to stand together and find a solution for the colour problem that could stand the test of time. 'With the awakening of Africa and the rise of the East the time factor is against us and the West.' After urging that it was necessary to accelerate all plans, it added: 'Adaptations must be made to the extent demanded by circumstances in order to transfer the right of self-determination gradually to the Bantu and other races, as they became ripe enough for it and reached the necessary level of welfare and civilisation.'[1]

The ideas of the new Afrikaner businessmen are reflected most regularly in *Die Burger*, the organ of the Cape National Party. Ever since Sharpeville this paper has been out of step on several issues with the other organs of government opinion. It has supported criticism of what the Afrikaner businessmen call 'pinprick apartheid': the laws that hurt Africans without achieving any practical purpose. It has questioned the tempo of the government's plans to get separate development working more effectively. It tends to take overseas criticism seriously. It calls for greater understanding of non-white attitudes. And it has cautiously given support to the idea of a proper partition scheme for the country. But *Die Burger* speaks for a minority group within Afrikanerdom, reflecting as it does the views of the less illiberal strands of Cape nationalism and the rising class of Afrikaner capitalists.

THE AFRIKANER WORKER

> Although nobody would argue with the postal workers —especially after the concessions to their railway colleagues—that their demands for higher wages are unfounded, it is cause for disturbed reflection when their leaders say: 'Our people are threatening to get out of hand despite the Sabotage Act, and we will not be able to restrain them longer.'
>
> *Willem van Heerden, editor of* DAGBREEK,
> *September 9, 1962*

The Afrikaner workers who came to the towns to escape from rural poverty were always the hardest group to bring under the control of Afrikanerdom especially if they belonged to the trade unions. Many of them gave up going to church, and the great majority stopped voting for the Afrikaner National Party. The Church and the Party came to look upon them as *verlore mense*, people lost to the *volk*. Up to 1929 their support went to the Labour Party and, after the formation of the Smuts-Hertzog coalition in 1933, to the United Party. They were not, however, an important electoral factor in the urban seats before 1938: the great inflow from the *platteland* gathered momentum only in the depression of the 1930s. Today, the Afrikaner workers' votes in the towns can influence the results in 29 of the Republic's 150 seats: enough to decide the outcome of a general election.

The Broederbond recognised the growing importance of the Afrikaner in the towns and took two steps which helped to change the Party's political fortunes. It persuaded Dr Verwoerd to leave Stellenbosch in 1937 to become editor-in-chief of the first National Party daily paper in the Transvaal. He had never worked on a newspaper before; but his skill as a propagandist made *Die Transvaler* a political success. The next move was to lay siege to the trade union movement, then controlled by the South African Trades and Labour Council. Its achievements had been to unify virtually all the unions —white, black and coloured; to maintain an easy relationship between Afrikaans- and English-speaking workers; and to maintain a less easy, but nevertheless viable, relationship between left and right. Even those Afrikaner trade unionists who supported the National Party opposed attempts to bring their unions into politics. In 1935 the Broederbond set up the Reform Organisation (helped by a gift of £10,000 from a wealthy Stellenbosch widow) and named Dr Albert Hertzog* to head its campaign to recapture the Afrikaners in the towns for the *volk*.

Its first target was the Garment Workers' Union whose white members are mostly Afrikaner girls from the *platteland*. But under the leadership of their then general secretary, Mr Solly Sachs, they staunchly maintained an inter-racial organisation which involved 'mixing' between whites and non-whites. Afrikanerdom was understandably perturbed about these rebel Afrikaner daughters. Although its campaign in the trade union movement had some success, the Broederbond never succeeded in controlling the Garment Workers' Union, not even after the government banned Mr Sachs from holding a trade union post.[1] But its campaign did achieve the division of the white trade union movement into two: the South African Confederation of Labour (SACL), and the Trade Union Council of South Africa (TUCSA).

* Dr Hertzog is now Minister of Posts and Telegraphs.

The South African Federation of Labour is itself divided into two: the Co-ordinating Body, and the South African Federation of Trade Unions (SAFTU). The former supports the government's apartheid policies uncritically; but it is by far the smallest of the trade union centres, with only three large affiliates: the *Blanke Bouwerkers* (White Building Workers), the Iron and Steel Workers, and the (white) Mine Workers Union. SAFTU does not accept apartheid as a policy, but strongly upholds the industrial colour bar. These divisions have robbed the trade union movement of any militancy, or even of real strength. However, the majority of its members fit quite comfortably into the present economic structure of white society. Their principal interest is to defend their rights as whites.

Although the Afrikaner workers now vote overwhelmingly for the National Party, they still form a comparatively weak link in its chain. As the least privileged of the white groups, they are continuously engaged in negotiations for higher wages, but with only limited success, particularly if they happen to work for the State, the country's largest employer of white labour. This makes for discontent. But, as the Afrikaner workers have failed to secure an integral part within the power groups of Afrikanerdom, as other groups have done, their major weapon remains the vote.

2: AFRIKANERDOM CHOOSES ITS WEAPONS

THE WEAPON THAT FAILED

> It is nothing short of a tragedy that the word [apartheid]...has become one of the ugliest political swear words in the world.
>
> DIE BURGER, *April 21, 1961*

Apartheid—the political weapon of Afrikanerdom to defend white supremacy—proved a great success with the white electorate. It offered them real *baasskap* over non-whites in place of the time-worn and obviously faltering policy of segregation. But its electoral success was no guarantee of its effectiveness as an instrument of national policy, and this for the very reason which made it so attractive to the white voters. To them it promised security and mastery, and demanded nothing from them in return. A government whose continued rule depended on fulfilling these expectations had little room for manoeuvre when the failures of this policy became too manifest to ignore. By 1959 apartheid had become a serious embarrassment to the government and the country.

South Africa first heard of apartheid in 1947, when the National Party published the findings of a committee of prominent Afrikaners. These became the Party's election manifesto.

> It is a policy which sets itself the task of preserving and safeguarding the racial identity of the white population of the country; of likewise preserving and safeguarding the identity of the indigenous peoples as separate racial groups, with opportunities to develop into self-governing national units; of fostering the inculcation of national consciousness, self-esteem and mutual regard among the various races of the country.

The following principles were laid down among others:

> In general terms our policy envisages segregating the most important ethnic groups and sub-groups in their own areas where every group will be enabled to develop into a self-sufficient unit. We endorse the general principle of

territorial segregation of the Bantu and the Whites....
The Bantu in the urban areas should be regarded as
migratory citizens not entitled to political or social rights
equal to those of the Whites. The process of detribalisation should be arrested. The interests and employment
prospects of the White workers in White areas will be
protected.[1]

In presenting this policy the Nationalists threw down a
challenge: 'The choice before us is one of [these] two diver-
gent courses: either that of integration, which would in the
long run amount to national suicide on the part of the Whites;
or that of *apartheid*.'

There were two serious flaws in apartheid from the beginning. The first was its unrealistic hope of separating millions
of people—who had been drawn together into a single economy over a long period—at a time when tremendous economic
expansion depended on the availability of black labour. The
second was that Afrikanerdom was divided over the true purpose of apartheid: should it work towards complete territorial
separation, or should it content itself with making more rigid
the laws intended to enforce social, economic and political
segregation? The commission which drafted the first apartheid statement had failed to agree within itself. It had therefore deliberately made its recommendation in favour of 'the
general principle of territorial segregation' as vague as possible
to allow the contending viewpoints to interpret it as they
wished. The Church, the Broederbond and SABRA (under the
influence of Dr Verwoerd and his chief lieutenant, Dr
W. W. M. Eiselen) interpreted it to mean territorial separation;
and this policy was, in fact, endorsed in 1950 by conferences
of SABRA and the Dutch Reformed Church. But the 'practical
politicians' in the Party rejected this interpretation.

The Prime Minister, Dr Malan, intervened with this frank
statement: 'If one could attain total territorial apartheid, if it
were practicable, everybody would admit it would be an ideal
state of affairs ... but that is not the policy of our party ... it
is nowhere to be found in our declarations of policy [*sic*].
On the contrary ... I clearly stated ... that total territorial
apartheid was impracticable under present circumstances in
South Africa where our whole economic structure is to a large

extent based on Native labour.'[1] Apartheid policy during Dr Malan's premiership is exemplified by the Group Areas Act, and amounted to little more than a rigid form of social, political and economic segregation, with strong control over the Africans' right of movement and a clamp down on certain types of political activity. The idea of separate homelands for Africans was not in the minds of the 'practical politicians' at that time; they in fact opposed it. Mr M. C. de Wet Nel stated emphatically in 1956 that 'the idea of a Bantustan must be rejected because it is . . . dangerous . . .'[2] He is now the Minister in charge of establishing them.

The wholly negative approach to apartheid pursued by Dr Malan produced considerable dissatisfaction within the ranks of Afrikanerdom. The *Broederbond*, SABRA and the Churches kept up their pressure for a more radical approach. Their efforts were helped by the increasing pressures within the country—notably through the Defiance Campaign launched by the African National Congress in 1951 which resulted in imprisonment for 8,500 people—and by the increasing hostility shown by the outside world. When Malan resigned in bitterness in 1954, the struggle for his succession lay between Mr N. C. Havenga—a 'moderate' leader who would have followed Malan's policies—and Mr J. G. Strijdom, then the leader of the militants. The power groups within Afrikanerdom strongly backed Strijdom. But once in office he, too, temporised on the question of territorial separation. However, he appointed the Tomlinson Commission to investigate 'the socio-economic development of the Bantu areas'. Professor F. R. Tomlinson was the nominee of Dr Verwoerd, who had been Minister in charge of Bantu Affairs since 1950.

When it appeared in 1955, the Tomlinson Report gave the *coup de grace* to the idea that the existing African reserves were capable of sustaining a large increase in population. It showed that at least one half of the existing inhabitants would have to be taken off the land to rehabilitate it. Looking further into the future it warned that by 2000 AD South Africa's population would have grown to 31,248,000, of whom only 5 millions would be whites; instead of comprising about one fifth of the total population the whites would have shrunk proportionately to one seventh. Even if all its recommendations for a vast expansion of financial and industrial development in the reserves were carried out, there would still be 10 million Africans instead of the present 7 million in the 'white' areas by the year 2000 AD. There was no question of getting all the Africans into the areas set aside for them, not even under the most ideal conditions. The Report's new contribution was the idea that Africans should be grouped into seven main ethnic divisions around separate 'heartlands': the Bantustans. It urged that £104 million should be spent on the reserves over the following ten years, and that European industrialists should be allowed to open factories there.

Now it became Verwoerd's turn to temporise. On doctrinal grounds he rejected Tomlinson's proposal that private 'white' capital should be allowed to industrialise the reserves; and because of political considerations he cut down the £104 million recommended to £36.6 million. But even on the main principle which he had formerly championed, he changed his ground: territorial separation, he argued, was 'the ideal . . . to aim at . . . the ideal must be total separation in every sphere, but everyone realises that today it is impracticable. . . . Everyone realises that such a thing cannot be attained within the space of a few years, nor even for a very long time to come'.[1] When his policy was challenged by SABRA (in which he had been a prime mover) he resigned from it; but within a year he succeeded in driving out his critics and had swung SABRA back into line.

The failure of apartheid—though presented by its propagandists as the failure of a 'word'—was of course the failure of a policy. It brought race relations to a dangerous crisis which compelled the white State to quintuple its defence budget in four years. It isolated South Africa in the African continent at a time when the Western colonial powers were withdrawing from it. It isolated the country within the world community, and made it the target for attack at the United Nations. It caused the Republic to withdraw from the Commonwealth. But, worst of all, it failed to achieve its immediate objectives at home. Afrikanerdom's confident boast that it would not only 'stop the black floods to the towns' but 'would begin to reverse this process', to make the 'white areas whiter', withered visibly as each new set of statistics appeared.

The latest census figures (for 1960) show that in the last ten years there was an increase of over one million Africans (45.2 per cent) in the urban areas, and nearly 1,300,000 in the 'white' rural areas (23.6 per cent). In the teeth of the ruthless efforts of the apartheid regime, 'white' South Africa has continued to become 'blacker'. Because none of the three governments— Malan's, Strijdom's or Verwoerd's—was willing to face the unpopularity of halting economic expansion or of providing more land for Africans in the reserves, each was compelled to try and achieve the limited task of accommodating apartheid to the existing social system by legislating for an impossible separation of races at every point of contact.

There is hardly an aspect of social and economic life— from the home, the school and the Church to the trade union, the factory and the political party—which has not been legislated for. As Professor D. V. Cowen has pointed out,[1] by providing for separate housing areas,* separate transport facilities and other public amenities,† separate education through the vernacular medium for Africans at the school level,‡ and separate higher education,§ by differential laws in industry denying to Africans the right to strike,|| and reserving skilled jobs for whites;¶ by restrictive legislation concerning land,** marriage,†† and other relationships,‡‡ by the rigours of a population register,§§ by pass laws,|||| and by a whole series of measures radically curtailing the basic human freedoms for non-whites—in short, by differentiating in the eye of the law between whites and non-whites wherever their paths cross, the exponents of apartheid have sought to arrest and devitalise the power of the forces of unity.

* The Group Areas Act, No. 41 of 1950, as amended and consolidated by the Group Areas Act, 1957; Natives (Urban Areas Consolidation) Act, No. 25 of 1945, as amended.
† The Reservation of Separate Amenities Act, No. 49 of 1953.
‡ The Bantu Education Act, No. 47 of 1953.
§ The extension (sic) of University Education Act, 1959.
|| Native Labour (Settlement of Disputes) Act, No. 48 of 1953, sec. 18.
¶ Native Building Workers Act, No. 27 of 1951, sec. 15; Industrial Conciliation Act, No. 28 of 1956, sec. 77.
** Natives Land Act, No. 27 of 1913; Natives (Urban Areas Consolidation) Act, No. 25 of 1945 as amended.
†† The Prohibition of Mixed Marriages Act, No. 55 of 1949.
‡‡ The Immorality Act, No. 23 of 1957, sec. 16.
§§ The Population Registration Act, No. 30 of 1950.
|||| Natives (Abolition of Passes (sic) and Co-ordination of Documents) Act, No. 67 of 1952.

The verdict of the International Commission of Jurists, which made an independent investigation of the Rule of Law in South Africa, provides a telling commentary on the consequent fate of civil liberties: 'While the deep sociological problems confronting the Government of South Africa certainly cannot be minimised, it is manifestly apparent that the pursuit of the present policy constitutes a serious encroachment upon the freedom of all inhabitants, white and non-white alike. There is strong evidence that the implementation of this policy is not supported by the entire white population. Indeed, constructive criticism of apartheid is clear and articulate.'[1]

IDEOLOGY AND GUNS

The South African [Afrikaner] should be the *baas* everywhere in South Africa.
                        General Hertzog (Prime Minister 1924–39),
                                        October 1912

The whites in other African territories to the north were changing more and more to the Nationalist viewpoint of the necessity of maintaining the *baasskap* of the white man in Africa.
                        Mr J. G. Strijdom (Prime Minister 1954–8)

Call it *baasskap* or call it leadership with justice, no serious thinker in South Africa any longer attaches the slightest value to it.
                        DIE BURGER, *October 17, 1961*

Dr Verwoerd's election to the premiership marked a decisive change in South African politics. If either of his rivals—Mr C. R. Swart, now President of the Republic, or Dr T. E. Dönges, now Minister of Finance and leader of the Cape nationalists—had been elected, they would have carried on where Malan and Strijdom had left off; only Verwoerd offered a new policy. Despite his lack of popularity among his own colleagues, he was elected because they had become aware of the failure of apartheid as applied between 1948 and 1958. It was Verwoerd who had foretold its failure: he was the prime mover in bringing about Malan's resignation and in trying to galvanise Strijdom's policies. Neither of those seasoned politicians thought the white electorate would be ready to accept the changes demanded by Verwoerd; and this was still a great doubt in the minds of those who supported him for the premiership. But they thought the situation had deteriorated so far that the gamble was worth taking. Immediately after Verwoerd's election a senior government whip confessed:[1] 'I have never voted for a leader with less pleasure. But what are we to do? Apartheid is finished. We might as well try something new before admitting defeat. But Verwoerd is not a man we can control. He will take the bit firmly between his teeth. We will either get somewhere, or end up in the dust.'

Unlike his predecessors, Dr Verwoerd does not believe that *baasskap* is a practical policy. He accepts that black nationalism is irresistible. 'Many derogatory things were said about black nationalism in particular, but world history showed that the desire of a group or a nation to become free could not be frustrated for ever.'[2] He thinks it desirable and possible to control and canalise African nationalism so that, instead of becoming a threat to white nationalism, it will become its natural complement. He rejects the view that Africans are inherently inferior to whites; they are at 'a lower level of civilisation', and they are culturally different; but they are capable of developing as fully as any other race. Because of these cultural differences and because of the disparity in numbers between whites and blacks, he rejects the notion that a fully integrated society should be allowed to develop in South Africa. On this point he is inflexible. 'Concession is surrender. White South Africans faced a simple choice between survival and downfall, and they would defend themselves in all ways, even with the rifle if it could not be otherwise.'[3]

Dr Verwoerd's new attempt is the policy of 'Separate Development'; as intended by him, it is not just a new word for apartheid. His plan is to reconstruct South Africa to allow for the growth of white and black states, these, in time, to find an accommodation in a 'commonwealth of South Africa'. The units of this commonwealth will be the Bantustans, the white part of the Republic, and the Coloured community. The Coloureds, however, will not have their own separate land unit; they will continue to dwell among, but residentially separate from, the whites. The Indians will have no distinctive role in this commonwealth. As for the white communities,

Verwoerd has reversed his previous position: he now accepts the need for a united white nation, though each of the two communities would retain its separate culture. He does not believe it is practicable under present circumstances to create complete racial or territorial partition. The great majority of Africans will continue to work in the white Republic; but they will have no rights there: all these will be exercised through the Bantustans with which they are ethnically affiliated. His remedy for unemployment in the reserves is to encourage 'white' industry on the 'white' side of the Bantustans' borders; and to build towns to house African workers on the 'black' side of the borders. This 'Border Industries' scheme would enable industrialists to draw on the pools of surplus labour in the Bantustans without making it necessary for Africans to settle in the white urban areas.

This is the essence of the Separate Development policy which Dr Verwoerd presented to parliament in January 1959 as the only way to ensure white survival without injustice to the non-white peoples. He envisages a transition period to achieve this reconstruction. During the transition 'the white man alone would decide on his future, which is safe only in the hands of the government with its policy of separate development.'[1] But 'while the white man, as in the past, will remain the ruler over white South Africa he, as the guardian of the black man, will see to it that their development takes place in such a fashion that, as they become free, they really become free. We will build up democratic freedom from the bottom upwards so that the masses will be ripe for it when freedom is attained.'[2] Such a policy, he recognises, will depend on the co-operation of Africans; and he believes this can be achieved through consultation with their tribal leaders in the reserves. In his eyes there are no other representative African leaders. The modern African nationalist leadership remains banned.

But this policy involves taking great risks since so many of the questions it raises cannot be answered with any confidence. What are the chances of winning African co-operation? What are the chances of avoiding serious internal violence? What are the chances that such a policy will be acceptable to Western leadership on whose understanding Dr

Verwoerd relies to buy enough time to implement his programme without the harassment of external pressures? Afrikanerdom, meanwhile, is leaving nothing to chance. While putting its faith in the ideology of Separate Development it is committed to defending its 'sovereign right' to carry out its own policies by creating one of the most powerful armies of any state not directly involved in war or in the cold war.*

BANTUSTANS OR BUST

> The Transkei experiment must succeed. Perhaps it is no exaggeration to say that the future of our country and of the white nation depends on it.
> *Dr A. L. Geyer, Chairman of* SABRA, *September 1962*

> The government wants to maintain the Transkei as an established undertaking. It wishes to hand it over to the Bantu like that when the time is ripe—whenever that may be—and as such it simply cannot fail. If the development of the Transkei fails it means the failure of the whole policy of segregation.
> *Dr J. E. Holloway, former Secretary for Finance, November 1962*

Despite all the evidence of the abuses and failures of apartheid —the coercion, the injustices, the humiliations and hardships —there are many who argue that it is the lesser of two evils. They contend that dividing South Africa into Bantustans and a white state offers the best hope for future harmonious relations between the races, and that whatever the 'transitional' hardships, it is wrong for both the Africans and world opinion to refuse to co-operate in making it a success. This argument is at the root of the government's case. It sees Separate Development as the alternative both to white supremacy and to integration which it rejects as leading inevitably to black supremacy. *Die Transvaler* summed up the basic motivation of Separate Development: 'Assuming that the worst happens, that the Bantustans become independent and hostile towards South Africa, it will still be a lesser danger than the one that would threaten us if the Bantu were to gain more and more political power together with the whites in the same political system.'[1]

* For a discussion of South Africa's armed forces see pp 204 to 212.

The assumption behind this argument is that the policy of Bantustans can be made to work. We intend to show that it cannot, and that those who put their faith in it are leading their own supporters into another *cul de sac*. It must be remembered that the Bantustan policy does not envisage partitioning the country between the races on any terms that bear the slightest relationship to numbers or resources.

Four questions need to be answered affirmatively if Bantustans are to hold out any hope of providing a workable alternative either to white supremacy or to complete integration. First: are they politically viable units, or could they become so? Second: could they satisfy African political aspirations? Third: how seriously is it intended that they should become truly independent of the Republic's white government? Fourth: can they become economically viable states able to sustain the populations they are intended to carry? The answers to these questions must, in the first place, be sought in determining the extent and the nature of the reserves which have been marked out as the units for the Bantustans. (See map *supra*, p. viii).

Politically Viable Units?

'When hostilities between black and white finally ceased at the turn of the last century there was . . . no such thing as the Union of South Africa. But, by then, history had . . . divided the whole of South Africa into white man's country and black man's country—into white and black homelands.'[1] History, it seems, was kind to the white man. At the end of the 'Kaffir Wars' he had been left with 87 per cent of the country's total land, as well as all the known mineral resources and harbours. What remained were some 260 widely scattered reserves, none of them, except the Transkei, with a coastline or the possibility of a port. They contain none of the major industrial or commercial centres, and have existed as overcrowded and underdeveloped areas of subsistence peasant farmers. At any one time, forty per cent of the adult male population are working as migrant labourers in the 'white areas'.

The Transkei is the only reserve of any size, but even it

is divided into three by intervening 'white' land. Mr P. S.
Toerien, a well-known apartheid supporter, gives this description of the Transkei:

> It is by far the largest continuous Bantu homeland
> covering an area of some 4,944,000 morgen*... A rela-
> tively small proportion of the total area, namely 32 per
> cent, is arable, and a large percentage, namely 74 per
> cent, has suffered the ravages of water erosion... There
> is an average density population of about 82 per square
> mile... a comparatively high figure considering the
> almost total absence of an urban population... Soil
> erosion [has] taken its toll of a very large proportion...
> especially in cultivated land; overgrazing has denuded the
> pastures, encouraged the growth of undesirable plants,
> weakened the springs and sponges and adversely affected
> the streamflow of rivers; natural forests and wooded
> glades, which were not protected, have almost disap-
> peared.[1]

There is no intention of consolidating the Bantustans
other than the Transkei into a single geographical unit. 'Dr
Verwoerd said the territory to be administered by the Zululand Territorial Authority was not in one piece... [But
they] would form one State—in the same way as the two
sections of Pakistan form one State—and would be governed
as one State by the Zululand Territorial Authority... Similarly in the Transvaal, the African territories would be governed by one Territorial Authority. Large areas would be
coupled where possible.'[2] Nor is there any intention of
increasing the size of the Bantustans. 'It has been laid down
unequivocally that what has always been white South Africa
will continue to be just that—the political domicilium of the
white nation.'[3] Replying to Chief Kaiser Matanzima's claim
to territory between the Fish River and Zululand, Dr Verwoerd told Parliament: 'The preservation of the existing
historical division ensures the greatest guarantee to the whites
that they will retain control not only between the Fish River
and Zululand but also in the whole Republic, and the same
thing applies to the Bantu as regards their areas.'[4]
There are three minimum prerequisites for a State's

* One morgen equals about two acres.

political viability: it must be sufficiently large or rich to offer the prospect of providing at least a subsistence livelihood for its population; its inhabitants must have sufficient community of interests to operate and benefit from a common political system; and its government must be able to establish effective authority over its subjects and effective central control over the area of its sovereignty.

These last two prerequisites are completely absent in all the seven proposed Bantustans. In all of them, the great majority of the intended subjects of the Bantustan political authority are forced to earn a living either permanently or for the greater part of their lives away from the Bantustans. Many of them have never seen the inside of the reserves and are completely detribalised. Many more seek to escape from tribal authority and rural poverty: they resent authority based on a traditional system, and have shown themselves ready to resist it. Nor is there any way in which the rule of the Bantustans can be extended effectively to the two-thirds of their total subjects who live in the 'white' towns or in the 'white' rural areas. Thus the writ of a Bantustan government will run only so far as its own borders, within which only a minority of its subjects dwell. Under these circumstances, it is hard to see how its legislative and executive institutions can serve the interests of all, or even most, of its citizens.

The South African Institute of Race Relations has pointed out: 'An analysis of the Transkei Constitution Bill makes it quite clear that "self-government" means a limited degree of local autonomy with the emphasis on problems of local concern. There will be no community of interest between those Xhosa living in the Transkei and the larger number living in rural and urban areas outside, who nevertheless will have to pay taxes to the "heartland" government.'[1] The Hon. O. D. Schreiner, a former Judge of Appeal, has said: 'There is clearly no scope for more Bantustans without a major reapportionment of the land, a vast increase in the share to be assigned to Africans, and large allotments to other non-whites. But the government has stated there is to be no increase in the area of the African reserves ... The Transkei is therefore likely to be the only detached part of South Africa to wear the trappings of independent statehood.'[2]

Moreover, since all the intended Bantustans—with the exception of the Transkei—will consist of several non-contiguous land areas, there is not the slightest chance of effective economic planning, let alone of political control. After examining all the potential Bantustans, Professor P. V. Pistorius has concluded that 'except for the Transkei, no further Bantustan is even possible without vast and arbitrary population resettlements, involving whites as well as blacks, and the purchase of large tracts of land ... These conditions are so impossible that they do not even merit argument.'[1] Nor, let it be added, does the government intend trying to fulfil these conditions.*

Thus, on at least two of the three basic prerequisites for political viability, Bantustans must fail; the third necessity, that of economic sufficiency, will be considered presently.

Political Aspirations?

Having established that the Transkei is the only potential Bantustan which covers a large and relatively contiguous area, the experiment there carries the whole burden of proof for the government that Separate Development is a feasible proposition. Since there is not the remotest possibility of successful statehood for the other Bantustans the second of our questions becomes narrower. Could the Transkei satisfy the political aspirations of Africans?

Its present constitution provides for a Legislative Assembly of 109 members of whom forty-five are elected and sixty-four are nominated chiefs, the latter paid by the Republic's government and subject to dismissal by it. The Assembly's legislative competence extends over Transkeian 'citizens' wherever they live (but excludes the whites living in the Transkei). Its powers, however, are limited to taxation, education, agricultural improvement, the lower courts, wills, registration of deeds, public works, the local authorities, traffic,

* On the single point of the sufficiency of land, it is worth quoting the report of a statement by Professor P. J. Schoeman of Stellenbosch, a supporter of apartheid: 'The existing Bantu areas were hopelessly inadequate to carry the Native population of the country. They would have to be enlarged by two-thirds if the Bantu were to survive as a separate people.' *Die Transvaler*, April 13, 1961.

certain labour matters, welfare services, vital statistics, elections, liquor, markets, game preservation and licensing of trading and business. It is precluded from legislating over military forces, the manufacture of arms and ammunition, foreign affairs, the right of entry or the presence of Republican police forces which might be needed for maintaining law and order and the preservation of internal security, post offices, railways and harbours, national roads, civil aviation, the entry of aliens, currency and public loans, customs and excise. Finally, even those laws which lie within its competence are subject to the assent of the President of the Republic.

The government may, of course, claim that what matters is not the present constitution but the ultimate system towards which this is only the first step. Nevertheless, it is relevant to consider what light these initial steps shed on the prospects for future development. The government's reactions to the Transkei's first elections in 1963, when the supporters of Bantustan were roundly defeated by the supporters of multi-racialism, are significant.*

The choice the Transkei leaders themselves put before the electorate was whether they favoured a purely black Bantustan or a multiracial state. But this latter alternative was ruled out from the start by the government. Mr de Wet Nel said in November 1963 that the government would not permit a multi-racial parliament 'because it clashed with the policy of Separate Development'.[1] The Secretary for Bantu Administration, Mr C. B. Young, had warned the Transkei Territorial Authority in 1962 that 'all talk of a multiracial parliament can be disregarded straightaway as a still-born conception'.[2] After the election results, *Die Vaderland*—reflecting the official view —said that whoever was elected Chief Minister 'cannot alter by one iota the constitution which the Transkei representatives† ... have themselves accepted'.[3]

The *Financial Mail* summed up this unusual feature of the election result by saying that if the multiracialist leader, Chief Victor Poto, had been elected Prime Minister 'one would have had the extraordinary situation of a self-governing terri-

---

* These elections are discussed on page 151.

† 'Transkei representatives' refer to the earlier Transkei Territorial Authority composed entirely of the traditional authorities.

tory ruled by a man whose declared aims are apparently in flat contradiction to the whole policy which is the only *raison d'être* for the granting of self-government in the first place'.[1]

On other and more immediate matters, too, the new Assembly's freedom of action is severely limited, not only by its constitution but by the poverty of the Transkei. A former parliamentary representative of the Africans, Mr Donald Molteno, QC, has shown that the powers devolved upon the Transkei Assembly are so wide in relation to the resources available to it as to put it in pawn to the Republic. 'The large measure of devolution contemplated is particularly undesirable in relation to a territory as economically backward and poverty-stricken as the Transkei. Despite wide powers of taxation conferred upon the [four South African] provinces by the South African Act . . . the poorer provinces have become progressively more dependent upon subsidisation by the central government . . . It can be predicted with certainty therefore that the Transkei will either be wholly dependent upon subsidisation by the Republic's government, or be reduced economically to the position of an even more stagnant backwater than it is now.'[2]

Another reason the non-resident Xhosa people of the Transkei have for rejecting Bantustans is that they are based on a return to a tribal past which many have rejected and which others aspire to abandon. The new leaders are modern men with modern aspirations and the capacity to fulfil them. It is clearly absurd to expect men of the calibre and sophistication of Professor Z. K. Matthews, Mr Nelson Mandela and Mr Oliver Tambo—all of them Transkeians by birth—to submit themselves to life in a tribal society. Yet this is what is intended for them. The new Transkei is founded on the Xhosas' 'traditional system of government which consists basically of the hereditary chief and a council of representatives . . . the Bantu Authorities' Act recognised and conferred the force of law on the traditional tribal institutions'.[3]

This approach is elaborately justified in terms of allowing the African 'to develop along his own lines' and in keeping with his own culture. At the same time even those who support Bantustans have come to recognise the need for a radical break with the past for the purpose at least of economic development—without apparently recognising the dilemma this poses for the mystique of 'traditional' political development. This failure to understand, or to accept, the basic conflict between the need for modern economic methods and the fossilisation, or reversal, of political systems is clearly shown in these statements by two prominent white supporters of Bantustans. 'It is a break with tradition which is needed to stimulate development in an underdeveloped community... New ideas and values generated in the [Bantu towns in the Transkei] will permeate the rural population, and in the process change the latter's attitude towards farming.'[1] 'Many of the Bantu traditions which, in fact, constitute their way of life, form very effective barriers to the introduction of a Westernised system of agriculture.... The resettlement of the population poses many problems because it implies a radical change from the indigenous pattern of living and infringes on rights recognised by custom. Resettlement entails the removal of people living in scattered fashion on the commonage into the recognised residential areas, and the reclassification of the members of the community as farmers and non-farmers.'[2]

The imposition of the Bantu Authorities system—a system of tribal traditional authority conceived by whites for blacks—aroused a normally passive peasant population to intensive political opposition. When it was introduced into the Transkei in 1959, it sparked off a minor civil war.[3] In April 1961, the Transkei Territorial Authority adopted a motion calling on the government to arm chiefs, headmen and all other 'recognised' people for their self-defence. Supporting this motion, one headman, Le Fleur Potwana, admitted that chiefs and headmen who were trying to enforce the law were 'very unpopular with the people and likely to be attacked at any time'.[4]

A state of emergency was declared in 1960 in one of the regions—East Pondoland—and the infamous *Proclamation 400*, containing all the important provisions enforced under a state of emergency, was extended to the whole of the Transkei. It remains in force still, and was not lifted even for the elections. It includes provisions for indefinite detention without trial, and a permanent ban on all public meetings for which specific permission has not been given.

The introduction of the present Transkei constitution met with renewed opposition. At every meeting called by Sabata Dalindyebo, Paramount Chief of the Tembu, the draft constitution was rejected. In 1962 when the former Transkei Territorial Authority was discussing the draft constitution prepared by the government, police patrolled the streets outside the place of assembly.[1] Chief Sabata's motion in the TTA that a decision on the constitution be deferred until after discussions with the people, was defeated. Hence, the present Transkei constitution was adopted without the people's having any effective voice in the matter. The elections provided the first opportunity for popular opinion to be formally expressed: two-thirds of the members elected to the new Assembly were opposed to the concept of black Bantustans.

The Verwoerd regime—for all its protestations to the contrary—is under no illusions about the extent of African opposition to Bantustans: but it seeks to blame it on 'hostile forces' ranging from the Liberal Party to Moral Rearmament.* To silence the voice of Liberals, several were banned and restricted over the election period: their vice-president, Mr Hammington Majija—himself a prospective candidate—was put under a ban which, inter alia, prohibited him from attending 'any gathering at which any form of State or any principles or policy of the government of a State is propagated, defended, attacked, criticised or discussed'. No wonder Chief Sabata told a meeting in Johannesburg: 'The freedom you are getting in the Transkei is a fowl run. A cattle kraal would be better.'[2] Summing up the government claims to support for its policies in the reserves, the Cape Times, said: 'Bantustan comes to birth, and a major constitutional change is made, against the background of one of the most curious laws in the modern world [Proclamation 400]. As this law seems designed to prevent the expression of any opposition, it would seem to make

* 'Even the less extreme influence like Moral Rearmament with its doctrine of equality might have a disruptive effect.' Dagbreek, May 19, 1963.

irrelevant Mr Nel's[1] statement that the Bantu in these parts favour Bantustans in general and Proclamation 400 in particular. If political disapproval cannot be expressed, is there much point in claiming political approval?"[2]

A careful examination of the facts in the Transkei must produce a negative response to the second question: can the Transkei satisfy the political aspirations of its 'citizens'? From the start, opposition has been widespread and disruptive. In 1963 alone—'the year of the first Bantustan'—592 Africans were placed under summary arrest in the Transkei under the provisions of Proclamation 400.[3] Opposition springs from the knowledge that Bantustans represent no more than an illusory compensation for the lack of political rights in the Republic itself. The policy can offer no real change in the power position in the country: indeed, in their less cautious moments this is admitted by government supporters. 'Self-government for the Transkei does not derogate from the sovereignty of the South African parliament in the whole country and also not in the Transkei.'[4] Every attempt to introduce similar 'freedom' in the other six reserves marked out for Bantustan status has so far met with failure. Despite government pressures and even threats, not even the minimum co-operation needed for the imposition of a Bantustan has been forthcoming. The Africans themselves refuse to accept that Bantustans can offer them political self-determination.

Future Independence?

To the third question—are the Bantustans intended to become independent of the 'white' State in South Africa—the government's answers are evasive. 'The idea of a Bantustan must be rejected because it is as dangerous, if not more dangerous, than integration. The Bantu, except for a few misguided agitators, also reject it.'[5] This was the view, in 1956, of Mr de Wet Nel, the Minister now engaged in setting up Bantustans. In 1951, Dr Verwoerd responded to a question in the Senate: 'A Senator wants to know whether the series of self-governing areas would be sovereign. The answer is obvious. It stands to reason that white South Africa must remain their guardian. We are spending all the money on

those developments. How could small scattered states arise?
The areas will be economically dependent on the Union. It
stands to reason that when we talk about the Natives' rights of
self-government in those areas we cannot mean by that to cut
large slices out of South Africa and turn them into independent
states.'[1]

Even today the government remains ambivalent. 'Independence' is sometimes mentioned, but 'autonomy' more often.[2]
The reason is clear: the prospect of independent Bantustans
on the borders of the Republic, and in the heart of the country
itself, frightens the electorate, and must therefore be played
down. In the debate on the Transkei Constitution Bill, Mr
de Wet Nel sought to reassure Parliament: 'The government
aims at eliminating racial friction . . . and in this it has the
co-operation of white as well as black. Though people might
cherish the ideal of totally separating the whites and non-
whites I have always believed that total separation was
impossible.'[3] Dr Verwoerd has recently produced the idea of
'a general consultative body—like a Commonwealth body'[4]
on which the Bantustans would eventually be represented
together with the 'white State' for discussions on matters of
common interest. But he was quick to add that matters
affecting 'the Republic as a whole' would continue to be dealt
with by the central parliament as presently constituted. The
South African Information Department is even vaguer: it
says there will be 'several autonomous Bantu nations in
co-operative association with the white nation.[5]

So before the ship of Bantustan is properly launched,
guide-lines are being fixed into position to ensure its proper
control and to diminish its freedom of navigation. There are
proposals even to remove important parts of its structure.
'With a view to South Africa's defences it may in future be
necessary to excise parts of the coast-line of the Transkei.'[6]
Mr de Wet Nel's earlier reference to similar excisions, moved
The Star to comment:

> Mr de Wet Nel was quick to give the assurance in the
> Assembly recently that there was 'no thought' of handing
> over areas like Port St John's, Kosi Bay and Sordwana
> Bay to independent (black) states. On the contrary,

Sordwana Bay was to be developed as an important white harbour, and would be linked to the white area by a white corridor. This is the kind of approach to the policy of Separate Development that must make its genuine supporters despair. If it is to have any validity and provide any solution it must live up to its professions of allowing... the Bantu homelands to develop to the limits of their capacity. They can only do this if they can make use of their natural assets, among the most important of which are obviously the potential harbours. Mr Nel... will have none of this. These attractive bays, embedded in the 'homelands' are valuable and therefore must be white, even if they have to be reached by a corridor through black territory. It is easy to imagine... what would happen if a rich gold mine were discovered in the heart of the Transkeii or Zululand.[1]

Ambiguous statements make it difficult to define the government's real intentions for the ultimate relationship of the Bantustans to the white Republic. But, in one sense, this is the least important of the questions with which we have to deal; for no one, least of all the government, pretends it is possible to grant either autonomy or independence to the Bantustans in the near future. The emphasis is on gradual evolution: 'The government's self-rule plan for the Transkei has a better chance of success than any other policy for the independence of the indigenous races of Africa. An important proviso, however, is that enough time should be granted for the gradual transition to independence.'[2] On this all-important question of time we shall presently see how little is left even by the calculations of the government's own supporters. Finally, 'independence' would, in any event, mean very little if the Bantustans had no possibility of becoming either politically or economically viable.

Economically Viable?

Bantustan supporters admit that 'the success of the policy of Separate Development... depends primarily upon the success of the economic set-up devised... to implement that policy'.[3] This brings us to the fourth and crucial question—can the Bantustans become economically viable units? The problem is vast: of this there is a mass of supporting statistics. The following, taken from the Tomlinson Report[1] are sufficiently telling: the average family in the reserves now receives only £43 yearly, of which £21 derives from the earnings of migrant workers. Thus, with these earnings, the average family income is only about two thirds of the minimum of £60 which the Tomlinson Commission estimated was required to support an average family. It further estimated that to give farmers in the reserves an economic holding, half the population (300,000 families or 1,500,000 people) would have to be moved off the land and provided with alternative means of livelihood. Professor Hobart Houghton of Rhodes University has shown from later studies that the *minimum* number which would have to be moved would be two-thirds of the present population rather than the half originally estimated.[2] Nor does this take into account the attempt to resettle in the reserves those Africans being expelled from the western Cape or from other 'white' areas under the influx control regulations; nor does it make provision for natural increases in the population.

It is not surprising, therefore, that the problem has already been found to be insuperable. There are two broad problems confronting the Bantustan planners: that of the farmers and that of the non-farmers. In a paper read to a SABRA conference, Mr P. S. Toerien reported: 'It has not been possible to adopt the economic farming holding (to produce an annual income of only £60) as a general basis for settlement, even though it formed the basis for planning. Had it been adopted it would immediately have created too large a surplus of non-farmers in every unit . . . *Through force of circumstances, the practice to settle only a token number of farmers on full-size farming holdings, had to be adopted.* It is expected that in the course of time some of the occupiers of half-size holdings will *eliminate themselves* thereby creating the possibility of gradually consolidating the holdings again.'[3] (Author's italics.)

So much for the farmers and their hopes of earning the minimum income necessary to support their families. What of the non-farmers—the 1,500,000 displaced from the land, not counting the millions who are to be displaced from the 'white areas' or the natural expansion of population? On the most optimistic figure for the ratio of capital investment needed per new job created,* it is estimated that £300 million will be needed to provide industrial employment for the 300,000 non-farmers alone. Even assuming that part of this were created internally through the 'multiplication effect' of capital invested, the minimum pump-priming capital involved is not even glimpsed in the proposed government programme of aid to industry in the reserves. The Bantu Investment Corporation has been established to provide capital to aspiring entrepreneurs in the reserves. Its 1963 report discloses that in its first four years of operations, 214 business loans were granted, amounting to a total of £333,000, of which only £144,500 has been actually invested. The Johannesburg *Financial Mail* commented: 'No doubt the BIC is doing a worthy job according to its lights and within its limits. But one can only point out that if this is supposed to hasten materially the day when the reserves can stand up as viable economic entities, capable of supporting their present populations and more besides, the government is merely deceiving itself. And if, in addition, it is supposed to justify depriving would-be African traders of the right to do business in the so-called white areas (which include of course the African townships in the urban areas) on the grounds that the Corporation is there to help them in their homelands, then the authorities are being crudely dishonest.'[1]

According to figures supplied to parliament in May 1962, only 20,592 people were in paid employment in the Transkei; of these 8,000 were in domestic service. The government's plan for remedying this situation takes the form of its Border Industries scheme. The theory is to take 'white' industry to the borders of the reserves so that African workers may live in their 'homelands' and venture daily to work in the nearby industries sited in the 'white' areas. Special inducements are offered to industrialists—including the right to pay lower wages to Africans—to implement what is put forward to them as a plan for decentralising industry. The theory is bad enough, involving as it does *not* the industrialisation of the

* A figure of £1,000 is generally regarded as the minimum needed in labour-intensive industries in underdeveloped countries.

reserves but decentralisation of 'white' industry based on even cheaper black labour. But the practice is even worse. Dr T. J. D. Fair and Dr L. P. Green have pointed out[1] that the areas selected for 'border industries' are those where the reserves already impinge on existing urban areas. Thus the degree of decentralisation is limited, and little or no new employment is created. The sham of the policy has been exposed by Professor P. V. Pistorius:

> We hear of large African towns being built. There is nothing of that in the Transkei since these towns are nothing more than the African townships around our cities to house workers. The only difference is that they are built on tiny reserves near the cities instead of on white territory . . . They are meant for border industries. The main ones are Garankuwa in Pretoria North, Kwa-Mashu near Durban, the one planned for Slangspruit near Pietermaritzburg, and the one in the reserves at the very gates of East London. Such towns have not the slightest bearing on the economic development of the Transkei or of any of the main reserves . . . That is how futile this policy of separate development is. It is definitely not separate, since it compels the Africans to leave their own areas and to come to the cities. Neither is it development, since by the embargos on [white] investment capital [in the reserves] all industrialisation is made impossible . . .[2]

What of the effects on the living standards of Africans who are supposed to benefit from these plans? 'The government is making South Africa a "cheap labour" paradise for industrialists . . . Large numbers of Africans are being settled in new townships close to some of the largest and oldest towns in South Africa. These white towns are being declared "border areas", and their factories will therefore qualify to employ Africans living in the satellite townships across the border—at wage rates far lower than those applicable elsewhere . . . For example, a clothing factory in the Hammersdale border area, between Durban and Pietermaritzburg, is permitted to pay a qualified machinist £4 a week compared with the legal minimum of £5-£7 payable in Durban only 27 miles away.'[3]

Since the government's main preoccupation is with providing housing for African workers for the 'border industries', very little of the capital voted for development is used in the reserves themselves. The announcement in 1962 of a £57 million Five Year Development Plan sounded impressive. But the sober truth is that £38 million is being spent simply on housing workers for this rather disingenuous scheme: it will contribute nothing towards improving the resources inside the reserves, or towards creating new employment opportunities, within the reserves or outside them. Thus two-thirds of the vote becomes a disguised subsidy for industrialists.

The next largest items in the Development Plan are £5 million on fencing, £4.5 million on afforestation, and £3.5 million on irrigation. But even these inadequate sums raise indignant protests from the white electorate who must be continuously reminded that the Africans are not being mollycoddled at their expense. Attempts at conciliating white public opinion have the unexpected result of revealing how much is in fact being spent on development for the 'white' areas by contrast with what is going into the 'black homelands'. 'In this year's Budget, £20 million was voted for all Bantu services. For the development of the white area in the next ten years £593 million will be spent on special undertakings like *Foscor, Sasol, Escom, Iscor,* the Orange River Development Project and the Pongola plan. Expenditure on the other normal developments would bring the total up to £1,250 million for the next ten years.'[1]

Thus our fourth question must also be answered in the negative. The Bantustans are not and cannot become economically viable units under the most optimistic possibilities afforded them by the government's present plans.

Two facts stand out clearly from the government's own statement of intentions about the Bantustans: 1) the experiment is to be confined *for all time* to only 13 per cent of the Republic which now constitute the reserves; 2) these already over-populated areas now hold no more than one-third of the total African populations. Nor is there any longer the intention that all the Africans should be domiciled in the Bantustans. The Minister of Bantu Affairs has declared that 'there will always be millions of Bantu workers in the white areas';[1] on a different occasion he said: 'South Africa's make-up was such that the whites needed the Africans and the Africans needed the whites.'[2]

It is clear, therefore, that what the government is offering the eleven million Africans in full and final settlement of their right to political self-determination is the possibility to control a little over one-eighth of the whole country in which there is room for little more than one-third of the black population; the remainder would be expected to live as alien migrant workers in the seven-eighths of the country reserved for whites. It should be self-evident that on political grounds alone such an offer can never be acceptable to the spirit of African nationalism in South Africa. Dr Verwoerd and his supporters are the first to admit that 'African nationalism is irresistable'. The two conclusions are clearly irreconcilable.

No people can be expected to accept the proposition that their political rights should be confined in states whose economy depends for all time on the export of labour to a neighbouring state. If it is objected that there are countries—especially in Africa—which can never hope to achieve full economic viability, the answer is that Africans in the prosperous Republic cannot be expected voluntarily to accept such a condition; since it would be the result of excising the non-viable parts of a rich country of which they form the overwhelming majority. It is equivalent to compelling the Scots in Britain to accept political rights only in an area north of Loch Ness, comforting them with the assurance that they could seek work, under permit, as unskilled labourers in the rest of Britain, and that, in accepting this fate, they would not be worse off than their fellow-Europeans in Sicily.

There is, therefore, no chance that the Bantustan policy could represent a real alternative to *baasskap* or racial integration. To the degree that it is enforceable, its total effect can only be to reverse two processes fundamental to the expansion of a healthy economy: a rising urban and a declining rural population, and a general rising of living standards. This latest version of apartheid attempts to compel the rural areas to absorb urban unemployed and sustain an already largely urbanised proletariat. This effort runs directly counter to the normal practice of draining rural unemployment into urban opportunities. And by trying to prise the black proletariat away from the traditional 'white' industrial areas, apartheid must inevitably achieve the result of reducing the standards of living for both.

But it cannot alter the present power position in South Africa. The only possible conclusion is that reached by Mr Justice O. D. Schreiner: 'Bantustans are places where votes can safely be exercised by non-whites without influencing the real balance of power in the country The ballot papers in a Bantustan might as effectively be dropped into a well as into a ballot-box, from the point of view of real legal power.'[1]

3: THE MOOD OF THE AFRIKANER

> We ask for a little fairness, a little human understanding from the nations of the world. We know very well that history has moved faster than our solutions. It is our most difficult hour. Those who call themselves our friends should not try to make it more difficult. Our struggle too is a liberation struggle.
>
> DIE BURGER, *March 24, 1960*

REACTIONS TO SHOCK

How do Afrikaners see the future beyond their guns and their plans to achieve racial harmony through Separate Development? Dr Verwoerd gives the impression of a man without doubts. But this is his public image; his own uncertainties are expressed by his closest colleagues. Mr Eric Louw, until recently Minister for External Affairs, warned in 1961: 'The people of South Africa should be under no illusions. The forces against it were growing stronger and stronger.... At present the battleground is the UN, but it may be extended soon.'[2]

The earliest warnings from within Afrikanerdom came, in fact, from Dr Verwoerd's own circle of colleagues connected with his paper, *Die Transvaler*. Their chief spokesman is Dr G. D. Scholtz, the paper's editor. His seminal work[1] raised the question whether the Afrikaners had a future. He was one of the first nationalist Afrikaners to insist publicly that there was no inherent difference in the capacities between whites and blacks—a view held until then only by liberals and 'reds'. In a later work[2] published by the South African Ministry of Information he wrote: 'As a result of all the indifferences and ignorance of the past the race problem has grown to become something casting a dark shadow over the survival of the whites. The men who have made this discovery* are thus far but voices calling in the wilderness. It appears that the overwhelming majority of the whites—even after all the warnings of the past half century—are still not aware of any danger.' In Die Transvaler he follows this line with the furious wrath of the prophets of old. 'We are still a nation of political introverts. It is remarkable how little interest is shown in international affairs. . . . What should be realised, though, is how harshly history deals with a people which has become so isolated that it no longer takes any notice of the prevailing currents in the world and does not have the necessary knowledge about them. Such a people will simply be overwhelmed by the great floodtides.'[3]

It required twelve years of apartheid and the huge African demonstrations which preceded and followed the shootings at Sharpeville in 1960 to produce a shock capable of arousing the whites to a realisation of the dangers building up. They were staggered by the unanimity of the world's reaction to Sharpeville. As hostility at the UN rose to the point where, in December 1963, South Africa stood alone in the face of the world's unanimous condemnation of its policies, they reacted with dazed incomprehension or truculent self-justification.

Meanwhile, there had been three other developments which helped to underscore the warnings of Dr Scholtz and of those who thought like him. An underground movement of violence and sabotage was begun in 1961. The Poqo† terrorist movement erupted in the killings of whites in 1962. The summit conference of African Heads of State decided at Addis

* An allusion to the Verwoerd-Scholtz circle, and to SABRA leaders.
† See page 179.

Ababa early in 1963 to mobilise African and world opinion to compel the isolation of South Africa, and to support the 'liberation struggle'.

The shock produced by the combined impact of Sharpeville and international hostility had a positive and a negative aspect. The positive was the first recognition by the leaders of Afrikanerdom that *baasskap* as they knew it was no longer feasible, and that not only personal but also political relations between the races must be changed. Dr Verwoerd called for 'a new constitutional partnership'. The negative aspect was the stampede, on the part of the electorate, into the military strength of the laager.* Thus the shock cracked Afrikanerdom down the middle, with the leadership recognising the need for radical change and the electorate clinging to its guns. Not surprisingly, it produced division and confusion in individuals as well: the same person will alternately urge military action and radical reappraisal, each as *the only way* to defend the white man's heritage.

South Africans use one of two images to convey their situation: that of the Voortrekkers on the eve of Blood River in 1838 as they confronted the black hordes of Dingaan; and that of a nation driven with its back to the wall by a hostile world, and with no possibility of surrender. These two images embody their fears of both internal and external enemies. 'The spirit of Dingaan to expel the white man with his civilisation from Southern Africa was growing in certain quarters', President Swart warned on the Day of the Convenant in 1962.[1] 'More urgently than ever before, South Africa called its people to stand together and fend off the dangers.' And the fear of the external enemy: 'The unadorned fact is that the world is driving South Africa with apartheid into a corner where the matter will have to be fought out, back against the wall—that is, unless the present government abdicates in the name of the white man'—which, by implication, is unthinkable.

* This is discussed on page 143.

THE SENSE OF URGENCY

For many years the whites have been subjected to a barrage of warnings about the imminence of the dangers they face. Reviewing the overseas front, *Die Burger* noted it was 'already past midnight'; it added that racial policies must keep pace with history. 'If we should fail in our internal policy, or fail to attempt such a policy, we will have to look forward to the permanent status of being the world's skunk,* with all the political and economic implications of such a situation.'[1]   In 1960 Dr Geyer had spoken of a decade of decision.   In 1961 this time margin was halved by the Minister for Economic Development, Dr N. J. Diederichs: 'It may be that the future of our people will be decided in the next five years.'[2]

Die Burger agreed: 'For us, time has shrunk tremendously.   What we wanted to do in fifty years we may have to settle in ten or five years.'[3]   A month later it lamented: 'The whole framework of ideas and conduct within which we could continue to exist lies in ruins around us.   Therefore the storms are howling around us, and therefore the new forces of non-white nationalism unleashed by the European abdication [in Africa] are concentrating on South Africa.'[4]   The country's internal problems, warned *Die Transvaler,* had been affected by the shrinking of distance in the modern world.   'It behoves every citizen to think deeply over this question [race relations] in the light of the disappearance of distance and the extreme sensitiveness that prevails in the world today about the race question, and to consider whether it were still possible to maintain the existing position.   If that were done, the answer could only be that it was impossible and therefore there must be separation between white and non-white.'[5]   Another editorial soberly stated that 'our hope lies only in the successful solution of our race problems, for even if the UN were to destroy itself our problems would not disappear.'[6]

A few months later it grimly commented that it was impossible to check 'the Revolution of the Twentieth Century, of which one of the most important elements was 'equalisation'. Anybody who tried to do so would be 'smashed'.   The answer was 'to create conditions under which the revolution would not

* Sometimes translated as pole-cat.

affect the Republic in its full fierceness, viz., separation of the races'.[1]

Thus there is no lack of realistic diagnosis in what the Afrikaners have heard from their leaders or read in their papers since 1960. Nor, however, is there any dissension about the prescription: push ahead as fast as possible with Separate Development. But in the meantime? Here the single voice has two tones: one laying more stress on guns; the other on single-minded implementation of ideological plans.

THE DOUBLE VOICE

In all this uncertainty, the predictable has happened: those who call for 'strong arm' methods have obtained a much larger following than those who try to teach sacrifice for the sake of their ideology. The effect has been to create a war psychosis, deepened by the warlike preparations and by 'blood and death' speeches regularly made by leading politicians. 'When fighting is necessary we will not hesitate. A time comes in a people's history when not only reason must speak, but also its blood. That time has now dawned.'[2] We will fight till the blood rises to the horses' bit—but I can tell them [the African leaders] that the blood won't be on the bits of our horses only.'[3] Addressing 3,000 schoolchildren the Minister of Transport, Mr Ben Schoeman warned: 'You are the coming generation which will have to defend South Africa, and you must be prepared to suffer everything—even your lives.'[4] Women, especially, have been gripped by this psychosis. At the conference of the National Party in 1963 a resolution was adopted in favour of their being given military training. 'Like the Voortrekker women of old we will stand shoulder to shoulder with our men,' a woman delegate said amidst great applause.[5] Ministers' wives are among the leaders of the women's shooting clubs. 'I can shoot moving targets easily— but don't give me standing targets,' boasts the wife of the Minister of Bantu Affairs and Development.[6]

Although Sharpeville had receded sufficiently for the Minister of Finance to say in the Senate in 1963 that it had been 'an ordinary police action which occurs daily in other parts of the world',[7] the repercussions of world opinion had, by then, begun to influence Afrikaner thinking. 'We are moving

toward dangerous abysses in our historical development,' said
the sober-minded paper, *Die Vaderland*:[1]

> World conditions are such that these [race] relations can-
> not be maintained for much longer if the Republic is to
> continue to exist in its present form. For that reason a
> change has become necessary. The political leaders have
> been aware of this fact for a long time but the question
> can be asked whether all whites also realise it.[2]

Two months later *Die Transvaler* returned to this theme.

> In so far as it is at present possible to look into the
> future, the whites here will only be able to survive if they
> are able in their own way to establish a new principle on
> which they can ensure their survival.... It was tragic
> that so many whites were ignorant of this cardinal fact.[3]

The Minister of Defence summed up the mood of 1963:
'South Africa is going through a difficult time when there was
confusion in people's thoughts. At one moment they were
full of courage; at the next they wondered "Can we?" People
said "I will live". At the same time they asked: "Can I?"'[4]
Mr Justice J. H. Snyman, who had inquired into the *Poqo*
movement, came to this conclusion: 'Inter-racial relationships
in this country must be put on a proper footing. There must
be a change in our attitude to the Bantu, and unless there is a
change, this country is doomed.'[5]

How do these years look to Dr Verwoerd? 'In a way
these five years (1958–1963) can be seen as the beginning of
our golden age. When one takes a look at world history one
realises that the golden ages of nations were never the easiest.
During the past five years we likewise experienced difficulties,
but have now reached the stage where we are riding on the
crest of a growing wave of prosperity.'[6]

HOW TO MAKE FRIENDS OR ENEMIES

> A white skin is no guarantee of continued leadership,
> but the attitude of the whites towards the non-whites
> will determine the future of the whites.
> *Mr W. A. Maree, Minister of Bantu Education and*
> *Indian Affairs, December 17, 1962*

Afrikanerdom today finds itself on the horns of an apparently
intractable dilemma. One horn is its leaders' acknowledge-

ment that total *baasskap* is impossible, and that black nationalism cannot be resisted. The other is its refusal to abandon the
hope of an exclusively white society. Separate Development
seems the only hope. It is admitted that this needs African
consent. 'The Government's Bantu policy can only succeed if
the co-operation of enough Bantu is obtained, and the key
point here is the Bantu in our cities and large towns.'[1] 'Every
white man should regard it as a moral obligation to contribute
towards better race relations by his or her personal conduct.
Only when that happens can there be any hope of securing the
white race.'[2] 'To ensure the future of the whites in this
country it is necessary to gain non-white friendship; by respect-
ing the non-white the white man would be increasing his own
dignity.'[3]

To achieve African goodwill, the leaders urge whites to
stop treating blacks as inferiors or as enemies. 'We must get
away from the wrong idea entertained by some people that
the non-whites are our enemies.'[4] 'We must not see an enemy
in every non-white.'[5] 'The spirit in the country must be set
right.... Any hatred there might still be against non-whites in
the hearts of whites must be eradicated. We must learn to
love and respect them.'[6]

The starting-point is to educate whites away from their
traditional racial prejudices towards better personal relationships. 'The Bantu are human beings like the rest of us, with
their capacity for emotions as deep as ours.'[7] 'White South
Africans must treat non-whites openly and fearlessly as equals
whenever merited. It has been done in the past and would be
inevitable in the future.'[8] 'There are still too many whites
who look upon the Bantu as "kaffirs who must be kept in their
place".... How do we treat our servants? Do we look upon
them as human beings with a soul and a body or as mere tools
—black muscles to be had to do the work we require of
them?'[9] 'There was nothing that could make a satisfactory
adaptation impossible if the spirit was right. And in many
quarters the spirit is not right. To tell the truth, the spirit is
in many places so wrong that there is need for a national campaign for good manners between the races.'[10]

At the same time it is realised that mere good manners
are not enough. 'We will be making a great mistake if we

assume that the problem and the task are merely a question of
the relationship between individuals. Good relationships between individuals cannot be disassociated from relationships
between communities.... The improvement of group relationships is a task which lies in the political sphere.'[1]

But here the dilemma leads to further difficulties: how
can Afrikaners be re-educated into treating the Africans as
friends when the country is arming to defend itself from
attacks by Africans? It makes for confusion. 'When relations between groups are strained, the question is not asked:
"How can we make friends of these people", but rather "how
can we best fight them?" '[2] 'It was wrong to say, as so many
whites did, that the salvation of the white man lay only in
military power. The army and police force were necessary
for defence and for the maintenance of law and order, but
could not be the basis of white preservation.'[3] 'Improved
race relations would be an even more effective deterrent than
the strengthening of our army. In the new era therefore our
race policy has also acquired a very practical military aspect,
which gives urgency and dramatic significance to what we are
doing or not doing in that sphere.'[4]

THE SENSE OF LOSING POWER

The leaders of Afrikanerdom understand that a decisive change
in political power is taking place in South Africa at the
moment when power is changing in the rest of the continent.
'Only a man totally blind to realities could expect that the
whites, who have become such a small minority, would still be
able to retain the political power in the changed circumstances.
... The race problem has grown to what it is today because of
the ignorance and selfishness of past generations.... To continue along the old paths is to consign the white race within a
generation or two to its ruin.'[5]

> White authority in Africa, with the exception of the
> Republic, had either disappeared or was on the way out.
> And to what extent South Africa would remain the
> exception was by no means certain any more.... Only a
> fool would imagine that it will necessarily remain inviol-
> able, and that relations of South Africa's white population
> on the one hand and our own non-whites and those else-

where in Africa could always be determined by the white man on the strength of his authority and power. That is why the policy of Separate Development has come into existence. On the one hand, we do not believe that the white man will always be able to keep the political power in his hands if we pursue the road of a multiracial society with a developed black majority. On the other hand, we believe just as little that a white minority, without possessing the political authority and therefore the power of governmental control, will remain proof against discrimination and repression by a black majority.[1]

While, therefore, it is now accepted by the leaders that it is impossible to maintain *baasskap* over the whole country, Afrikanerdom is as determined as ever to keep a large part of the Republic white. 'We reject an integration partnership because our white nation desires to remain free from black domination, and we reject permanent white *baasskap* because we recognise the Bantu's basic right to freedom.... We find it difficult to see how we, even were it in our power, would want to maintain elsewhere a colonialist order of more or less permanent *baasskap* which we consider neither moral nor practical, in South Africa. Assuredly, we cannot help others to defend what we reject for ourselves.'[2] A government spokesman described the same idea in this way: 'We believe in the *baasskap* of the white in the areas that are traditionally his, but we must also be prepared to acknowledge the *baasskap* of the Bantu in areas that traditionally belong to him. That is the only valid interpretation of the concept [of *baasskap*].'[3] These attitudes reflect the views of Dr Verwoerd himself. 'With developments in the world and in Africa, the whites must realise that eventually they could only set themselves the aim of ruling *their* territory. They could not say that they would always remain the rulers of other groups.'[4]

There are influential voices today which even question whether Afrikanerdom can maintain its mastery over the whole of the presently designated 'white areas'. The Minister of Finance, Dr T. E. Dönges, has said: 'We prefer a smaller South Africa with the political power in the hands of the white man than a bigger South Africa with the political power in the hands of the black man.'[5] Dr A. L. Geyer, chairman of

SABRA, was even more specific: 'It must be accepted that the area of white South Africa would eventually be considerably smaller than was now comprised within the border of the Republic.'[1] And this from a man Dr Verwoerd chose to guide SABRA!

THE GREAT GULF

> Whatever the voter's problem today, one fact will have to be driven home to him, and that is that *baasskap* is as extinct in the modern world as the quagga.
> DIE BURGER, *August 28, 1962*

A gulf has opened up within Afrikaner leadership, and between the leadership and the mass of its supporters. The leadership—more especially that provided by the intellectuals, the Church and the Broederbond—is no longer under any illusion about the rapidity with which they need to move towards the fulfilment of Separate Development if it is to have any hope of achieving the results they expect from it. But Afrikaner electors refuse to accept the financial burdens and the additional land concessions which will be necessary to accomplish what the intellectuals have in mind. They still view the programme of Separate Development either as propaganda to conciliate the outside world and African opinion, or as a plan that can be carried out over a long period of time. This attitude gives rise to serious doubts in the minds of the leaders: 'Is public opinion ripe for political separation with all that it implies, at a tempo that will ensure that the Separate Development movements will remain in the lead? Or will other developments overtake South Africa while we are still wrestling fruitlessly with thinking in terms of a past that is long done with? These are questions that we cannot avoid facing.'[2]

A survey of Afrikaner attitudes on the *platteland*, undertaken by a well-known journalist, Jan Burger, in 1961,[3] shows the anxieties and confusions that exist. 'God led us through Blood River. He will do the same in another Blood River', was the philosophy of one farmer. He went on to say: 'I am taking my wife and daughter to the pan near our farm once or twice a week to teach them to shoot straight. If the kaffirs do not want to behave themselves after all we have done for them, they must be made to feel it. They are making a big mistake if they think they are going to start a Congo or an Angola here.' At Pienaarsriver, a hamlet of about a hundred whites, Mrs Maria Harding said that she read a number of Afrikaans magazines but whenever she saw an article on Africa 'and the revolution going on there', she simply skipped it. 'My husband feels that I should not read such things. Whenever I ask him what the situation is like with the blacks, he glosses over it.' The butcher's wife at Warmbaths confessed: 'When they had the trouble at Warmbaths* I packed a pistol under my pillow every night. I am worried about what is going to happen to my grandchildren [sic]. I never thought anything would be upside down so soon in Africa.' Jan Burger's survey led him to two conclusions. First: there was little 'rethinking' going on among the Afrikaner voters; local leaders confided 'that they were greatly disturbed by the hardening in attitudes among the farmers in their area'. Second: 'I doubt very much whether Dr Verwoerd, even if he wanted to steer a new course, would be allowed to do so by his *platteland†* followers. All these Defence Force preparations... suit the attitude of the *plattelanders*. They see in them a silent hint that the Government may have come round to their approach—the strong arm approach.'

Verwoerd's policy has produced two types of rebellion among his supporters. On the one hand, many intellectuals have resigned from the Party over the failure to adopt a sufficiently practical approach to Separate Development. On the other hand are those who feel the government has become 'too liberal' in its attitudes to Africans and who are frightened of Bantustans. 'The government's policy is a danger to white survival', is the view of a former Nationalist Senator, Hennie Smit, the chairman of a new 'Save South Africa Organisation'. Its vice-chairman, Dr S. Swanepoel, a former Nationalist MP, says: 'In the classic right-left classification, I regard the Verwoerd Government as lying to the left of the Liberal Party. On the left of the Verwoerdists lie the Communists.[1]

Neither of these rebellions has seriously embarrassed the Verwoerd Government. Their real significance lies within

---

* Demonstrations by Africans in the local township.
† *Platteland*: the rural areas.

Afrikanderdom. The division between those who seek a basis for co-operation with Africans, and those who see no alternative but to 'rule by the gun' is bound to grow sharper as the struggle deepens. Meanwhile, the leadership itself is engaged in trying to get its own supporters to understand why more needs to be done for Africans to win their co-operation. 'Everything we are doing for the non-whites we are doing for our eventual self-preservation', Dr Verwoerd has said in reply to his critics. 'We are buying our safety with it. Much more, for example, is being spent on white than on Bantu housing.' The chairman of the Natal National Party went further: 'Every bit of ground, every housing scheme and every facility given to the black man is not given merely out of love for the non-white but out of love for the white man whom we want to preserve.'[1]

The leadership, however, is far from sanguine about its efforts to re-educate the electorate. *Die Transvaler* wrote at the end of 1962 that 'it was a tragedy that there were still so many whites who had not the vaguest idea of the change in Africa and who did not realise the need for adaptation. The Bantu simply would have to receive that degree of freedom which their development enabled them to enjoy, and this meant separation. Were the whites prepared for this degree of adaptation or did they place their economic interests higher than their survival as a people?'[2] And Mr Willem van Heerden drove this point home more strongly: 'Now the words "we will sacrifice what you ask"[3] are beginning to acquire practical definition. Money and support for Bantu homelands and defence are among the necessary sacrifices asked for—it sounds different from the "sacrifices" which are flung about so liberally in public speeches without the audience knowing what it means or what it will bring.'[4]

THE SENSE OF ISOLATION

> The wind of change is blowing very cold for South
> Africa. . . . Probably not one of the nations stands so
> isolated in the coldest and loneliest corner as we. . . .
> *Mr D. C. de Villiers, editor of* DIE HUISGENOOT,
> *October–November 1960*

Gnawing away in the Afrikaners' minds is the constant fear
that the West might one day abandon its equivocal support for
the Republic, and that this would bring about their complete
isolation. Their reactions to isolation vary considerably: at
one extreme is an almost masochistic pleasure in the romantic
idea of a small, proud nation embattled for survival against a
greedy hostile world; at the other extreme is the realistic
apprehension of those who know what lies in store for a tiny
group which defies not only the majority at home but world
opinion as well. The romantic, masochistic mood has two
hero-images: the Voortrekkers who in their day withstood
both the Africans and the British; and Israel, which they mis-
takenly see as standing alone in a hostile Arab world.*

'We stand alone', said Dr Albert Hertzog, the Minister of
Posts and Telegraphs, after the Sharpeville shootings in 1960.
'The world is against us. But we have stood alone before—
belied, slandered and spied upon. Courage and strength
carried us through in the time of the Voortrekkers, and they
will do so again.'¹ Israel's example is extolled by the Defence
Minister, Mr Fouché: 'They stand alone in the world, but they
are full of courage.'² *Die Burger* draws a similar analogy:
'We in South Africa would be foolish if we did not at least
take account of the possibility that we are destined to become
a sort of Israel in a preponderantly hostile Africa, and that fact
might become part of our national way of life . . .'³

In 1962,⁴ SABRA declared: 'Indigenous white South
Africa does not want to, and dare not become, an Israel in a
hostile Arab world. . . .' The official government line is to

---

* Those who draw this analogy between South Africa and Israel over-
look three crucial differences: that Israel has many friends both in the
West and in the Afro-Asian world; that its own Arab population is a comparatively small minority and not actively subversive; and that Israel's
moral right to exist in its present state is not challenged except by its
implacable Arab enemies.

deprecate talk of the Republic's being in danger of isolation.
The lengths to which they go to disprove this threat is shown
in this report of a speech of the Prime Minister's. 'Dr Verwoerd said it was untrue to say South Africa was completely
isolated internationally. She was *universally* attacked on her
race policies because the great powers were committed to
multi-racialism as part of their struggle against communism.
But South Africa's relations with the great powers over *other
matters* remained excellent.'[1] (Authors' italics.) On the very
next day, however, he was reported as saying: 'Even if we
are accused of isolating ourselves, it is our first duty to look
after our own interests and ensure our survival because that
way we can perhaps be able to provide the world with a
remedy for its own sickness.'[2] This same uncertainty is
shown in the editorials of the pro-government papers. 'Our
policy has not failed just because it has been rejected in certain
circles', *Die Transvaler* wrote.[3] 'We haven't been ship-
wrecked on an island. The world ideological current is indeed
flowing strongly against us, but we still have many friends.'
Yet only three months before it said: 'If South Africa has to
be isolated ... as a result of her race policies, then her strength
lies in her isolation.'[4]

ATTITUDES TO THE WEST

Afrikaner anxiety about the effects of losing Western support
altogether makes for frantic ambivalence. Sometimes they
heap insults on the West. 'I say the world is sick. I say that
the West particularly is sick.'[5] 'It sometimes appears as if this
decline of the West can no longer be halted. The proud white
race which dominated the world for so many centuries and
which bent others to its will, today confronts its former subordinates as if it were on its knees, and pleads with them, only
to be told what it should do to carry out their wishes immediately. Never before has the West found itself in a more
deplorable situation.'[6] 'Every day we see how the West is
degrading itself and, through loss of faith in itself, is renoun-
cing those nearest to it for an illusion of temporary advantage.'[7]

Often it is the same leaders or papers who argue most
persuasively for the need to maintain good relations with the
West. 'Nothing has happened to diminish the estrangement

which has developed between us and our European and American blood and culture relations. This gap which has come between us and our Western background must again be bridged, if only because we as a Western nation will not be able to survive in Africa without leaning against that background.'[1]

Their hopes rest almost entirely on the premise that the Republic is essential to Western interests. 'In Western strategy Africa's southern end occupies an increasingly important place; and in diplomacy and politics, survival and one's own interests are of the utmost importance.'[2] 'We can ride out the storm in the knowledge that it is the solid core of Western interests, threatened by all this recklessness, which we are maintaining and strengthening.'[3]

Although the Afrikaner leadership had misgivings about Western support after Mr Harold Macmillan's 'wind of change' speech in Capetown in 1960, they continued to believe that if the worst came to the worst, the West would act as a buttress between themselves and a coalition of the Afro-Asian world and the communist states. But the unanimous vote in the UN in December 1963 began to shake their confidence. They go on hoping, but they are no longer so sure.

ATTITUDES TO AFRICA

Attitudes to the independent states swing similarly between expressions of sober realism and angry denunciation. After commenting that the average South African knows little of the continent he is living in, *Die Burger* added: 'We South Africans are in Africa and of Africa. We shall have to work out our salvation in peace and friendship with the new States which have already become such an influential group in the various world bodies.'[4] Just over a year later it commented that happenings in Africa showed that the idea of giving human rights and human dignity to the new black African states through the granting of political freedom was naïve.[5] In its official policy statement in 1963 SABRA took the view that:

> White South Africa will have to prepare itself for, and adjust itself to, this unprecedented new situation (of independence in Africa). On the one hand the black peoples

of Africa will, in the interests of all, have to accept the white South African nation as a permanent part of the population structure of Africa. On the other hand, the whites of South Africa will have to accept that their destiny is most closely interwoven with the rest of Africa south of the Sahara, and with its inhabitants, and that for all time they will have to live and co-operate with the other independent peoples of our continent.[1]

Dr Verwoerd has consistently upheld the view that co-operation is essential, and has offered to meet with heads of African states provided they did not expect him 'to abandon policies for the survival of the nation'.[2] But Dr Verwoerd has also referred to the leaders of the African states as 'ducktails' (teddy-boys). His Commissioner-General for the Transkei, Mr Hans Abraham, took up this cue: 'The black states of Africa, still living under the intoxication of an independence beyond their understanding, had become the leaders of world opinion, and the spirit of the jungle ruled the council halls of the peoples.'[3]

Statements by government spokesmen usually follow the theme that the African states will soon start warring with each other, they will collapse into economic chaos, they will become footholds for the communists, and the West will lose patience with them. In that moment of sanity South Africa will again be seen to be the only 'stable friend the West has in Africa.'[4]

But whatever their feelings concerning the black States, few of the leaders make the mistake of under-rating the importance of what is happening in the continent. 'The forces gathering against us in Africa are not of an ephemeral nature. If things go on as they are doing, we should very certainly be forced into permanent and total preparedness such as that in which some other controversial states and areas have to live today.'[5] Another pro-government paper commented:

Whatever differences and disputes there might be between the various states, there was the greatest unanimity on one particular matter. And that is that the slightest trace of white authority must disappear from Africa.... How soon an attack will come on the position of whites in the southern end of Africa one does not know. What one does know is that for these whites there is not the slightest reason to remain in ignorance about the conditions in the rest of Africa. That, however, is precisely the position in which many whites today find themselves. Their ignorance results in their having a false sense of security and in their not worrying in the least about what is happening north of the Limpopo.... He who today thinks of maintaining the white race and its civilisation in the Republic must bring the whole of the African continent within his range of vision.[1]

ATTITUDES TO THE UNITED NATIONS

The embodiment of Afrikanerdom's enemies is the United Nations. They see it as an organisation completely dominated by the Afro-Asians and the communist bloc. On the anvil of the UN, the West is seen to be at its most vulnerable, submitting under the hammerblows of the majority to all manner of humiliating defeats. The continued existence of the UN is therefore regarded as the direst threat to the future of the Republic and the West. Every time the UN meets to discuss apartheid in South Africa or South West Africa, anxiety rises in the Republic: on the surface there is irritation and anger; but there is always a strong underflow of concern. Paradoxically, the ardent wish is not to be expelled from the UN: such an act, the government knows, would signal the moment of the Republic's complete isolation. Although Dr Verwoerd shows his concern over this possibility, it does not stop him taunting both the UN and its Afro-Asian members: 'It may be regrettable that the UN no longer embodies the hopes of mankind. Everyone must face the fact, however, that since young duck-tailish nations practically took charge, by determining the majority vote, the UN commands little respect. It is now a platform for their display of juvenile aggressiveness and their inferiority complexes.'[2]

Superficially, there is little sign of understanding of the reasons why the Republic comes under such continuous and universal attack. 'By now, every delegate at the UN outside of the Afro-Asians and the communist blocs must be completely fed-up with the inexhaustible obsession with the question of South Africa.'[3] 'What makes the United Nations so tiresome is that it is such a unanimous chorus of doom. From Accra to Washington, from Washington to Moscow, from Moscow to London and from London to Delhi, there is only one refrain and one note: Apartheid is a curse and a distress and has to be wiped off the face of the earth.'[1]

However, it would be a grave mistake to suppose that what happens at the UN has no effect on Afrikaner thinking. Elsewhere we shall deal in detail with the effect of UN influence on South African opinion. Meanwhile these two statements serve to show that Afrikanerdom is much less sure of itself than its public attitudes might lead one to suppose. After the 1962 UN session, Mr Willem van Heerden wrote: 'For South Africa it was necessary to get the West to preserve it as a Western nation and for Africa to accept it as an African nation. The debate and the voting at the UN indicates that we have made no visible progress.... The reconciliation of background and aim necessary to make us acceptable to both sides is lacking. And for that white South Africa is undoubtedly as much to blame as any other element and circumstance. The sooner we realise it and stop blaming others only for our difficulties, the sooner shall we be able to plant our feet towards the ideal projected by Mr Eric Louw'[2] (i.e., that South Africa would become the ideological link between white Europe and Black Africa'). Writing of the same debate, *Die Transvaler* warned: 'The UN has tightened its pressure on South Africa to the breaking point. In the process something must break, and it would be advisable for South Africa not to view the situation with absolute indifference.'[3]

THE DIVIDED MIND

It would be superhuman if we did not experience moments of surging rage, alternated with moments of dejection, even of a cringing feeling of impotence, in the face of the apparent world-wide venom against our race policy.... But truth will overcome lies.... We dare not yield to the temptation to abandon our high fortress of calm purposefulness and descend into the mud of our slanderers. Nor dare we disturb our friendship, patience and sincerity towards the black man in our midst by the brutality and barbarity rampant in black states.

DIE VADERLAND, *July 13, 1963*

South Africa is today the horror and scandal of the
whole civilised world. We are condemned and without a single exception by all the nations. We are what
Die Burger has called the stinking polecat of the West,
loathed and denounced by every member of that civilisation we are supposed to be defending. Yet we are
already smugly establishing the myth that 1,000 million
people are wrong, and that we are right. They do not
'understand' us. We can ignore them. Thus does the
schizophrenic nod, grin, grimace, blow upon his fingers
or test with his thumb the point of the dagger which,
later, when his frenzy seizes him, he will run into
himself or his nearest victim.

CAPE ARGUS, *April 8, 1960*

Afrikanerdom has reached the dreaded moment in the life of
a nation when it begins to realise that power is slipping from
its fingers. Fearful of the future, it clings desperately to the
greater certainties of the past. It creates hero-images to stem
its draining courage. It seeks desperately after scapegoats to
explain its own failures. It whips up patriotism to still
doubts. It goes in search of new allies: thus the exclusiveness of Afrikanerdom is enlarged to make room for English-
speaking South Africans as well as foreign imigrants—both
enemies of the past. It alternately chastises and beseeches its
former friends. Feeling the foundations crumbling underfoot,
it endows its leaders with qualities of granite. It utters shrill
warnings of the disasters that lie ahead, and in the very next
breath it indignantly denies that there is anything seriously
amiss. Its years of gathering darkness are cloaked in the
garments of a Golden Age.

The problem now facing Afrikanerdom is how to achieve
the ideals it holds for itself in a situation which robs them of
all reality. An individual whose ego-ideal conflicts totally
with reality becomes a schizoid personality: the divided self.
To nurture his ideal he must deny reality: the harsh facts of
the world must be bent to allow him to indulge his dreams.
That is the final state of schizophrenia. But before the point
of irretrievable psychosis is reached, there is a stage in which
the mind moves rapidly from one state to another: at one
moment it recognises reality; at the next, when the picture
becomes too painful, it blots it out and lapses into unreality.

Afrikanerdom has reached this pre-psychotic state. Its leaders are capable—as we have seen—of displaying a remarkable sense of realism; but they are equally capable of deluding themselves utterly. This duality makes it hard to draw a clear-cut picture of the current mood of the Afrikaners.

Afrikanerdom has entered a friendless twilight; sick with torments of doubts; tortured by anxieties of being betrayed by its friends; lacerated by the unfairness of being the victims of a history which sowed the seeds of the whirlwind which threatens to uproot it. And in its own sickness, its leader releases the nation's tensions by projecting these anxieties on the outside world. 'I say the world is sick . . . I say that the West particularly is sick . . . South Africa's duty is not to be drawn into this sickbed.'[1] The contradictions can best be shown by juxtaposing the two moods—the realistic and the unrealistic.

In a groping frustrated world, the speech of the State President . . . is a model of positivism, a clarion call to our allies and enemies alike from a free nation which knows what it wants, and which offers a more peaceful and happier pattern of society and coexistence than any other country, large or small, in this world-shaking era of the 1960s.

DIE VADERLAND[2]

Inter-racial relationships in this country must be put on a proper footing. There must be a change in our attitude to the Bantu; unless there is a change, this country is doomed. . . . We must not only change our attitude but we must also find a policy acceptable to the black man or find a way to make them acceptable to him. These attitudes must be broken down in less than 300 days.

Mr. Justice J. H. Snyman[3]

*   *

To direct attention away from what they are doing in Africa, the Western nations are using South Africa as a handy scapegoat. This is why South Africa is meeting with so much enmity from those with whom in the past we have co-operated.

Dr Verwoerd[4]

We refuse deliberately to take cognisance of our own weaknesses, and then we blame others. We sit under an umbrella and shield ourselves from the colour question, the enmity of the black States, the United Nations and liberalism. Now we want to spread the shadow of the umbrella still wider by blaming our short-comings on communism.

Caspar Greyling, National Party MP[1]

*   *

South Africa is making progress in the international sphere and the nations of the world are getting to understand its problems better. Proof of this are the thousands of letters received from all over the world.

Dr Verwoerd[2]

The Minister of External Affairs, Eric H. Louw, conceded that it would be difficult to find a world leader well disposed towards South Africa.... Not long ago Mr Louw admitted to parliament that he had been unable in fifteen years to convert a single country to a sympathetic view of South Africa's policy of apartheid.

New York Times report[3]

*   *

In both old and new countries, the picture is one of conflict between nation and nation, group and group, person and person. The picture is better and happier in South Africa. There is a government which has been in power for fourteen years and is still growing in strength. There is stability and security, and the expectation that the government will remain in power for a long time to come. The government here achieves this support because its policy is based on principles and there is no doubt about its course.

Dr Verwoerd[4]

The storm might now have blown over but it is inconceivable that it will go on blowing over if we go on having trouble with the rest of the world in the way trouble has piled up year after year since 1945. No one could suffer from the illusion that South Africa would be able to go into laager and continue living for generations in a hostile Africa, and maintain itself inside and outside by force without a real solution ever being found for this problem of maladjustment.

Mr Willem van Heerden[1]

II

ENGLISH-SPEAKING SOUTH AFRICA

I should diagnose the English South African's reluctance to co-operate [with Afrikaners] as follows. He
has plenty of colour prejudice, and fears and suspicions.
These, however, run counter to his political and moral
traditions. The Englishman has never had much faith
in racial theories. How can he? His is the classic
example of the bastard race. His conscience is
genuinely worried about apartheid, and—perhaps more
important—his empirical horse-sense tells him it simply
won't work. He may in a moment of panic submit to
his prejudices and get into a white laager, but he'll be
no more happy there than anyone else.

Professor Guy Butler, 1961

*   *   *

1: SOCIETY, ATTITUDES AND POLITICS

About one millon white South Africans are of British descent.
They form 38 per cent of the total white population, but only
36 of the 160 members of the present parliament are English-
speaking. Almost exclusively townsmen, they predominate
in Natal and in the Eastern Cape Province; their largest concentration is in the Cape peninsula and on the Witwatersrand.
They still dominate the world of business, industry and mining,
as well as the liberal professions. The English-speaking
workers are principally higher grade artisans or technicians,
or else white-collar workers. As a group they form the
upper layer of the white aristocracy: an elite of the privileged.
    Leading very rich or comfortably middle-class lives,
English-speaking South Africans lack the stimulus that gave
the Afrikaners their fierce political passion: their enthusiasm
is for financial success, material comforts and sport—
especially golf. In the days of the old Unionist Party and the

South African Party (1910–1933), the English-speaking group was actively engaged in politics and in the trade unions, contesting the Afrikaner at every point; but with the coming together of the South African Party and the Nationalist Party to form the United Party coalition government in 1933, their interest in politics declined.   A jingoistic attempt to rally them behind Colonel C. F. Stallard's Dominion Party flickered briefly and died quietly during the second world war.   This abdication of political responsibility to the Afrikaners turned the scales in the post-war years.

English-speaking attitudes in the crucial 1960s have been joyfully lampooned by an anonymous versifier who prefers to be known simply as *One of Them.*

A Broker will get you seven per cent,
There's dancing at Kelvin Grove,
The elf are running at Rooikrantz again,
Which all of it goes to prove,
Though the Nats are in, they are not so bad,
Rough-tongued, but they mean no harm,
For our world goes on as it always has,
And there's no real cause for alarm.

We hear that they're out to convert our youth,
And they've got control of the school,
That they're out to pattern the English child,
To the Christian National rule.
It's tough on the chap who isn't well off,
But his choice, like mine, is still free.
*My kids go to Bishops and Michaelhouse,**
So it's nothing to do with me!

The rule of Law has gone for a loop,
And there's no appeal to the Courts,
But we couldn't care less while the football's on,
For the Nats are darn good sports.
We all play rugby together, you see,
And we all have a beer and a chat,
The game's much bigger than politics,
And they won't interfere with that!

They've stopped our news from the BBC,
And they're out to muzzle the Press,

* English-speaking public schools in South Africa.

They've sacked the Chief of the General Staff,
And they've changed the Navy's dress,
But they're only too pleased if we earn our keep,
And collect our dividends,
And they let us play in the Springbok sides,
Which shows they want to be friends!

The infuriating accuracy of this lampoon should not be allowed to obscure the existence of a vigorous minority element in the English-speaking community which is creative in literature and science, radical in politics and religion, and bravely dedicated in the liberal professions and in journalism. Their lack of numbers is to some degree balanced by the quality and the courage of the contribution they make to creative thinking and to the struggle for civil rights.

It is misleading to think of 'the English' in South Africa as if they were an extension of Britain. For the most part, the only active link between people of British stock in the Republic and 'the home country' is that they share a common tongue. English-speaking South Africans, allowing for exceptions, have more common interests with the Afrikaners than with the British. Their loyalties lie with Pretoria and not with London: if they do not approve of Afrikanerdom and if they cherish their separate cultural traditions, they are no less South African and no less capable of working closely with—and, indeed, accepting the leadership of—those Afrikaners who also reject the narrower tenets of Afrikanerdom.

This distinction between the British and the English-speaking South Africans is important to understand. Politically, they are as separate from Britain as are the Americans. The fable of 'the British in South Africa' has persisted for two bad reasons. The worst is that it suited the purpose of Afrikanerdom to maintain the image of an alien English race, loyal to the Queen, the Union Jack and 'home' rather than to South Africa. Now that this political distortion no longer suits the purpose of Afrikanerdom, its leaders are strenuously wooing the English South African to the cause of white unity. 'This South Africa—the land opened to us by Afrikaner Voortrekkers and British settlers—is our own country, our one and only homeland', the President of the Republic, Mr Charles R.

Swart, said in a recent appeal for a 'union of hearts'—of white hearts. Yet President Swart was the man chosen by the leaders of Afrikancrdom to discredit General Hertzog in 1940 in a particularly ugly political campaign: one of the charges made against Hertzog at that time was that he stood for co-operation with 'the English'.

Afrikanerdom's campaign against 'the alien English' was helped by the exclusiveness of an unrepresentative minority of English-speaking South Africans—mainly those concentrated in Natal and parts of the Eastern Cape. They invented and sustained a militant snobbery on the basis of a spurious 'Britishness'. They despised the Afrikaners and looked down on their less jingoistic compatriots as *Englikaners*, hybrid Englishmen. It was this attitude which gave rise to the idea of a 'Natal Stand': the assertion that Natal would stand out against the rest of the country if it ever became a Republic. But when the Republic was born, it became all too clear that the 'Natal Stand' is the lamest of all the country's lost causes. Though Natal is predominantly English-speaking, it is one of the most racially-minded provinces: its victims are the Indians who form a numerically important element in Natal.

Contrary to the pretentious reactions of the jingo minority to the propaganda of Afrikanerdom, the fact is that the majority of English-speaking South Africans have their roots as deeply in Africa as the Americans and the Australians have in their continents. Their feelings and attitudes on South African questions are closer to Afrikanerdom than to Britain. On the crucial political test of white rule the majority of both communities stand together. The characteristic attitude of English South Africans is not liberal on the racial issue. Their dislike of apartheid stems less from their disapproval of its motives than from their belief that it is impractical and too rigid in application, that it is harmful to the economy, and that it isolates the Republic. But the majority thoroughly approves of its basic segregationalist philosophy.

Certain qualifications to this broad statement are necessary. It obscures the important fact that most English-speaking South Africans are political pragmatists, whereas most Afrikaners are rigid doctrinalists. When Dr Verwoerd insists 'there must be no concessions because concessions will lead to defeat', he is applauded by most Afrikaners; but the English-speaking group is irritated. It believes that limited concessions are necessary and could be effective. It shows a degree of flexibility as opposed to the 'granite-like determination'* of Afrikanerdom.

A second important difference is the radical tradition kept alive by a minority of English-speaking South Africans, and today supported by an even smaller, but no less militant, minority of Afrikaners. This radical tradition at least enables Africans to distinguish between 'good whites' and 'bad whites'. It is in a real sense the 'conscience' of white South Africa. In the 1961 elections 71,500 white voters supported the Progressives and the Liberals: the two parties which reject the notion of white supremacy. Although their number represents only about seven per cent of the electorate, it marks a considerable and healthy increase in the number of whites willing to champion an 'integrated society'.

Politically, the radicals operate through the Progressive Party, the Liberal Party and the communist-dominated Congress of Democrats. But their greatest contribution lies outside party organisations. An oustanding example was the struggle fought by the English-speaking universities to retain their status as 'Open Universities' allowing non-whites to enrol as students. They lost the fight after seven years, when the government despaired of persuasion and threats and legislated for racially exclusive universities. Even now, the academic staff and the student bodies miss few opportunities to take a stand against compromise. An impressive number of the staff of Rhodes University boycotted a function to honour President Swart; and virtually the entire staff of Natal University has threatened to resign if any of its members are arrested under the ninety-days' Detention Law. The most militant university opposition, however, came from the predominantly English-speaking National Union of South African Students (NUSAS). At its 1962 Congress, NUSAS accepted the role a students' organisation must play in establishing 'a democratic society in which a non-racial educational system could develop'. It also unanimously accepted the 'duty to speak

* Dr Verwoerd's favourite phrase.

and act against those measures of government, not necessarily concerned with education, but which . . . seek to destroy the democratic rights of opposition'.[1] It is not surprising that the Minister of Justice regards NUSAS as 'a cancer to be eradicated',[2] and that he should have hinted at direct action against them if the students failed to amend their policies.

The two outstanding movements in the field of civil rights are the Institute of Race Relations (to which SABRA forms Afrikanerdom's counterpart) and the Black Sash. The Institute champions the cause of 'a shared society'. Its chief merit lies in the excellence of its publications based on careful research and painstaking documentation. Its reasoned representations to the government exasperate Dr Verwoerd quite as much as an effective parliamentary opposition might have done if one existed. The Black Sash, an all-women's organisation, is not only a splendid moral force, but a brave band of ambulance workers tending to the casualties of apartheid. Its members—many of them wives of cautious business and professional men—have defied angry mobs as they stood in silent vigil outside Parliament and in the main civic centres, wearing the broad black sash of mourning for South Africa's loss of constitutional government and civil rights. Their campaign of adult education about human rights has done much to awaken the liberal conscience. But their outstanding contribution lies in their willingness to identify themselves with the victims of apartheid; these are helped in practical ways, notably by arguing their cases before the authorities, and by keeping a watching-brief at the magistrates' courts.

The voice of radical protest is heard abroad most effectively through South Africa's writers: Alan Paton, Nadine Gordimer, Dan Jacobson, Guy Butler, Anthony Delius—and at home through its journalists. The English language press —almost entirely controlled by two large groups dominated by mining and business interests—is without exception opposed to the government. But with two exceptions they support the United Party. The exceptions are the *Rand Daily Mail* (Johannesburg), edited by Laurence Gandar, and the *Evening Post* (Port Elizabeth), edited by John Sutherland: they support the Progressives—not because their proprietors necessarily approve, but because the editors insist on their right to make policy. Both Gandar and Sutherland have had to defy not only the government but also many readers who dislike some of their more radical campaigns: a good example is Gandar's exposure of the hideous truth about malnutrition among non-whites in the Republic, and his attack upon the South Africa Foundation in 1962.* Among the weeklies, the *Financial Mail*, edited by George Palmer, is perhaps the most effective critic of apartheid economics. Of the political commentators, the government's two *bêtes noires* are—for the best of reasons—Anthony Delius of the *Cape Times* and Stanley Uys of the *Sunday Times* (Johannesburg). What upsets the government is not so much what they write for local papers but their reports for the overseas Press: for they cannot be accused of the blanket crime of 'failure to understand the true problems of the country'.

THE CHURCHES

One of the saddest features of the English-language Church in South Africa† is that its hierarchy so often speaks for a small minority of its members. The political climate might have been very different if the attitudes of English-speaking Christians had been those of leaders like the former Archbishop of Capetown, Dr Joost de Blank; the former Bishop of Johannesburg, the Rt. Rev. Ambrose Reeves; the Bishop of Natal, the Rt. Rev. Vernon Inman; and the Roman Catholic Archbishop of Durban, Monsignor Denis Hurley. But these men do not talk for all of the hierarchy, let alone for their Synods or members. They have spoken as much against the entrenched prejudices of their own flock as against the official upholders of the policies of apartheid.

The Reverend Christian Molefe, African rector of a mission church in Johannesburg, caused considerable anxiety and heart-searching with his statement: 'The Anglican Church in the Diocese of Johannesburg would like the world to know that there is no colour bar within its ranks. But in point of

* See p. 112.
† Anglicans (1,230,000 total; 416,500 whites); Methodists (1,364,000 total; 219,000 whites); Presbyterians (277,000 total. 100,700 whites); Roman Catholic (684,000 total; 141,300 whites). There are also 108,500 members of the Jewish faith.

fact there is in this Church not only a colour bar, but colour prejudice of the worst kind. I have worked in this diocese as a full-time catechist and priest for twenty-six years. During all these years it has always been most painful to attend Synods and to observe the outward multiracialism of the Church when in reality this was not so.'[1]

While these criticisms apply in some measure to all denominations, the Roman Catholics and the Methodists are perhaps the least susceptible. Membership of the Methodist Church is already overwhelmingly black, a fact recognised by the recent election of an African to its head.

These general strictures upon the Church do not, however, derogate from the importance of its leadership; if anything, they emphasise the courage of those men who refuse to submit to the dictation of their own supporters on issues they recognise to be of fundamental importance to the bearing of the Christian witness in a multiracial society. It requires an act of exceptional courage for Bishop Inman to endorse completely for South Africa these views of the presiding Bishop of America: 'Men, women and children are today risking their livelihood and their lives in protesting their rights. We must support and strengthen their protest in every way possible rather than give support to the forces of resistance by our silence.' Bishop Inman added: 'To all the foregoing I say "Amen" and I hope you do it as well.'[2]

THE UNITED PARTY

The Prime Minister is changing the land position to the advantage of the non-white.
Mr Douglas Mitchell, Natal leader of the United Party,
1962

The United Party tries to win support from nationalists by behaving like the National Party.
Dr Verwoerd, 1961

Apartheid is opposed not only by the non-whites but also by the majority of whites—a point usually overlooked by apologists for the South African government. In the last elections, held in 1961, 51 per cent of the white electorate voted against apartheid. But though the government polled only 46.26 per

cent of the votes, the weighted rural constituencies resulted in
their gaining 105 seats against the opposition's 51 (United
Party 50, Progressives 1).*

The United Party opposes apartheid, and is even more
strongly against its latest version, Separate Development.
Nevertheless, it stands firmly for 'the maintenance of white
leadership for the foreseeable future', with the vague qualification that 'the fruits of Western civilisation should be shared
with non-whites capable of joint responsibility in administration, and that there should be respect for individual dignity,
regardless of race'. Its leader, Sir de Villiers Graaff, believes,
like General Smuts, that the party's policies must be based on
'realistic considerations' of what the white electorate is likely
to support. Its alternative to apartheid is 'race federation':
a central federal parliament uniting communities rather than
territorial units. Each racial group would have a defined
share in government; the Coloureds ranking as equals with
whites. The basic rights of individuals, groups and areas
would be entrenched constitutionally. The first step would be
to restore the vote to the Coloureds; the second to negotiate
with Indians to determine their place 'as a permanent part of
the community'. A distinction would be made between permanently urbanised Africans and those living in the reserves:
the former would be represented by white MPs. A considerable measure of self-government would 'eventually' be granted
to the reserves, and rural Africans would have an, as yet,
undefined form of parliamentary representation.

Because the United Party competes with Afrikanerdom
for electoral support, it often tends to rival the government's
own reactionary policies. Typical of its opportunism is its
criticism of the Verwoerd government for too much spending
on African development. Its right-wing is led by Mr Douglas
Mitchell, the spokesman for Natal, a leader as steeped in
racial thinking as any of Verwoerd's supporters. In its public
attitude to the UN, the Afro-Asians and other international
critics of South Africa, there is little difference between the
United Party and the government. On the other hand, the

* The other four seats are open to the Coloureds in the Cape who
elect white MPs.

essential pragmatism of its rank and file preserves the party from imitating the paranoid and crusading approach of Afrikanerdom to its overseas critics, and there is little doubt that, under duress, the United Party would sooner make an accommodation with the international community than would the government.

Most of its support comes from English-speaking voters, but its membership includes a sizeable minority of Afrikaners. The United Party is favoured by the big mining, industrial and financial interests, with the notable exception of Mr Harry Oppenheimer,* the head of the Anglo-American Corporation, who supports the Progressive Party.

THE PROGRESSIVE PARTY

> Dr Verwoerd says we would rather be poor and white than rich and mixed. I believe that most South Africans will opt for the latter once the time of decision comes.
> *Mrs Helen Suzman, Progressive Party* MP, *1963*

> Whites have been caught up in the vice grip of their own prejudices.
> *Dr Jan Steytler, leader of the Progressive Party, 1964*

The Progressive Party was formed as a break-away reaction to the growing illiberalism of the United Party. On seceding in 1959 the group had eleven MPs, but the number was cut to one in the general election of 1961. Under present conditions, the party falls between two stools: it is seen as too liberal by the whites, and as too conservative by the non-whites. By the same token, of course, its programme could, under different circumstances, provide the starting-point for an inter-racial constitution. It has attracted many outstanding people. Its leader, Dr Jan Steytler, is typical of the younger generation of Afrikaners who have moved out of the camp of Afrikanerdom. Its supporters include Mrs Helen Suzman, its brilliant, solitary MP; Mr Donald Molteno, QC, a notable champion of civil rights, who chaired its Constitutional Commission: Dr Ellen Hellmann, an internationally recognised student of race relations; and Professor P. V. Pistorius, former

* See p. 116.

professor of Greek at Pretoria University, and one of the party's most telling political writers. Its best known supporter is Mr Harry Oppenheimer, who rebelled against the United Party's 'race federation' plan.

The Progressives are pledged to 'the maintenance and extension of the values of Western civilisation, the protection of fundamental human rights, and the safeguarding of the dignity and worth of the human person, irrespective of race, colour or creed'.[1] To this end it advocates radical reforms to establish a non-racial qualified franchise, a federal parliament with an entrenched constitution embodying a Bill of Rights, and an unusual and ingenious plan for an Upper House or Senate. Membership of the latter would be limited to individuals who had gained a substantial measure of support from all races; this, combined with the necessity for senatorial assent to legislation, is designed to ensure that no discriminatory legislation is passed into the law.

THE LIBERAL PARTY

> A fact that must be faced by everybody is that liberalism is one of the greatest threats to the survival of the Republic of South Africa.
>
> DIE TRANSVALER, *October 30, 1962*

The Liberal Party is the only political movement which stands for universal suffrage and which is still allowed legal existence in the Republic. Several of its active leaders are under restriction. Mr Alan Paton, author of *Cry, the Beloved Country*, has had his passport withdrawn; several others, including two journalists—Mr Randolph Vigne and Mr Peter Hjul—and a prospective candidate in the Transkei elections —Mr Hammington Majija—are restricted by banning orders; while its principal African spokesman, Mr Jordan K. Ngubane (himself a prominent journalist and author), is in exile following a banning order.

The Liberals are a small band of crusaders who refuse to trim their policies to make themselves acceptable to the enfranchised electorate. The result is that in the 1961 elections they polled only 2,461 votes—0.31 per cent of the total poll. But this paltry vote is offset by their moral and educational influence, which is considerable enough for them to be under constant attack by the government, which equates them with communism. 'The liberal trend of thought is today the best propagandist for communism, and liberalism is nowadays a powerful front organisation for communism', said Dr Carel de Wet, former MP, now ambassador to London.[1]

The Liberal Party stands for 'one man one vote' without qualification. It asserts 'that it is not possible at this stage to foresee the precise circumstances under which the (political) change will occur'; but it aims 'to have the idea of a universal franchise and a Bill of Rights accepted by the people of South Africa, and to bring about the change with the minimum possible dislocation'.[2]

2: THE BUSINESS MEN

> In the developing world of Africa, but not in Africa alone, the challenge to the business world and to the business leader ... is far-reaching: it remains for the future to decide whether modern enterprise, with its complex structure, can at all survive the possible breakdown of government, or at any rate, meet the triple challenge of nationalism, and racialism, and communism. . . . The business leader must now think in terms much wider than those formerly appropriate or necessary ... he must consider public opinion, and even if he cannot bend it to his will, he must at least attempt to influence and persuade.
> *Sir Theodore Gregory:* Ernest Oppenheimer and the Economic Development of Southern Africa; *1962*

BIG BUSINESS MINDS ITS BUSINESS

If the Marxists were right in their analysis of where power lies in society, Afrikanerdom would not today be ruling the Republic. The key 'means of production, distribution and exchange', and the most important section of the press, are in the hands of English-speaking South Africans. The disparity between capitalist power and political power in South Africa is clear. English-speaking South Africans control 99 per cent of mining capital, 94 per cent of industrial capital, 88 per cent of finance capital, and 75 per cent of commercial capital. But the political interests they support have no chance of achieving power as things stand today. Nor can this disparity be explained in terms of the diffusion of capitalist power: the bulk of it is controlled by seven financial houses. Between them they control over a thousand of the largest companies, with combined financial resources exceeding £1,000 million. Their policies are co-ordinated through the Transvaal and Orange Free State Chamber of Mines. This great financial empire's interests are further interlocked through overlapping directorships with powerful financial interests in the West.

In its early struggles to achieve power, Afrikanerdom caricatured this powerful financial complex as 'Hoggenheimer' —the 'foreign, imperialist, capitalist octopus'. It looked upon this fat, cigar-smoking, diamond-studded, hook-nosed, oligarch as the heir of Cecil John Rhodes, still regarded as Afrikanerdom's greatest enemy. In their years of opposition, the Nationalists accused the 'Randlords' and their Chamber of Mines of forming 'a state within a state'. At one time the National Party talked of nationalising their mining interests: a threat periodically revived by Dr Albert Hertzog, a senior member of Dr Verwoerd's Cabinet.

The Randlords, for their part, tended to look upon Afrikanerdom with distaste and anxiety, and provided financial support to arrest its growth. They backed successively the Unionist Party, the South African Party (led by Generals Louis Botha and Jan Smuts), and the United Party (led by Generals Hertzog and Smuts). But their strongest support always went to General Smuts, the leader they really trusted. It is a well-known fact that in order to stop Afrikanerdom from winning the 1948 elections, Big Business subscribed more than £250,000 through the Unity Trust Fund. The English-language press, which commands about 80 per cent of national readership, was unanimously opposed to apartheid. South African big business, therefore, played a very different role in the rise of Verwoerd from that of the Ruhr barons in Hitler's rise to power. 'Hoggenheimer' was the main target of attack in Dr Verwoerd's paper, *Die Transvaler*.

The victory of Afrikanerdom was acknowledged by big business to be a serious setback to their own interests: they feared its effect on overseas financial confidence; they were concerned that apartheid would interfere with the efficient use of labour; they were apprehensive about the dangers of sharpening racial conflicts; and they did not relish the idea that the seats of power would no longer be filled by their own friends. All they could hope for was that 'the government would trim its sails': instead, it is they who have had to compromise.

Although the 1948 election defeat was one of the worst political setbacks big business had known, it was by no means their first defeat. They were never altogether satisfied with the policies even of those governments they had supported in the past. Usually their disagreement was over taxation of gold-mining profits, but their fundamental fight was over the industrial colour bar. The ending of the colour bar would have enabled them to reclassify jobs reserved for the more highly paid white miners, and replace some of them with lower-paid African workers. It was their attempt to force Smuts' hand on this issue that led to the 1922 Rand Revolt. It ended not only in the defeat of Smuts' Government but in even more rigid industrial colour bar legislation—the so-called 'civilised labour policy'. Moreover, the successor Nationalist-Labour government of 1924 embarked on a policy of protecting local industries and establishing a state-owned iron and steel industry—both against the bitter opposition of the Chamber of Mines. There are many other examples of governments over-riding the interests of the Randlords. A recent one was Dr Verwoerd's quashing of the Oppenheimers' plan to end the system of migratory labour through the creation of a permanent labour force for their new mines on the Free State Goldfields.

There is a simple explanation for the limits set on the power of big business in South Africa. No government can afford to legislate against the wishes of the white electorate, which, on racial questions, conceives its interests as different from those of the Randlords.

By no means all of big business in South Africa is controlled by the corporate members of the Chamber of Mines, notwithstanding their large stake in industry. Many

industrialists and business men are entirely independent, or
linked with overseas companies. Their interests are watched
over by the Federated Chamber of Industry and the Association of Chambers of Commerce. These two Chambers are
also regarded with some suspicion by the government, because
they have in the past declared themselves opposed to apartheid.
It prefers, on the whole, to listen to the views of their rival,
the *Afrikaanse Handelsinstituut* (started on Broederbond
initiative); its former director is now the Minister of Economic
Development.

After almost sixteen years of ineffectual protest against
apartheid, the country's business leaders have come increasingly to 'mind their own business'. They do not see this as
an abdication of power or responsibility. They have come to
rationalise it as the most effective contribution to be made
towards securing the defeat of apartheid. They argue that,
since apartheid cannot be defeated politically, it must be made
increasingly unworkable economically, until it collapses, irrespective of the wishes of politicians or the white electorate.
This can be achieved, they argue, by expanding industry so
that its economic thrust will become more effective than the
restrictions of apartheid. 'However important politics may
be, South Africa's racial problems are not going to be solved
by political parties but by industry.'[1] This is the view of the
leading Afrikaner business man, Dr Anton Rupert. It is
shared by Mr Harry Oppenheimer and by most English-
speaking business men. Mr Lief Egeland, a director of the
Union Corporation, speaks for them when he says: 'South
Africa's problems are going to be solved more and more by
industrial and commercial development and less through
politics.'[2]

This *leit-motif* communicates itself easily to the overseas
investor. 'I think the economy of your country will *automatically* enforce a solution to most of your pressing problems', Sir Aynsley Bridgeland (chairman of Humphries Ltd,
the £40 million firm of British contractors) told South Africans
in 1963. 'I do not think the political side will be a factor *at
all*.'[3] (Authors' italics.)

It is undoubtedly true that the Republic's economic expansion has been an important factor in limiting the application of

Separate Development, particularly in respect to the government's failure to reduce the numbers of Africans in the 'white areas'. But it is equally true that, were it not for the country's economic buoyancy, the government would have found it less easy to survive. It would not have been possible to finance the administrative machinery to enforce apartheid while at the same time expanding the police and defence forces, and still satisfy the electorate by generous subsidies to farmers and small but steady increases in wages to white workers. Nor would it have had the money for its important state-sponsored industrial programmes and for expenditure on arms, both of which helped to give the economy a considerable boost at a time when it had begun to flag. The result is that, even if economic expansion has put a brake on the implementation of some aspects of apartheid, it has been a strong factor in creating the confidence at home and abroad which is vital to the government's survival. It is merely wishful thinking to suppose that economic activity is a substitute for political action in overcoming apartheid. At the same time, it is fair to ask what one might expect big business to do in the situation in which it finds itself in the Republic.

It is in the nature of big business to make its accommodation with the government of the day, unless presented with an active threat to its survival. Apartheid is not at present seen as such a threat, though its economic effects are held to be seriously prejudicial to economic development and long-term stability—and even perhaps to the nation's moral well-being. The main political concern of business leaders is to bring about changes in the apartheid regime without seriously threatening the existing order. If they must choose, they prefer the *status quo* to revolutionary change. They fear that militant African politics might be more disruptive of their interests than apartheid, and they especially fear international intervention. This fear of possibly uncontrollable change makes big business and Afrikanerdom bedfellows in the struggle against 'the liberation forces' and world opinion. The bed they share is the South Africa Foundation.

THE SOUTH AFRICA FOUNDATION

> The South Africa Foundation is an association of
> leaders in every sphere of national activity who have
> come together with a single objective: to present to the
> world a true picture of South Africa.
> *The Objective of the South Africa Foundation, 1961*

> It is idle to pretend that the dislike of South Africa's
> policies abroad arises merely from misunderstanding.
> *Mr Harry Oppenheimer, Chairman's Address to the*
> *Anglo-American Corporation, 1961*

The South Africa Foundation has brought together a strange
gathering of men, ranging from Harry Oppenheimer, a leading
Progressive, to prominent Broederbonders, like Dr F. Meyer
and Mr M. S. Louw; from anti-apartheid crusaders, like the
Reverend J. B. Webb, a Methodist, to die-hard upholders of
apartheid, like the Reverend W. Nicol of the Dutch Reformed
Church. Its one hundred trustees read like a studbook of the
most powerful directors in the Republic: they include men of
all the political parties (except the Liberals), and of both white
communities. Their leader is a former British general.

Major-General Sir Francis W. de Guingand, KBE, CB, DSO,
Legion of Honour (France), Order of Kutzov 1st Grade
(Russia), Order of Orange Nassau (Holland), came to South
Africa at the end of the war He had served with great
distinction as Chief of Staff to Field Marshal Viscount Mont-
gomery. A resourceful soldier in search of a new career, he
made South Africa his home. He is the chairman of Tube
Investments (S.A.) and holds directorships in a dozen compan-
ies. The South Africa Foundation is largely his brainchild.
He runs it like a military engagement.

It has Man-to-Man sections. This is its international
goodwill organisation which—to quote from its own literature
—is designed to enlist the support of South Africans of foreign
origin to promote its objectives 'in their own countries'.* It
defines in direct terms The Problem to be tackled: 'South
Africa faces a mounting wave of world criticism, coupled
with threats of boycotts, sanctions and even possibly military

---

* One might have supposed that, if they were South Africans, the
Republic would have been their 'own country'.

action.' It has its Enemy and its recognised battlefield: 'The international vendetta against South Africa is a reality, well organised and well financed, and should be recognised for what it is—nothing less than another manifestation of the cold war against the West.'[1] It has a Special Field of Operations in this cold war: 'In a turbulent continent, coveted by the Soviet Union and its allies, South Africa stands implacably opposed to Communism and is a vital factor in the economic and military strength of the Western World.'[2] It has clearly defined weak points from which attention must be diverted: 'It must be quite frankly admitted that South Africa's race policies are rejected by almost every other country in the world. Whilst it is true that these policies are the product of a unique situation and, moreover, are usually not thoroughly understood by the rest of the world, the fact remains that they are generally not acceptable—because they do not accord with doctrinaire ideas of freedom and democracy. The fact that European conceptions of these great principles appear to be impractical in semi-civilised communities is largely obscured or ignored.'[3] Finally, it has a Mission: To Tell the World. 'We South Africans ourselves have failed to appreciate the facts of the South African success story, and have failed to realise that, while political differences are legitimate in any democratic society, *they cannot and must not be projected into the outside world* [Authors' italics]. As a result, most people in Europe, America and elsewhere have a seriously distorted image of South Africa, the product of ignorance, indifference, or an unbalanced presentation of the realities of the South African situation.'[4]

Simply described, the objectives of the Foundation are 'to promote international understanding of South Africa'. Facts about the Republic are collected and disseminated internationally. The Foundation has branches throughout South Africa, and special representatives in Western countries. Its international ramifications are discussed in Part Two. It is paid for mainly by big business through a system of corporate membership. The Foundation sells itself to potential members by stressing that its purpose 'must encourage better conditions for business enterprises and, therefore, greater prosperity for everybody'.[5] It has raised over £500,000 from the business community. A firm not joining it is represented as lacking in patriotism. We know of business men who have joined because, as they have frankly admitted, 'it would be bad for our business if we refused to do so'.

De Guingand's greatest achievement has been to bring together into a single movement both the forces which support and those which oppose the government: they contend with each other at home, but defend the country collectively abroad. Their differences over whether or not Afrikanerdom should dominate the country, whether South Africa should be inside or outside the Commonwealth, and whether apartheid is right or wrong, are no concern of the Foundation: these belong to politics. One of its most prominent members, Dr Harry van Eck* said recently: 'In the past, we have emphasised and exploited our petty differences far too much. By his leadership, Sir Francis has shown us how we can, through the Foundation, overcome these little differences by having a great common objective which can lead our nation to greatness.'[1]

How truly does the Foundation serve South Africa's interests? Its sharpest critics are to be found among moderate South Africans. The conservative Johannesburg *Star* (itself owned by men who form the backbone of the Foundation) allowed itself to remark cautiously at the time of its launching in November 1960:

> This formidable enterprise, underlining as it does the comparative futility of the government's own information services abroad, would have been superfluous if the image of South Africa had not been sadly tarnished by events in this country. No great exertions are needed at this time of day to tell the outside world of South Africa's natural assets, her achievements and potentialities. But by the same token the world also knows perfectly well that there is a good deal wrong with her human, social and political relationships. It is this knowledge that has thwarted the best efforts of those who have tried hitherto to 'sell' South Africa overseas.[2]

Mr Laurence Gandar, editor of the *Rand Daily Mail*, wrote a penetrating analysis of the weaknesses and the dangers

* See p. 42.

of the Foundation in 1962. 'It has no non-white members and is thus not able to show that it speaks for all South Africa*... It is predominantly a business man's movement. Eighty per cent of its founders and trustees are leaders drawn from commerce, industry, finance and the marketing side of agriculture.... This is a distinct handicap, for its efforts will only too readily be interpreted abroad as those of Big Business rallying to the defence of its economic interests.' He raised the crucial question of whether the Foundation was not simply a whitewashing agency for the government and for apartheid. While he was satisfied that it did not originally set out to do this, nevertheless 'the Foundation almost automatically adopts the posture of champion and apologist for the *status quo* in South Africa'. He quotes de Guingand as saying: 'I do not agree with those who say that the Foundation has an impossible task unless our racial policies undergo a major change. We can't afford to chuck away what has already been achieved.' Gandar saw 'a very real danger that the entire business leadership of the nation will find itself politically immobilised through enrolment in a movement which is ostensibly non-political but which is nonetheless committed to the defence of the existing order.' Instead of resisting change, Gandar argued, the best way to help South Africa was to work for change, and to be seen to be doing so.

> I believe that what would most positively influence world opinion in our favour would not be the efforts of any army of defenders in South Africa, but the sight and sound of an army of dissenters. There is plenty of evidence that the one thing which has heartened our few remaining friends abroad and encouraged counsels of moderation in the United Nations has been the knowledge that there is a strong body of opinion in this country against the racist policies presently in vogue. Let us give the impression of being solidly behind the government and race discrimination, and our moment of greatest peril will have arrived.

The fears of the Foundation's critics have been only too

---

* A recent announcement by the Foundation suggests that it is hoping to meet this objection: it will be interesting to see what type of African leaders will join this front.

well founded. Its role as fact-finder and fact-provider ties it closely to the chariot-wheels of the largely ineffective government Information Service. It interprets its 'non-political' role as depriving itself of the right to speak on political questions.* What did it have to say about the infamous General Law Amendment Bill ('the Sabotage Act') which was vigorously assailed by South Africa's legal profession? Addressing itself to the Foundation, the *Natal Witness* wrote: 'To state clearly that this Bill makes a murderous assault on the civil liberties of all South Africans must surely be essential to promoting international understanding of South Africa, of her problems, and to advancing the welfare of all her peoples.'[1] But the Foundation remained silent; its silence drove the Progressive Party to attack it openly. Dr Zac de Beer, the Progressive's chairman, said that because the Foundation 'never by any chance' criticised the government, 'the tendency was to create the impression elsewhere in the world that all leaders of commerce and industry in the Foundation did, in fact, support the very policies of which the world was suspicious'.[2] But though his party attacked the Foundation, Mr Harry Oppenheimer continues to serve as one of its trustees. This ambiguity appears even stranger if one compares the Foundation's declared purpose with his opinion presented in the headpiece to this section.

---

* 'Being non-political and having no connection with the government, the Foundation has refused to be dragged into the political arena': Mr John Pascoe, Chairman of the London Committee of the South African Foundation, in a letter to the *Guardian*, July 13, 1962.

THE ROLE OF MR HARRY OPPENHEIMER

Defending the Broederbond in the Assembly, Dr Verwoerd said he could mention another mighty machine: the whole combination of businesses known as the Oppenheimer group.... Mr Oppenheimer could exercise tremendous influence if he so wished, and his was a more dangerous machine than ... the Broederbond.

THE STAR, *January 25, 1964*

Mr Harry Oppenheimer is the best example of the big business man who strongly rejects apartheid, but whose methods of fighting it are conditioned by the need to defend his important economic interests. No financier has done more than he to maintain international financial confidence in South Africa, and none has attracted as much foreign capital into the country. And yet he is regarded by the government as its worst enemy among business men. Nor does government distrust of Mr Oppenheimer remove the distrust with which African political leadership in South Africa regards him.

Harry Oppenheimer is not an easy man to place. His great financial power invites suspicion, and his policies are sufficiently ambiguous to raise questions about his motives. His vast interests are spread over a number of African states, besides Europe and the United States. His empire even reaches into the Soviet economy: Russia's diamond exports are marketed through his Diamond Syndicate—the world's only monopoly sales organisation If the term 'international financier' did not exist, it would have had to be invented to describe the Oppenheimers.

When Sir Ernest Oppenheimer died in 1957, Harry Oppenheimer inherited not one but three separate empires: De Beer's, Rhodesian Anglo-American, and the Anglo-American Corporation of South Africa. Through these interests he controls the world's diamond market, the world's largest gold-producing group, and about half the copper output of Northern Rhodesia—equal to 15 per cent of the world's output. Uranium, lead, zinc, vanadium and coal mines, breakfast foods and cereals, cold storages, real estate, railways, bricks and tiles, ranching, fertilisers, chemicals, ceramics, explosives and munitions—Oppenheimer has interests in them all. His ninety-odd companies have a market value of more than £500 million; they produce between £15 and £20 million in profits a year.

This opulent empire rests on a tripod with politically vulnerable legs: gold and diamonds in South Africa; copper in Northern Rhodesia; and the international diamond syndicates. The real problem facing Oppenheimer is how to survive in today's white-ruled South Africa; in the new South Africa after the inevitable changes have occurred; and in black-ruled Northern Rhodesia. It is a position in which most financiers would choose to behave with the utmost caution. But this is not Oppenheimer's style.

When he returned to South Africa after the second world war, he went to Parliament as a member of General Smuts' opposition United Party, representing Kimberley. In 1961 he quarrelled with the present United Party leader, Sir de Villiers Graaff—mainly over the rejection of Oppenheimer's proposals for a federal constitution which might have made an integrated society possible—and helped to form the Progressive Party. He proclaimed his political beliefs in his resignation speech: 'South Africa's moral standing among the nations of the world will not be restored until we make it clear that in apportioning rights and responsibilities, we look primarily to the ability and standards of the individual man rather than to the average ability and standards of the racial groups to which he belongs. It is respect for individual worth and dignity that is the true mark of civilisation.'[1] Again, at the launching of the left-of-centre Progressive Party in 1959 he warned that South Africa was 'in grave danger' and urged support for the party best qualified by its policies 'to get us out of this dangerous situation'.[2]

Mr Oppenheimer—who was a great believer in the multi-racial partnership experiment which failed in the Central African Federation—put his faith in winning over black and white moderates to join in a common front. 'The first thing we need is to encourage an important body of reasonable and moderate non-whites who are anxious to work with the white man. And I am ... convinced that we shall be unable to do that as long as we persist in granting political rights on the basis of the colour of a man's skin.'[3] While wishing to establish a non-racial voting system, he insists that the universal franchise is a goal to work towards: to apply 'one man, one vote' immediately would, in his view, necessarily lead straight into a one-party state. He accepts the 'desirability' of one-party states for African countries where literacy is low and tribal loyalties strong, but not for South Africa or Southern Rhodesia. 'It seems to me that Africans in South Africa or Rhodesia who insist on "one-man-one-vote" are really (consciously or unconsciously) demanding the end of all parliamentary opposition and the concentration of power in the hands of a single African nationalist party. This is something that no substantial European population will accept, or ought to be asked to accept. They might (as in Southern Rhodesia) agree to abandon their position of domination, but they will fight, and rightly so, to maintain their political liberties.'[1] His quarrel with the African nationalists and the Liberals goes further than this disagreement over the franchise. Like the leaders of the Central African Federation, he equates African nationalism with extremism and racialism; and like the Tory peers who support Lord Salisbury—and unlike Verwoerd —he rejects the idea that African nationalism is necessarily irresistible.[2] It is these views that bring Oppenheimer into conflict with both the right-wing and the radical forces in Africa. 'I am afraid that I find myself becoming increasingly lonely,' he confesses; but he remains unrepentant. He is opposed to apartheid because he thinks it is morally wrong and unworkable; in the end, he says, it will have to be abandoned. But in favour of what? 'I still believe that a policy of racial partnership in Southern Africa is right and practical. I do not mean by that, however, that I think that the white population should surrender its interests or its mission—for it still has a mission. The whites have undertaken a work of civilisation in Africa and they are determined to complete it. It would not, however, be true civilisation unless Africans were associated with it to the full extent of their ability and will to co-operate. This sounds old-fashioned, of course, but where have the new fashions taken us in Africa?'[3]

Mr Oppenheimer's statements contain bewildering ambiguities. There are times when he speaks in the urgent tones of a reformer who clearly sees the danger of delaying change;

at other times he goes out of his way to damp down talk of impending crisis. In 1961 he told Anglo-American shareholders: 'I have no doubt that at present the government is capable of controlling the situation by force. Perhaps it can be held in this way for a long time, but only at the cost of a perpetuation of racial conflict, which must become progressively more embittered. And while this conflict lasts, it will be impossible to restore confidence in the future of the country, and the economy will be threatened with stagnation.'[1] A few months later he was telling a Progressive Party meeting that South Africa was 'in a dangerous situation'.[2] But early in 1962, at a Paris exhibition of 'The Diamond in Industry', he declared it was nonsense to claim that South Africa stood on the brink of catastrophe. 'On the contrary, we may indeed provide a model of inter-racial co-operation to other countries. We have much more time than people are prepared to admit to achieve a reasonable solution.'[3]   Much more time?   A year earlier he was saying: 'To obtain racial peace, what we need above all else is time: but we will not have the time we need if we persist in a policy that is condemned on moral grounds by the nations that have been, and want to remain, our best friends.'[4] Nothing in the intervening twelve months had weakened the application of apartheid.

Equally puzzling is the inconsistency of these two views: 'The truth is that the fundamental principle upon which South African policy is at present based is morally unacceptable to practically all the nations of the world, European as well as non-European. No amount of provision of social services for non-Europeans, no amount of development in the native reserves, nor the granting of local self-government or even full independence in African tribal areas will reconcile the world to a policy under which African, Indian and Coloured people, no matter how high their individual capacity or character may be, are denied on grounds of race and colour alone, rights of citizenship in the country in which they live.'[5]   And in 1963, at a lunch attended by the US ambassador in South Africa: 'It is important for Americans to realise that apartheid is neither as vicious nor as stupid as it might appear. The government is trying to solve its problems in a reasonable and fair manner, even though I am far from happy with these policies.'[1]

But it is not only these ambiguities which blur Mr Oppenheimer's image as a leader of opinion. Nothing did more to shake the confidence of 'moderate' Africans than his decision in 1963 to spend £10 million to build three munitions factories to make South Africa's armies independent of imports. Obviously, if the company with which he is prominantly associated, African Explosives, did not build these factories somebody else would: there is enough profit in munitions in the Republic today to attract many industrialists. But why Oppenheimer? It may be good financial practice; it may even be that African Explosives' powerful board—its deputy-chairman is Paul Chambers of Imperial Chemical Industries—over-rode his own wishes. Whatever the reason, it has done more than anything he has said to undermine African confidence.

At times Oppenheimer has troubled even his colleagues in the Progressive Party. His decision to sponsor the South Africa Foundation* at its inception may be explicable in terms of a need not to isolate himself completely from his colleagues in the business world. But his refusal to resign after the Progressive Party had denounced its role, cannot be so easily explained.

Yet it is not altogether surprising that Oppenheimer's policies and actions should put him in such an equivocal light. As a financier his job is to ensure the survival of his empire during a dangerous transition period; as a radical-minded man he accepts the need to defeat apartheid, and to produce a different kind of society in South Africa. In both these roles he is naturally concerned that the methods adopted should neither disrupt the economy nor shake international confidence in South Africa's future. It is this concern which nullifies his contribution as a radical politician. Only once has the Verwoerd Government looked like being in serious trouble: after the Sharpeville shootings in 1960 morale was low, capital was leaving the country—no less than £81 million in 1960—and investors were holding back to see what would happen. The economy slumped; the atmosphere was thick with speculation

* See page 113.

about a possible change of government. Despite the personal efforts of the Minister of Finance, overseas capital remained frightened. It was only when Mr Oppenheimer personally went to arrange a £10 million loan for one of his companies in the United States that new capital began to find its way back into South Africa. He was careful to say at the time: 'Plainly being able to borrow money in this manner is no substitute for investment confidence.'[1] But the importance of his achievement was that capital again began to flow into the Republic instead of draining out. Since then the economy has bounded forward. Nobody believes that Mr Oppenheimer stepped into the breach to save the Verwoerd regime: that would be absurd. His concern was for the country's economy because his company's financial interests are so closely bound to it. His role as financier dictates his actions in doing all he can to help maintain international confidence; and because nobody carries as much authority in the world of finance, his word counts for a great deal.

Verwoerd depends a good deal on Oppenheimer's unique ability to maintain the confidence of international finance in the Republic. This explains why Afrikanerdom dare not act against Oppenheimer's empire despite their bitter mutual antipathy. And Oppenheimer needs to maintain international confidence for the interests and policies which he is committed to supporting—even if the result assists Verwoerd. This is Oppenheimer's real dilemma: the more successful he is as a financier, the less successful he is as a radical politician.

Oppenheimer, understandably, cannot see his dilemma in this way. He explains his policies by arguing that the Anglo-American Corporation has something to contribute 'to foster and sustain inter-racial understanding and sympathy, and to keep open the possibility of a solution to our problems based not on superior forces but on compromise and reason'.[2] Nobody would quarrel with such intentions; but how are they to be achieved? The party Mr Oppenheimer supports has precisely one member of parliament. It is perhaps not surprising to find that he no longer attached much importance to 'political action'.

In a statement to Anglo-American shareholders,[3] he outlined the three stages he felt should be taken to produce a new society in the Republic. The first step is to establish 'on the personal level attitudes of respect and affection for people of other races'. The second step is to extend these attitudes 'to the level of industrial and other organisations'. Only at the third step does he consider 'political policy'. He argues for 'a change of heart' at a time when political forces operate consistently to harden race attitudes. To relegate political action to the third priority is to stand reason on its head and to contribute to disaster.

But there is another twist to the irony of the situation in which Mr Oppenheimer finds himself: instead of regarding him as a valuable ally, the Verwoerd Government loses no opportunity to flay him. Dr Albert Hertzog, the Minister of Posts and Telegraphs, is the main spearhead of their attack. He was recently reported to have said that Mr Harry Oppenheimer is one of those whose financial ambition 'would cause the whites in Africa to be sacrificed'. He accused Mr Oppenheimer of belonging to 'the United States and British international capitalist bloc competing with the Russians for Africa's riches'.[1]

Mr Oppenheimer seems to be able to please nobody: no wonder he complains of feeling lonely. But this would be unimportant if one could be sure that his political judgement were sound. This is the crucial question, because few South Africans carry so much weight in influential Western circles. How realistic is his judgement? On the most important recent test—the experiment of partnership in Central Africa— Mr Oppenheimer's judgement led him wildly astray. He was among the first to support the 'partnership' of the Central African Federation, and he gave it every support. Long after Sir Roy Welensky had been abandoned by most of his backers, Oppenheimer continued to believe that the Federation could be saved. And even after shrewd industrialists like Sir Ronald Prain and the Rothschilds of the Rhodesian Selection Trust had foreseen the collapse of the Federation, Oppenheimer continued vigorously to uphold Welensky. The result was that his company had to begin to mend its broken fences in Northern Rhodesia at the last possible moment. Fortunately he found in Dr Kaunda a tolerant and forgiving antagonist. In future, other opponents might be less so.

3: INTERNATIONAL FINANCE IN THE REPUBLIC

The business man's almost total disregard of the forecasts of the political pundits is based on one thing. And that is the fact that the country has never had it so good in pounds, shillings and pence.
PERSPECTIVE, *Journal of the South Africa Foundation,*
December, 1963

Our trade and bilateral agreements need undergo no change. They include the maintenance of preferential trading agreements, South Africa's membership of the Sterling Area, defence agreements, etc. This is a comforting assurance. We need each other. With friendship and so many interests so intertwined to our mutual benefit, this is wise policy and will, I trust—and have reason to believe—become wise practice.
Dr Verwoerd, at a dinner in London on March 17,
1961, when South Africa left the Commonwealth

THE BRITISH STAKE

British investment in the Republic stood at £909 million at the end of 1962. On that figure, Britain had a 60 per cent interest in the £1,500 million of foreign investment in the Republic; this compared with the United States' 11 per cent, Europe's 15 per cent, and other countries' 8 per cent.

The British stake in mining amounts to about £250 million; in manufacturing to over £250 million; in wholesale and retailing, £125 million; in insurance, £21 million. Britain's earnings from capital in South Africa (£18.9 million in 1961: £400,000 more than the previous year[1]) is second in importance only to its earnings from the United States (£25.3 million in 1961).

Ever since Cecil John Rhodes opened up the Kimberley diamond fields in the 1890s, British financiers and other investors have provided the lion's share of the voracious capital needs of South Africa's economy. The Republic is now able to provide 90 per cent of its own new capital requirements for normal growth, but its unrequited appetite for expansion makes huge demands on foreign capital. The City of London remains its biggest supplier of foreign capital; but large as it is, it would unquestionably be greater still if it were not for the doubts about Verwoerd's policies that persist in some City circles. The attraction for British investors is easily explained. Tax on dividends deductible at source is only 7½ per cent compared with Australia's 15 per cent, Germany's 30 per cent, Switzerland and the United States' 38¾ per cent.

Private enterprise is supported by all the leading white political parties. Industrial peace is ensured through the Industrial Conciliation Act applied to white workers and a total ban on strikes by non-whites. The economy is inherently strong and expansive; as Mr Oppenheimer once said of it, 'it takes a very bad manager to ruin a good mine'. The State is proposing to spend something like £1,350 million on new projects over the next ten years. Gold production is booming, and munitions' spending is reaching unprecedented heights. The only serious complaint is the artificially created shortage of skilled labour which, with boom conditions, presents a grave threat.

But the British role is not only that of the investor of capital: there is hardly a major British company which does not have an associate or subsidiary company in the Republic. In many cases they form a substantial part of the interests of the parent company. Nor are these interests confined to the giants of British industry: there are over 330 British companies with a stake in the Republic. Many of these have started subsidiaries since the apartheid government took power. The incentives are expanding opportunities and special taxation advantages. All this activity helps to establish an active British financial and industrial 'presence' in South Africa; and because these large financial interests have so much at stake, their pressure on British policy is predictably strong. How they exercise their influence is discussed in Part Two. Here we give only a general impression of the extent of British interests in the Republic.

The 'Golden Houses'

Direct British investment in the gold-mining industry amounts to more than £200 million; but the City of London is strongly represented in the board-rooms of the Rand's seven 'Golden Houses'. It was as late as 1962 before the Union Corporation

Limited moved its headquarters from London to Johannesburg because of taxation advantages. Its total assets amount to about £60 million, largely concentrated in mines, industry, property and trust companies. Four of its ten directors are British, and its president was, until recently, Sir Charles Hambro, the banker. He reassured shareholders by telling them he has 'not lost confidence in South Africa's ability to solve its problems in the long-term future of the country'.[1] He added that 'one of the best ways of strengthening Western civilisation in Africa is to strengthen South Africa'.

The Rand Mines Limited (assets £18 million) has three British directors out of thirteen; its chairman, Mr Charles Engelhard, is American. The Gold Fields of South Africa (assets £8 million) has three British directors out of eight. Anglovaal (whose assets have a market value of £13 million) has no British directors. The General Mining and Finance Corporation Limited (with assets of £27 million) has three British directors out of thirteen. 'Johnnies'—the Johannesburg Consolidated Investment Company (total assets £51 million) has three British directors out of eight. Despite its name, there is very little American money in Oppenheimer's Anglo-American Corporation; roughly one-third of its capital is British and two-thirds South African. It has a separate London board of directors.

The City of London derives other direct advantages from the Republic's gold and diamonds. Its gold exports are marketed exclusively through the Bank of England; 80 per cent of the world's diamond output is sold through London under the system operated by the Diamond Syndicate.

The Financiers

Two of South Africa's four largest commercial banks—Barclays DCO and the Standard Bank—are incorporated in London; Standard Bank's total assets in the Republic are more than £288 million; Barclays DCO does not publish separate accounts. Nearly all the leading British insurance companies and many building societies have a share in the Republic's £680 million building society movement (the fourth largest in the world), and in its insurance societies whose assets exceed £400 million. Lloyd's of London has twenty-one agents or underwriters working in the Republic. Mr Harold Drayton, whose Investment Trust is one of the largest in the United Kingdom, has large and multifarious interests in the Republic, from coal mines to credit finance companies.

The Giants

The giants of the British industry are heavily committed in the Republic. Imperial Chemical Industries is a partner in Oppenheimer's African Explosives and Chemical Industries Ltd, which makes everything from explosives for the mines and chemicals for industry to munitions for the South African army: £10 million is invested in three new munitions plants alone, and its total post-war investment comes to £45 million. Courtaulds has invested on its own account more than £6 million, apart from its partnership with the Industrial Development Corporation in the £10 million South African Industrial Cellulose Corporation, which exports £7 million of rayon pulp a year. Unilever has spent £6 million on fixed assets alone since 1945: recently Mr George Cole, its chairman, said he wished its capital investment was even larger because its business in the Republic 'is showing a greater proportionate increase than elsewhere'.[1] Dunlop Rubber has an investment of nearly £4 million. International Combustion, Metal Box, and the English Electric Company are among other large investors.

The Shippers

Shipping is virtually an Anglo-American preserve, with the British dominating the closed circle of *The South and South-East African Conference Lines*. Its chairman, Sir Nicholas

Cayzer, is also the chairman of the British and Commonwealth Shipping Co, a group of eight shipping companies which include the Clan Line, Houston Line, King Line and the Union Castle; this last ccmpany holds the valuable mail contract between the Republic and Britain. Sir Nicholas has a third chairmanship as well: the London Committee of the South Africa Foundation. His view of those who complain about the lack of competition in shipping is that 'it is perhaps fortunate that the long-term interests of the shipping company and the country it serves are the same'.[1]

The shipbuilding firm, John Brown and Co, builds not ships but machine-tools in its two South African subsidiaries; it is also building the gas transmission and distribution system for the South African Coal, Oil and Gas Corporation. John Brown's chairman, Lord Aberconway, has reported encouraging success for the firm's efforts to 'obtain a substantial portion' of the market for mining tools. The Clelands Shipbuilding Company of Wallsend builds ships at its own yards for the Republic. Its chairman, Mr Kenneth Craggs, in an attack on Mr Harold Wilson in 1963 said: 'Our socialist politicians do their best to upset South Africa with their continual chorus of woe concerning the methods of government in that country 6,000 miles away, of the problems of which they know nothing. ... What worries all of us here connected with business in South Africa is that it is damaging to the tremendous reciprocal trade of which shipping is a most vital part.'[2]

Sugar, Chocolate and Biscuits

When South Africa left the Commonwealth, the special preference under the sugar agreement was extended for another $3\frac{1}{2}$ years, partly because sugar from the Swaziland protectorate (almost entirely owned by South Africans) is included in the Republic's quota. South Africa is the world's seventh largest producer of cane sugar. Its largest sugar concern, Sir J. L. Hulett and Sons, is partly British-owned. One of its four British directors is Lord Lyle. Last year, Hulett's interests were bought by a consortium of seven sugar companies assisted by two merchant banks, one of which is a subsidiary of the City bankers, Philip Hill, Higginson, Erlanger, Ltd. Among the leading British chocolate manufacturers is Cadbury-Fry which has recently expanded its interests. The firm tries, as in Birmingham, to adopt liberal employment practices; but as African trade unions are not recognised under law, its African workers elect headmen through whom they discuss their problems with management.

One of the confectioners who has recently moved into South Africa in a large way is the Canadian multi-millionaire, Garfield Weston, who controls the £90 million Associated British Foods. In 1963 he paid £5 million for the Premier Milling Company, which absorbs a quarter of the country's flour milling, and two fifths of its maize milling and feed-stuffs, besides producing one fifth of its baking products and being the second largest producer of oils and fats. 'I am enormously impressed by the growth and possibilities of the South African economy, by the quality of its business men, and the stability of the government,' Mr Weston said in support of his decision. 'Of course there are problems and difficulties—do you know any country without them? But South Africa is a great country with strong leadership. I believe in it.'[1]

The Liquor Merchants

'In the field of investment the Republic of South Africa is still the safest bet,' says Mr George McWatters, chairman of Harveys of Bristol Ltd, one of the many British wine and spirits firms with substantial local interests. 'Reports of underground activities are disturbing, but I have concluded that any likelihood of a change based on violence in this country need not cause potential investors any sleepless nights,' he added.[2] Booth's Distilleries opened its first distilling plant in late 1962 when its managing director, Mr Michael B. Henderson, said: 'I have great faith in the future of South Africa and believe it has excellent potential as an increasingly important market for "High and Dry".'[3] A director of Philip Hill, Higginson, Erlanger, Ltd, London is the chairman of its South African Board. W. & A. Gilbey Limited of Great Britain has expanded its interests by taking over one of the leading local firms, Santhagen's. Even Guinness's of Dublin broke its golden rule of always brewing in one of its own plants by agreeing to its stout being made by South African Breweries.

The Car Makers

The British motor car industry* has the largest share of the 110,468 cars assembled and sold in the Republic (1963) and of the £60 million of motor vehicle imports (1960). It ousted the Americans from their former top position in the provision of cars; the Germans are its closest rivals now. Six British car firms have established assembly plants in the Republic. Leyland Motors Ltd, Lancashire, with an investment of £8 million, is further consolidating its interests in Verwoerd's Republic— and, impartially, in Castro's Cuba as well. Its chairman, Sir Henry Spurrier, has said: 'We back our belief in that country [South Africa] with a big stake.'[1]   The Rootes Group of London and Coventry increased its investment by £750,000 in 1962. Its managing director, the Hon. Brian Rootes, called this 'the first instalment of what will ultimately be a big investment in that country'.[2]   British caravans, too, have found a rich market; Sprite Caravans of Newmarket, Suffolk, manufacture 1,200 a year in Natal.   The booming motor car industry has meant great expansion for the accessories and components provided by companies like Joseph Lucas Ltd of Birmingham and London.

Oil and Chemicals

South Africa's oil needs have quadrupled in fourteen years to 3,376,000 tons in 1961.   Both Shell and B.P. have a large share in this market.   Shell's investment rose from £3 million in 1939 to £22 million in 1961, and £24 million in 1964.   These two competing companies have combined through Consolidated Petroleum Company to build a £20 million oil refinery near Durban, which is nearly completed; its annual capacity will be three million tons.

Chemicals and fertilisers—with a gross output in 1960 of £116 million—are among the country's fastest growing industries.   Apart from the bigger firms like I.C.I., Courtaulds and Fisons (which has built a £2.5 million fertiliser factory), there are many smaller ones like Hickson and Welch of Castleford, Yorkshire, which makes a valuable copper chemical for the huge citrus industry.   The Beecham Group of

* Counting whites only, the number of persons to a vehicle in the Republic is 2.6, second only to the United States (counting *all* inhabitants).

Britain has recently completed its new £300,000 plant. Federated Paints of Glasgow is one of a number of British paint manufacturers with an important share in the paint market. British Titans Products, in partnership with African Explosives and Chemical Industries (linked with I.C.I.) has built a new titanium plant worth £3 million.

The Engineers

'I believe that, in the end, an apartheid policy will not be in the best economic interests of South Africa', Mr William Fraser, chairman of British Insulated Callender's Cables Group of Lancashire, said at the same time as he announced a decision to enlarge its interests. 'Business', he added, is 'remarkably resilient'; as an optimist he feels 'a solution will be found'.[1] Stewarts and Lloyds have an investment of £20 million.

British Oxygen of London recently voted another £480,000 to increase its oxygen and argon production. The Associated Electrical Industries and the Automatic Telephone and Electric Company have embarked jointly on a £2 million expansion programme. Standard Telephones and Cables of London has built a new rectifier plant. Scottish Cables' assets in 1962 amounted to £1.3 million. Turner and Newall, which has established two new factories costing £1¼ million, has brought technicians from Britain to get the new plant started. The Earl of Verulam, chairman of the Enfield Rolling Mills Ltd of Middlesex, is one of the newest arrivals on the scene with a company investment of £750,000. British Mitchell Cotts —its subsidiary in the Republic is already the largest manufacturer of welded steel—is spending £300,000 in further expansion.

Dorman, Long and Company of London and Middlesbrough—a large manufacturer and exporter of railway waggons—was given a £2 million contract by the South African Railways in 1962.

The expansion of two of the largest state-controlled enterprises—*Sasol* (the South African Coal, Oil and Gas Corporation), and *Vecor* (the Vanderbijl Engineering Corporation), the largest engineering works in Africa—has provided rich fields for harvest. Vickers Ltd and Associated Electrical

Industries have a large financial stake in the £8 million *Vecor* works; they also have technical aid agreements to assist in developing technical and electrical equipment. Other British firms with similar agreements include Duncan Stewart and Co of Glasgow, George Fletcher and Co of Derby, Iddon Brothers of Leyland, the Davy-Ashmore Group of Staffordshire, Babcock and Wilcox of London and Renfrew, and John Shaw and Sons of Salford. *Sasol* chose the Simon Engineering Group of Stockport for a £3 million contract which includes supplying them with the know-how and designs for the synthetic development of nitrogen fertiliser.

'As soon as there is a greater understanding between the different [racial] groups, the confidence of the rest of the world, particularly Britain, will be restored in the Republic',[1] Sir Walter Puckey, a director of International Computers and Tabulators Ltd of London, concluded at the end of a survey of prospects in the Republic. . However, many smaller British engineering firms have preferred not to wait for the kind of understanding mentioned by Sir Walter Puckey. Parkinson Cowan Ltd of London, Birmingham and Manchester has increased its manufacturing and distribution facilities. Williams and Williams Reliance Holdings of Chester has enlarged its aluminium window plant. Three British firms—Securex Ltd, Lodge Plugs Ltd, and Glacier Bearings Ltd—have combined to share administrative, clerical and tool room facilities in a new £325,000 group of factories in Natal. A. Reyrolle and Company of Hebburn-on-Tyne has increased its capital investment to £300,000.

'South Africa is today manufacturing more drill steel than the rest of the world put together',[2] was the jubilant endorsement given by Mr R. P. M. Holliday, managing director of Wickman Ltd of Coventry, to his firm's decision that all its exports of integral drill steels will be made only through its subsidiary in the Republic. The Adamson-Alliance Company of London has started building cranes locally, and the Birmingham firm of Cope Allman and Co has acquired control of a number of industrial companies.

Sir Aynsley Bridgeland, chairman of Humphries' Ltd (Britain's oldest firm of contractors) is the business man who believes that the economy will automatically solve all the countries most serious problems.*   His firm's investment stake in the Republic is £3 million; but he envisages further expansion.   A British firm, Universal Grinding Wheel Company of Stafford, and an American company, the Carborundum Company, have joined to step up production of grinding wheels. The world's largest makers of door-closers—William Newman and Sons of Birmingham—has taken over a local company.

The Manufacturers

No matter how distinctive his personal fancies and favourites, the chances are that the British consumer will find the same products under the same trade names made by the same firms in South Africa—whether it is Walls ice-cream, Horrockses cottons, Beechams pills, Beehive, Jenny or Lister Lavenda wools, or Meridian vests.   Like the engineers, British manufacturers think the risks are worth taking.   'There are first-class prospects for more business in South Africa, provided you have internal peace', was the careful verdict of Mr O. M. Stroud of Riley and Co, Bradford, announcing a limited expansion of his Port Elizabeth plant which makes interlinings and tie-linings for the clothing industry.   'If the non-whites get more money and buy more suits, it comes back to us.'[1]

South Africa's textile industry, with 200 firms employing 41,000 workers and producing £67 million worth of goods annually—nearly 4 per cent of the total value of the manufacturing industry—has lured many textile manufacturers. The biggest is the Lancastrian, Mr Cyril Lord, whose successful bargain is described on page 136.   The Calico Printers' Association of Manchester has an equal share with the state-controlled Industrial Development Corporation in the £4 million Good Hope Textile Corporation at Zwelitsha.   Here 3,000 African workers are supervised and trained by 200 whites—many of them Lancashire cotton workers.   This 1,000-loom mill produces more than half the country's cotton and rayon fabrics.

Horrockses Crewdson and Co of Preston is associated with Berg River Textiles in a £1 million expansion plan started in 1962.   Paton and Baldwins Limited of Darlington have joined with the Belgian spinners, Jean Tiberghien, to manufacture

* See page 110.

their famous range of 'Jenny' wools. The Lindhurst Group
of London manufactures fabrics in partnership with another
well-known British firm, Braitex Ltd. Towles, Edgar Jacobs
Ltd (formed by Towles Ltd of Loughborough) has been spec-
tacularly successful with its TEJ products. Having doubled
its initial £100,000 investment by a capitalisation issue in one
year, it put a further £100,000 into development in 1962.
James North of Hyde, Cheshire, doubled its productive capacity between 1956 and 1962 and now meets the country's
entire needs for protective gloves.

'The African treats clothes as a status symbol', says Mr
Gordon Bignall, managing director of the hosiery firm of
Meridian, Nottingham, which has had connections with South
Africa for fifty years. 'The special emphasis of the African',
Mr Bignall adds, 'is on the possession of a hat, but underwear
is considered very important, and many Africans already wear
Meridian.'[1]

The trend among British firms is to export technical staff
as well as plant, designs and capital. Thousands of British
technicians lead the life of Riley as supervisors and trainers in
some of the Republic's most salubrious areas. The Bentley
Group of Companies of Leicester, is one of the firms which
adopts this policy. Its managing director, Mr William Bentley, believes that 'South Africa has one of the brightest
industrial futures of any country in the world':[2] a view apparently shared by Lister and Co, of Bradford which decided in
1963 to step up their local production of Lister Lavenda
knitting wools.

The boot and shoe industry has kept step with clothing
and textiles; output has risen to nearly twenty-five million
pairs annually. Invested British shareholding forms a considerable part of the capital of £8½ million. British United Shoe
Machinery of Leicester alone has an investment of £3 million,
and its associations with South Africa go back to 1912.

Warning Voices

It is impossible not to detect behind the British business
man's infectious confidence about the Republic's economic
future the undertone of anxiety about its political future.
Optimism is being qualified: 'if internal peace can be main-

tained' or 'provided a solution can be found for the racial problems'. These doubts are not sufficiently strong to halt investment; but they slow down the potential volume of fresh capital which unqualified confidence would undoubtedly bring. This view is reflected in the warning given by Mr Peter Runge, the president of the Federation of British Industries, in a speech to South African industrialists in Johannesburg. 'I would be insincere—nay cowardly—if I were to leave you with the impression that the tremendous achievements of South African industry are the *only* factors which colour the views of industrialists at home, or which influence their confidence in your future. There is a fear that South Africa is isolating herself from the outside world behind barriers of hatred and suspicion. And there is a belief that progress and isolation are contradictory terms.'[1] An equally forthright opinion came from Sir Harry Pilkington (chairman of the TV committee of inquiry), whose glass firm Pilkington Brothers Ltd, has a stake in the Republic. After an absence of thirty-two years, Sir Harry returned to South Africa at the end of 1963 'prepared to write down' the reports about the political scene he had read in England. 'After being here for a while I feel that those reports are certainly not inaccurate.' Dismayed by this discovery, he was nevertheless surprised to find the country's economy in 'such a healthy state'.[2]

Nobody can deny the resilience of South Africa's economy: the only doubt is about the resilience of its political set-up.

Mr Lord's Black Paradise

> In the same position as South Africa I would do exactly the same as the Verwoerd government. South Africa may have to make some concessions, but she will bargain from strength.
>
> *Mr Cyril Lord*, EVENING STANDARD, LONDON,
> *October 5, 1963*

Before he came to power, Dr Verwoerd was a vehement critic of General Smuts' policy of encouraging British immigration and of tying South Africa's economy closely to Britain's. Now, his government pursues these policies with more vigour than ever did Smuts. It does all it can to smooth the way for thousands of immigrants, mainly British, and it arranges special terms for new foreign investors, often British. These terms make even South African industrialists envious. It is, therefore, both easy and profitable for industrialists to expand their activities to the Republic: how much more so for a Lancashire mill owner in a dwindling industry with everything to gain and little (except possibly some old plant) to lose.

Mr Cyril Lord is a cheerful Lancashire textile millionaire, and his success in South Africa provides an outstanding example of what Verwoerd's policies have to offer British industrialists. Mr Lord's fortunes were made when Lancashire's textile industry was still flourishing; its decline has caused many textile tycoons to seek new opportunities abroad. The Republic's Bantustan policies have brought Mr Lord and Dr Verwoerd's government together in a remarkable financial partnership. To provide employment for the hundreds of thousands of Africans who are, or will become, unemployed through population removals and influx control, the government embarked on the 'Border Industries' scheme.* Local textile industrialists, with heavy commitments in established areas, look with disfavour on this scheme. They fear the establishment of low-cost industrial rivals in the 'border areas', sustained for political reasons by important economic concessions, including the right to pay considerably reduced wage-rates. The government has therefore had to rely largely on the state-owned Industrial Development Corporation to pioneer the 'Border Industries'. It has made available £22½ million to start new textile factories. It was this opportunity which attracted Mr Lord. He became a partner with the IDC in a £2½ million textile mill near East London which will initially employ 1,200 Africans and 217 whites. Most of the whites are skilled Lancastrians who have been transported, *en famille*, to the 'borders' of Bantustan. Eighty-eight houses have been provided for the immigrants at a total cost of over £250,000.

Mr Lord's partnership has enabled him to obtain terms which considerably upset the established industrialists. His contribution to this partnership—apart from his own know-how and the technical skills of his immigrant labour force—is

* See page 70.

the plant no longer profitable in Lancashire: its value is £2 million. The rest of the capital is provided by the IDC. In return for what the government demanded—an integrated spinning, weaving and finishing plant with a capacity to expand to 15 million square yards by 1968—he obtained a special duty rate on imported loomstate cloth which, he insisted, should not be granted to previously established textile mills: an unprecedented monopolistic concession. The agreement is, of course, wrapped up in a way that makes it appear non-monopolistic: but this is its effect, as has been pointed out in the Johannesburg *Financial Mail.*[1]

Mr Lord and Dr van Eck, the chairman of IDC, provided their own enlightening commentary to this arrangement when their new poplin factory was opened in 1963. 'Mr Lord quipped that he had abandoned a sinking ship (the Lancashire industry) and was now going to help sink it (by depriving it of a South African market). Dr van Eck's joke was that Mr Lord had not only succeeded in jumping clear himself, but had also managed to salvage a lot of obsolete machinery: "And the IDC fell for this racket! The machinery works!", he said.'[2]

OTHER EUROPEAN INTERESTS

> When I woke up in Johannesburg, I found I was not in Africa but in Europe. There is practically nothing to distinguish your way of life.
> *M. Pinay, former Prime Minister of France, 1963*

Western Europe's interests in the Republic, apart from considerable trade, amount to a capital investment of £229 million —one quarter the size of Britain's investment in South Africa. Compared with Britain's, Europe's stake tends to take the form of minority rather than controlling shareholding; well over half of it (in Britain's case under a third) are minority shareholdings in mining, insurance and finance, and in loans to public authorities. The largest shares of these holdings are held by companies and individuals in Switzerland, France and Western Germany. Relatively few continental industries have gone into business on their own account. Notable exceptions include Philips of Holland, Siemens of West Germany, and the Hotchkiss-Brandt Engineering Company of France.

Most of the leading continental motor car firms share in local arrangements for manufacture, and a number of European shipping lines have an interest in the Shipping Conference. Eleven major industrial undertakings in the Republic rest on Swedish technical skill and capital; but these are largely operated by South Africans—only fourteen of the fifty-four directors are Swedish; they employ 3,000 people (1,750 of them whites) and have a yearly output of £8.5 million.

West Germany has in recent years taken a keen interest in industrial activities; but its main concentration is still on trade—up from under £250,000 in 1946 to over £124 million in 1962. The French have been exceptionally cautious about venturing into South Africa; their investments are concentrated largely in the shares of Paris-favoured mines. The Swiss share with the City of London the role of 'banker to the Republic'.

AMERICAN FINANCIAL INTERESTS

We have not given the racial situation any thought whatsoever, either in short- or long-term planning.
A manager of General Motors in South Africa,
June 1963

Mr Adlai Stevenson, the US representative at the UN deplored apartheid as a 'bitter toxic'. The white South African now calls it 'Separate Development'. The American investor calls it 'politics' and hastens to point out that his decisions are 'business decisions'.
NEW YORK TIMES, *August 18, 1963*

The American financial stake in South Africa is relatively small. The latest available figures show American investment in mining as £65 million, in manufacturing £40.5 million, in insurance and finance £18 million, in commerce £28 million. in miscellaneous interests £25½ million, and in loans to Public Authorities £119.5 million—a grand total of £293.5 million, rather less than one fifth of the total overseas investment in the Republic.

Nevertheless, it is large enough to mobilise an influential lobby of American big business interests in defence of their South African stake. Their chief spokesman is Mr Charles

W. Engelhard, multi-millionaire chairman of the Rand Mines, one of the seven 'Golden Houses'. Its total assets are valued at £18 million. Mr Engelhard's personal stake (primarily in mining and forest products) is estimated at about £12 million.*

There are about 160 American concerns doing business in the Republic. The largest are the motor car and farm implement manufacturers, and the oil companies. But chemicals and pharmaceuticals, mining and mining equipment are also important. General Motors, Chrysler and Ford run their own assembly plants. Ford's have by far the largest individual share of the motor car market—almost 24 per cent. Both Ford and General Motors—facing tough British, German and Japanese competition—have recently decided on extensive increases in their capital investment to enable them to manufacture car and truck engines in South Africa instead of importing the component parts for assembly. This decision has been welcomed by the government as it speeds up their plan to produce 'the All South African Car' by several years.

The Standard Vacuum Oil Company owns a large refinery in Durban; together with Caltex it has been asked by the government to expand its storage facilities. There is a suggestion that Caltex might also start its own refinery.

The American mining groups with the largest interests are American Metal Climax, Inc. (also associated through the Rhodesian Selection Trust in the development of Northern Rhodesian copper) and the Newmont Mining Corporation. They jointly hold most of the stock in the Tsumeb Corporation (South West Africa), and are likely to be involved in the new copper development in the Northern Transvaal as well. 'We know the people and the government and we back our conviction with our reputation and our dollars',[1] says Mr M. D. Banghart, vice-president of Newmont. He pointed out that US firms could make an average profit of 27 per cent in South Africa—considerably more than they can at home. Armco Steel Corporation—a leading American steel manufacturer—has started producing corrugated steel pipe at its new factory near Johannesburg. It will consume more than

* The role of Mr Engelhard and of the American lobby is discussed in Part Two, Chapter Four.

5,000 tons of steel annually from the state-owned *Iscor* works.

Americans are well to the fore in the new diamond rush which has started in South West Africa as a result of the discovery of vast new diamond deposits both on the land and on the sea-bed. This development has attracted to the Skeleton Coast some of the world's most powerful companies. They have formed a complex structure of alliances which link together Oppenheimer's De Beers, several of the Rand's 'Golden Houses', Paul Getty's Tidewater Oil Company of America, and the Broederbond-inspired *Federale Mynbou*. The pioneering genius of sea-bed diamond mining is a Texan millionaire, Mr Sammy Collins, who controls Establishment Collins International. He holds a 40 per cent interest in the Southern Diamond Corporation—a company with an authorised capital of £1 million which holds extensive tidewa*er and sea-bed concessions—and twelve million of the 14,315,0 '0 Sea Diamond Corporation's shares; this Corporation, in its turn, has a 44 per cent interest in the £5 million Marine Diamond Corporation. All these companies pay from 5 to 12 per cent in royalties to the South African government.

Mr Paul Getty's Tidewater Oil (wholly owned by the Getty Oil Company) has the dominant interest in the Diamond Mining and Utility Company of South West Africa. It holds concessions to mine diamonds and all other minerals in South West Africa's Diamond Area No 2, as well as the foreshore and offshore to the continental shelf over a distance of 250 miles. These interests are developed through Getty's locally registered Veedol Minerals, which is also associated with De Beers.

JAPAN'S RISING STAR

Just as Hitler's Nuremberg laws were waived to allow the Japanese to be treated as 'honorary Aryans', so in South Africa they have been granted exemption from the Republic's racial laws against Africans and Asians. This concession has made it possible for Japan to become one of South Africa's most important trading partners. Since 1956, trade between the two countries has increased by 500 per cent; exports to Japan went to about £35 million in 1963, and are even higher now; imports from Japan are well above £25 million. The Japanese are mainly interested in maize (£5.5 million in 1961), wool (£7.5 million) and base metals (£7 million). Yawata Iron and Steel has a £90 million contract to take five million tons of pig iron over ten years.

Japan looks like ousting the United States as the Republic's second biggest trading partner, after Britain. South Africa is already Japan's twelfth biggest supplier of raw materials.

But the Japanese are not content simply to be trading partners. They are opening up factories in the Republic. Within eighteen months of entering the field of light truck manufacturing, Datsum, Toyopet and Mazda succeeded in capturing almost one fifth of the total market.

4: THE MOOD OF ENGLISH-SPEAKING SOUTH AFRICA

Those who have tears for South Africa prepare to shed them soon. For inexorably we are moving into the twilight that precedes the night.

Laurence Gandar, Editor of RAND DAILY MAIL,
March 14, 1962

I would not be surprised if gallant, loyal and British Natal of all provinces should be in the van of any 'English' stampede into the white laager.

Scott Haigh, political columnist of SUNDAY TRIBUNE,
Durban, September 1, 1963

It is not easy to discuss the mood of English-speaking South Africa because it is both diffuse and variable. Right-wing, moderate and radical attitudes compete for influence: each represents an important strand in the local English culture, and all help to condition attitudes and morale. The dominant attitudes at any time are strongly influenced by prevailing conditions within South Africa and by international opinion. Economic prosperity, combined with an absence of sabotage and violence at home and a diminished threat of international intervention, produce a mood which is relaxed, if not optimistic. At such times it is felt that 'time is on our side', and that 'the worst will never happen'. Thus negatively expressed, there is some hope that a solution will present itself, and that 'given enough rope' the government will hang itself. This mood is translated into propagandistic clichés like 'given enough time', and 'if we are only left alone, everything will be all right'.

But this mood is sharply reversed at times of overt crisis, deriving either from overseas threats or internal violence. Then opinion is divided. The right wing takes the view approximating closely to Afrikanerdom's that a tough government is needed to handle the situation; the moderates are less sure and so waver between this position and that of the radicals who argue that the changes are caused by the inflexibility of the government itself. The right wing is articulately in favour of 'white unity' when the apparent threat comes from black Africa. Others see Pan-Africanism and the eruption of violence to the north as evidence of the need to adapt to the new African situation. Mrs Helen Suzman, MP, said of the government's reactions to the mutinies in East Africa in 1964: 'Foolishly they gloat about disasters in the rest of Africa. How shortsighted can Members of Parliament be?'[1]

Nothing more profoundly affects attitudes than the fear of estrangement from the West. However irritated and defensive, English-speaking South Africa as a whole is strongly realistic about the need to consider world opinion. The *Natal Mercury* sums up these fears. Describing world opinion as 'an irresistible force' and the Verwoerd Government's racial policies as 'an immovable object', it warns: 'If neither gives way there can be only one end—an explosion, probably violent.' It adds that there is an ever-present doubt that [Afrikaner] Nationalism is being too rigid and implacable in its racial approach to current problems. This obduracy in high places could be South Africa's Achilles' heel. It is losing for us friends we need in a hostile world.'[2]

Not surprisingly, the mood induced by growing awareness of danger produces conflicting recipes: one is for all the whites to join in a single laager; another is to oppose the government's policies much more strongly. 'Loyal Natal' is particularly receptive to the laager idea, but it is by no means alone. Yet it would be wrong to conclude that a realignment of forces has already taken place. Although the number of English-speaking voters who support the government is growing, it still remains only a small proportion.

Except among the radicals, morale is low. This appears from the generally passive submission to the Afrikaners' growing cultural and political domination; the increasing willingness to compromise on Dr Verwoerd's terms; the characteristically apathetic support given to the United Party; and the pessimistic acceptance of the view that a change of government is very unlikely in the near future. These attitudes reflect a fairly general acceptance of reactionary policies among English-speaking voters, and recall an opinion expressed by General Smuts in 1948: 'Reaction has struck its roots very deep in this country; just how deep few people yet realise.'[3]

The morale of the radicals is sustained by their passionate sense of the need to present a positive alternative to the government's policies, and of keeping in touch with modern political trends. They are encouraged in these beliefs, not by the expectation of becoming electorally strong, but by the sense of providing the 'conscience' of white South Africa and by the hope that, in the long run, they may provide a political bridge to reconnect the white and the non-white communities. Their crusade to defend civil liberties and the rule of law is waged consistently and with little regard for the consequent decline of electoral support. They are not easily intimidated by coercion and threats. They fight both the government and the United Party in the spirit that their cause is essentially similar to that of the anti-Nazi forces which resisted Hitlerism. 'Nationalists and United Party supporters do not understand the psychology of free men, but they do understand the psychology of neo-Nazism', the leader of the Progressive Party, Dr Jan Steytler, declared in a recent speech.[1] And the Liberal leader, Mr Alan Paton, has said: 'South Africa is not a Nazi country, but it is not a bad imitation of one.'[2]

One problem common to all the predominantly English-speaking parties is the problem of establishing a common front with the African nationalist movement. They can admire individual African leaders—and especially the calm dignity and integrity of Chief Lutuli—but all except the Liberals reject the basic demand of the African leadership for the universal franchise. This dilemma is described by the *Pretoria News*: 'All parties now know that they must come to terms with African aspirations while holding firmly to their own. The question the Lutuli affair [the award of the Nobel Peace Prize for 1960] raises, is whether anyone has tried to use his qualities to achieve this end. The [Afrikaner] Nationalists have locked him up, the United Party has ignored him, and the Progressives have pretended not to notice that he is not saying what they are saying.'[3]

With the exception of the radical minority, therefore, uncertainty and pessimism prevail in the English-speaking community. Even those who have joined the laager lack the crusading conviction of their Afrikaner colleagues. The rest seek an uneasy accommodation with Afrikanerdom through organisations like the South Africa Foundation. In this way they have linked their economic power to the political authority of Afrikanerdom in an uneasy and unequal partnership to ensure that, whatever else changes, the economic *status quo* is upheld.

III

THE AFRICANS

Non-whites, under the minority rule of 'whites only',
have for decades suffered and continue to suffer a
repression that not only impoverishes them, but is a
most humiliating affront to their person and dignity.
Chief Albert Lutuli, 1962

*   *   *

1: AFRICAN SOCIETY

South Africa is not the only authoritarian society in the world,
but it is the only racial autocracy. It is this which sets the
Republic apart from all other contemporary states.

Although Africans outnumber whites by eleven to three,
they have no say whatever in making the laws by which they
are expected to live. Not even when it comes to planning
their future under the projected Bantustans—supposedly
designed to enable them to develop their own separate societies
—are they allowed to discuss its fundamental principles. The
Bantustan idea was thought up by white politicians, its laws
drafted by white civil servants, approved by a white cabinet,
debated by a white parliament, and submitted for approval to
a white electorate. When the fundamentals of Bantustans
were established, the draft plan was discussed with Africans—
but only with tribal leaders in the reserves. They represented not only the most backward part of the African community but also a minority of the population, for almost two
thirds of the Africans no longer live in the reserves. Moreover these tribal elements were consulted only on the narrow
question of how to apply the white-made laws. They may
bargain over details but have no right to reject the substance.
At no point in this process of law-making has the African
majority the right of consent on the issues which affect it.
This is one of the stark realities of South Africa today.

It will be asked: why, if the Africans are so numerous and so deeply dissatisfied with their lot, have they not long since revolted as did the Kikuyu in Kenya, or the Algerian Arabs? Up to 1906 they did fight back, but their capacity for physical resistance was effectively broken at Blood River in 1838 with the defeat of the Zulu armies. After 1910, when South Africa ceased to be ruled by a colonial power, the forces in control were locally based. They were committed to maintaining their rule in the same way as they had established it—by relying on their superior weapons, and by denying these to Africans.

REACTIONS TO CONQUEST

> Seen in retrospect it was clear that the greatest disservice ever done to the Bantu was that the whites had helped to disintegrate his tribal life. It had been done for most part by people who did not have the welfare of the Bantu in mind but who had some political or economic objective to serve. They wanted to use the Bantu for their own selfish ends.
>
> DIE TRANSVALER, *March 9, 1962*

Conquest was not just a matter of military defeat; nor did it cause only the disintegration of traditional society. It yoked Africans to the white economy and forced the majority into the white social system. There were broadly four types of reaction. Most of those who remained in the reserves sought to preserve as much as they could of their old ways, segregated from whites except for officials and missionaries; these were the conservatives; some of them spend much of their working lives in the 'white areas' as migrant labourers, but their roots remain in the reserves. Those who changed life on their own land for work on the white man's land passively accepted a master-servant relationship in conditions of rural poverty. Those who gave up their tribal lands and settled in the towns and accepted urbanisation and detribalisation became a black proletariat in a white capitalist society. Finally, there were those who chose Christianity and education as a challenge to their own abilities to become a part of Western society; for these, acculturation was a deliberate choice. From this group the new elite sprang.

The conservatives in the reserves complained that 'at first we had the land and the white man had the Bible, now we have the Bible and the white man has the land'[1]. But the committed African Christian claimed the Bible as his weapon to regain the land.

This oversimplified but not inaccurate picture of the way Africans reacted to their conquest bears comparison with the experiences of the American Negro. With the exception of the conservatives in the reserves who clung to their old ways, the majority of black South Africans, like the Negroes, accommodated themselves to a Western society and tried in their different ways to adapt to it.

One answer, then, to the question why there has been no 'black revolt' in South Africa since 1910 is that the Africans, like the Negroes, have spent the last fifty years struggling to find their place in an alien society. It was left to a minority, the elite, to foster the struggle for the dignity of full citizenship. It is they who founded the first African nationalist movement. Their aim has never been to 'push the white man into the sea', but to compel the white society to open its doors to Africans who wished to join it.

These leaders of the African political struggle are strikingly similar to the American leaders of the Niagara movement and the NAACP. They, too, are professors, clergymen, teachers, journalists, lawyers and doctors. Almost without exception the leaders of the African National Congress have been committed Christians. There are other striking parallels: the great importance attached by both movements to the status of higher education; their firm belief in constitutional methods of struggle, and their rejection of violence; their treasured belief in an elite leadership; their ambivalent relationships with white liberals and with marxists; their apparently unshakable confidence in the ultimate 'reasonableness' of the white rulers; their insistence on the virtues of moderation; and their eager desire for co-operation between the races.

Those who fail to understand the similarities between the American and the South African societies find it hard to understand why African political leaders have behaved as they have and for as long as they have. But the temper of the African nationalist movement, like that of the Negro, has begun to change. The old elite is becoming discredited; Christianity is being regarded as a dangerous soporific; moderation is felt to be weakness; the need for violence is accepted as inevitable and necessary; and racism is beginning to find its supporters, especially among the youth. These are the new trends. It is less remarkable that these should have grown up than that they should have been so long delayed.

AFRICANS IN THE RESERVES

> Referring to the Bantu Authorities Act (1951) and the Promotion of Bantu Self-Government Act (1959), the Prime Minister said in parliament on January 23, 1962, that there had been no true Bantu leaders in the past and certainly no leader of all Bantu nations. Through these Authorities it was now possible to know what the Bantu themselves wanted.
>
> STATE OF SOUTH AFRICA YEARBOOK, 1963

The reserves, comprising 264 blocks of land scattered over the country, cover about thirty-three million acres of land. They hold over four million Africans. By any standard they are the least developed parts of the country.* The income of the average family in the reserves (estimated at six to a family) was given by the Tomlinson Commission† as £43 per annum. Agriculture in the reserves produced a *per capita* income of £12.9 compared with £99.4 for the country as a whole. According to the Commission, the real income of the reserves remained unchanged between 1936 and 1952, while *per capita* income naturally declined. Generations of overstocking and overcrowding (the Transkei's population density is eighty-two per square mile) have reduced the reserves to conditions of chronic soil erosion. The Tomlinson Commission estimated that about £25 million would have to be spent in ten years on stopping soil erosion alone, and that half the present population would have to leave the land permanently and settle in 'rural villages': only then would there be any prospect that the rest might earn £60 a year on 'stabilised land'. These wretchedly poor areas are to become the Bantustans of the future. They are not only intended to become the focus-point

---

* For a more detailed description of the reserves see pp. 58–59.
† See page 69.

of African political development; they must also receive the Africans expelled from the 'white areas'.

Many of those expelled include politically conscious 'trouble-makers'. Thus the reserves—which for most of this century have drowsed in the backwaters of rural poverty—are being churned up by contesting sets of political ideas and modes of life. The chiefs have been catapulted into the political arena by the Bantu Authorities Act and the Bantu Self-Government Act, which give them a central place in the new territorial governments. Chiefs who support the policy of Bantustan come under attack not only from other chiefs who oppose it, but also from dissenting tribesmen. In this way, chiefs have been set up against chiefs, and tribesmen against the chieftaincy. These disagreements are turned into vicarious attacks on the central government by opposition to those chiefs who support government policies.

The government's commitment to 'separate development' presents two major risks. The first is its decision to try to steer African nationalism into the reserves from the towns: a crucial decision taken by Dr Verwoerd with his eyes wide open. One of his propagandists, Mr J. J. J. Scholtz, carefully underscored this risk in a series of articles he wrote for the government paper, *Die Burger*, in 1962. The 'Black Nationalists of the Transkei', he wrote, were now co-operating in implementing the Transkei plan, but it should cause no surprise when in a year or so, they began to insist on human equality, even if only at first for those whom in their opinion had a claim to it. 'Let us make no mistake: it is essentially the same Black Nationalism which has swept everything before it elsewhere in Africa.... The striving for equality is perhaps the main element in the expressions of Black Nationalism elsewhere in Africa. It cannot be expected that the Transkei will prove an exception.'[1] If Verwoerd's supporters understand this danger, why have they let themselves in for the experiment? The answer is that they believe the only chance of keeping African nationalism weak in the 'white areas' is by giving it an outlet in 'the Bantu homelands' where, they hope, it might be easier to guide and control.

The second risk is the government's decision to put its future in the hands of the chiefs by relying on them to make the Bantustan policy work. If the chiefs fail, the whole edifice of apartheid fails. Who are these chiefs on whom the government has decided to rest its power? A few are leaders of great authority who feel themselves accountable to their own people, and command loyalty among the tribal peasants. Among them are paramount chiefs Sabata Dalindyebo of the Tembu, Victor Poto of the Fingo, and Cyprian Bhekuzulu of of the Zulus. Chiefs like these cannot easily be dismissed by the government because their authority is strong, and because their supporters would not easily accept substitutes: to dismiss them would produce grave administrative problems such as occurred among the Ba-Pedi of Sekhukuniland and in Pondoland.

Others are chiefs appointed by the government to establish new centres of tribal authority, or to replace traditionally elected leaders dismissed for non-coöperation or incompetence. There are many of these—men like Chief Kaiser Matanzima of Emigrant Tembuland. Their authority depends to a considerable extent on the support of the central government. But most of the chiefs are of little real consequence, controlling weak tribes or being subordinates to Paramount Chiefs. The chiefs are salaried by the government: £2,218 for the Paramount Chief of the Zulus, £1,500 for other Paramount Chiefs, £1,000 for Chief Kaizer Matanzima, and from £600 downwards for others. They must act as agents for government policies, and they can be dismissed by the government. The only chiefs who count in terms of real power are the senior leaders of the larger tribal groups who have been elected by traditional methods. One feature common to all chiefs is their role as intermediaries between the white authorities and their own people. When unpopular government decisions have to be enforced, they find themselves pushed by the authorities to be strong and even ruthless, and resisted by their own people who expect them to intervene with the government for relief. But as the majority of chiefs have no real power, it is to the government that they must listen in the end, or accept their consequent dismissal.

The chiefs reacted in various ways to the government's offer to 'reconstitute tribal authority'. The conservatives among them were often ready-made clients for Bantustans.

Others accepted passively simply to avoid trouble with the government; others opposed from the start. A number of these last were dismissed or banned. The majority played for time, neither accepting nor rejecting it, but asking for a postponement of decision. It was only when the government, having chosen the Transkei as the first Bantustan, insisted on the scheme going through that the majority of the chiefs there submitted to the inevitable; even so, many accepted with the intention of adapting the policy to their own purposes.

These different attitudes were brought out in the clash of forces in the Transkei after the decision to turn it into a Bantustan. Chief Kaiser Matanzima, trained as a lawyer and with considerable experience of radical nationalist politics in Capetown, emerged as the leader of those chiefs who accept Bantustan because they feel that it offers them an opportunity to reject white domination and to create a segregated black society. Explaining Matanzima's policies, his secretary, Mr T. E. K. Tshungwa, said the chief had 'consistently followed a policy of Bantu nationalism'; it was a policy accepted by the Transkei people as a 'counterblast to white domination'. The Bantu should base their economic construction on industrial development as a 'counterpoise to white capitalism and the exploitation of the poor that will lead to permanent enslavement of the black man'.[1] Matanzima's black racism is the complement of Verwoerd's white racism. One recalls how the American Negro, Marcus Garvey and the Ku Klux Klan made common cause over Garvey's wish to lead the Negroes 'back to Africa'.

Matanzima's aim is to exploit his value to Verwoerd to get as much as he can to enable him to make a reality of his rule in the Transkei. Against Matanzima's view is that of the two most powerful Paramount Chiefs in the Transkei: Sabata Dalindyebo and Victor Poto. But although they accepted the Bantustan Territorial Authority as inescapable, they reject its philosophy. They insist that if the Bantustan idea is to lead to eventual African self-determination it should be on lines determined by Africans whose choice is to turn 'Bantustans' into multiracial societies. The ticket backed by Sabata and Poto won a convincing two thirds majority of elected members in the first elections for the new Legislative Assembly in 1963.

Whether this result should be interpreted positively as a vote for multiracialism, or negatively as a rejection of Matanzima, is open to argument. What it does show is that an overwhelming majority of Africans rejected the candidates identified with the government's policies.

The result was a blow to the government's prestige. It contradicted the tireless assertions of the Minister of Bantu Affairs and Development that the government knew what the Africans really wanted. It made nonsense of the assertions of the chief spokesman of his Department, Mr Chris Prinsloo, that 'a referendum among Bantu in South Africa would show that 85 per cent of them approved of the policy of separate development'.[1] The Transkei election, at least, proved no such thing. Having ascertained (in Dr Verwoerd's words) 'what the Bantu themselves wanted', how did the government react? Before the election results became known, the government had announced that it would not tolerate the 'multiracialism' advocated by Sabata and Poto; and when they won, it immediately declared that there was no question of their being allowed to implement their election promises. So much for democracy in the Bantustans.*

But though the Transkei experiment had got off to a bad start, the government quickly recovered its control. The popular majority won by Sabata and Poto became a minority in the Territorial Legislature through the votes of the nominated chiefs—who outnumber the elected members. Even so, the chiefs were not easily suborned. From accounts of the pressures applied by Matanzima and the government's representatives on chiefs reluctant to stand out against the Sabata-Poto majority, it seems clear that not even the traditionalists are happy about the way tribal authority is to be imposed. It will be interesting to see how Matanzima and the government attempt the downfall of Sabata and Poto—as they certainly will. It will not be easy: their removal could produce a revolt such as the one which led to a state of emergency in 1959 in one of the Transkei's important provinces, East Pondoland. Now, five years later, the whole of the Transkei is subject to the infamous 'Proclamation 400' permitting indefinite deten-

* For a discussion about these issues, see 'Bantustans or Bust', p. 57.

tion without trial and forbidding the holding of meetings without permission: this amounts to a perpetual state of emergency.

Meanwhile, none of the other projected 'homelands' has yet acceded to the Bantustan experiment in their territories. The government has marked out Zululand as the next of the Bantustans; but the Zulus have so far resisted the white man's dream of restoring tribalism to the glories of the days of Dingaan before Blood River.

AFRICANS ON THE PLATTELAND

My humble opinion is that there will be millions of Bantu workers in the white areas. It is however my policy and that of the government to canalise the best labour into agriculture. I feel convinced that such a policy is in the best interests of our economic development.
Mr M. C. de Wet Nel, Minister of Bantu Affairs and Development, 1960

'Farmers would shortly find that the wind of change blowing in Africa was a cold reality,' said Mr H. H. Odendaal, Administrator of the Transvaal. 'The demonstrations we had last year (Sharpeville, etc.) were confined to the urban areas, but you must not for a moment imagine that the urban Bantu and the platteland Bantu can be kept separate. The Bantu in the town has merely taken the lead and will carry his brother on the farm with him.'
DIE TRANSVALER, *April 27, 1961*

There are two striking features of social and economic life in the 'white rural areas'—the *platteland*—which cover roughly three quarters of the Republic. They hold only 17 per cent of the total white population, but almost 40 per cent of the African population. There are about ten times more blacks than whites (5 million to 506,000) on the platteland; of these nearly 3½ million are on white farms. The trend of population movement shows a steady decrease in the number of whites (605,000 in 1941; 571,000 in 1951; 506,000 in 1960), and a rise of over 20 per cent in the number of Africans between 1951 and 1960.

Reporting on the rapidity with which the platteland was 'going black', the Du Toit Commission in 1960 found that up to 83 per cent of the farms in parts of Natal and up to 25 per cent of the farms in the Orange Free State were occupied by non-whites. Commenting on this report the pro-government paper, *Die Burger*, said that town and country were facing the same challenge: how to keep 'the white part of South Africa for the white man'. It added: 'In some parts of the country there are farmers who have no white neighbours. According to present trends . . . it seems as if it is an accomplished fact that the platteland has become black.'[1] Another pro-government paper[2] commented that if this trend continued 'we may foresee in a measurable time that the owners of the farms will be sitting in the towns while the farming class will consist of Bantu'.

The second striking feature is that agriculture contributes only slightly less to the value of the Republic's exports than the combined industrial and mining sectors, excluding gold. But there are only 66,000 whites employed on 106,220 white farms as against 717,000 Africans* and over one quarter million Coloureds and Indians. Thus the Republic's important agricultural wealth is as dependent on a non-white labour force as its mining, industry or commerce. The size of the African farm population is partly the result of government policy, which ensures cheap labour and therefore a relatively low degree of mechanisation. The various Pass Laws, the Urban Areas Act, the Masters and Servants Act and the laws governing squatters and contract labour have created a complex web binding farm labourers to their employers. 'Surplus' labour in the towns is simply shunted out to the white farming areas, unless it finds accommodation in the already crowded reserves. A survey conducted in the Eastern Cape[3] points out that 'the legal position . . . is that it is virtually impossible for an African farm worker to be anything other than a farm worker all his life, and the same applies to his children and their children'. The effect of legislation controlling influx to the towns, together with the saturation of the reserves, is to create 'in the true sense an exploited working class [who have] no alterna-

---

* The apparent discrepancy with the quoted figure of 3½ million Africans on white farms is explained by dependants and migratory workers.

tive but to accept employment on farms on any terms which the farmer likes to determine'.

At best, relations between white farmers and their workers is paternalistic; at worst it is medieval and scandalous. Periodically, the country is shocked by evidence of particularly brutal abuses. Until 1961 farmers were allowed to maintain private prisons to which Africans arrested for technical offences were sent in lieu of trial and judicial punishment. In 1959 the government appointed a commission to investigate conditions, especially in the notorious Bethal area where scores of farmers have been tried for crimes including murder and brutal assault of labourers. The report has not been published, but the system was suspended.

There are no reliable overall statistics showing wages and conditions of farm labour. The Eastern Cape survey referred to above indicated an average monthly wage in cash and kind of £9 per family. Of this the greater part was in kind; and since the mean wage for an adult male was between 25s. and 30s. a month, the achievement of £9 per month depended upon most members of the family accepting employment. A senior officer in the Department of Agricultural Economics and Marketing indicated in 1959 that the average cost of a farm labourer was £60 per annum.[1]

It is hardly surprising that African farm labour is the most passive group in the African political spectrum. Trade union or political activity is impossible in such vulnerable conditions. Complaints against employers go through official channels, and these rarely result in redress of grievances. The crux of the farm worker's position is that the government's laws have reversed the normal economic processes in an expanding industrial society: the rural areas are being expected to absorb the urban unemployed, and not *vice versa*. The result is the creation of a permanently depressed class of workers, with no alternative to existing employment. To the familiar conservatism of rural workers is added the apathy bred by hopelessness.

AFRICANS IN THE TOWNS

The Native in the towns, in the industries of South
Africa . . . remains a weapon aimed at the economy and
the order of the country. That this Native in the mass
can be peace-loving and law-abiding if he is left in peace
does not alter the fact. From outside and from
within the country, he is being incited to assert himself
until his demands are granted to the very limit of what
his political leaders can conceive.

DIE BURGER, *April 5, 1960*

About 61.5 per cent of the non-white population live in
white areas where they come daily into contact with
whites. Is it not profoundly deplorable that we stand
detached and cold towards them and live in separate
worlds? Must we not let these people feel that we not
only have big gaols to lock them up in, but that we can
also appreciate much that is good in them? Why must
some of them never hear anything but cold commands,
harsh swear words and curses from the lips of white employers and foremen? If this process cannot be made to
stop, the wind of change could indeed become a cyclone.

DIE KERKBLAD (*organ of the Dutch Reformed Church*),
March 25, 1960

The government's policy is to extend the authority of the
tribal-based African leadership into the urban communities
through a system of 'tribal ambassadors'. Each of these is
intended to act as a link between the Bantustans, his own
tribe in the town, and the government. This policy has two
objectives: to encourage the growth of separatist nationalism
among the different African ethnic groups, and to fix a political
lodestar in the reserves to rival the modern urban leadership.
These efforts have so far borne little fruit; the 'ambassadors'
find themselves under the same pressures as the chiefs: be-
sieged by their clansmen in trouble, and coerced by the
authorities to enforce discipline.* The tendency today—
spurred by government policy—is rather the other way: urban
ideas are taking root in rural minds.

There are over 3,500,000 Africans in the urban areas—an

* One of the findings of a SABRA commission in 1961 was that 'Bantu
born and raised in the cities showed little loyalty to tribal captains and
were unwilling to submit to the authority of men of whom they thought
very little. In general, urban natives were not in favour of a system of
captains' representatives in the cities.'

increase of more than a million since the Afrikaner Nationalist government tackled its self-imposed sisyphean task of stemming the black flood to the towns. There is no town in the Republic where non-whites do not predominate; and the larger the town the greater the preponderance. Because the government is unwilling to curb South Africa's economic expansion it cannot curb the influx to the towns. Instead, it imposes drastic restrictions on the terms under which non-whites can live in 'the white areas'. This policy is guided by three principles: Africans have no right under any circumstances to the privileges of citizenship in 'white areas'; they are to be regarded 'for all time' as temporary sojourners there; and they have no right to live in these areas unless their labour is specifically required by the 'white' economy.

Guided by these principles the following measures are applied to control urban Africans:

No African is automatically entitled either to seek work or to remain in employment in any area outside the reserves. Every work-seeker requires permission to enter and remain in employment in all 'white' areas. Before the passage of the Bantu Laws Amendment Bill of 1964, an African could 'qualify' to remain in a 'white' urban area if (a) he was born there and had resided there lawfully ever since; or (b) he had been in continuous employment there for fifteen years or (c) he had worked there continuously for the same employer for ten years. Such 'qualifications' can no longer be earned. Any African, whatever his previous record, can be 'endorsed out' of an area if, *inter alia*:

1. The Minister has decided that the number of Africans in the area concerned exceeds its reasonable labour requirements.

2. The African concerned comes from an area from which the Minister has decided no more labour is to be recruited to the 'white' area concerned.

3. The African concerned is deemed to be 'idle' or 'undesirable'.

4. It is deemed not to be in the interests either of the employer or the employed, or in the public interest, that the contract of service shall continue.

Wives and other dependants of Africans working in the 'white' areas may not live with their husbands and fathers unless they have 'ordinarily resided' together *in the same area* previously. The position of a newly married couple remains legally obscure, since the assumption is that they have not ordinarily resided together before the marriage. Certainly, a man who marries a woman from another area must have express permission for her to enter his area of employment, and this *may* be granted only if he fulfills one of the three conditions mentioned above. If permission is not granted for man and wife to live together, the wife may visit her husband without permission for periods of up to seventy-two hours; but if she is picked up by the police during that time, the onus is on her to prove she has not been there for longer than seventy-two hours.

The official in charge of the 'labour bureaux' responsible for considering requests by Africans to enter 'white' areas or take up employment there, are designated 'peace officers'; as such they have the power of arrest and the right to search premises. 'Aid centres' are being established to which Africans arrested on charges of contravening these 'influx control' regulations may be sent. Those arrested without warrant may not be detained for more than forty-eight hours, unless a warrant is subsequently obtained. Courts are to be held in the 'aid centres', but persons brought there may be released without charges being brought against them.

This new legislation can only be described as a blueprint for a system of direction of labour. No African may take a job or live in any 'white' area unless the authorities sanction it. The government will be able to determine the supply and distribution of labour to all parts of the country   Residential and employment rights for Africans are linked entirely to the labour needs of the 'white' economy. Africans have lost the last vestige of security in the 'white' areas. No African's job or home is safe from official decree.

How do all these laws affect the personal lives of Africans? This is just one typical case described by a social worker in Capetown.

Kaiser M. . . . is a married man with a worry—one which

non-Africans should know about. Kaiser has been married for eight years and has never lived with his wife, never had a home. The law has not allowed it. That is the literal truth, and it applies to the vast majority of African marriages, as family life is normally lawful only under the starvation conditions offered by the reserves. Kaiser goes home from Capetown to the Transkei on unpaid leave for three months every few years, and occasionally Patience, his wife, visits him in the location in Capetown. But they don't live together—they have no *right* to live together. Kaiser has worked for sixteen years, barring holidays, for a big department store in Capetown; but that does not give his wife any right to live in the area. If they want another baby, they must arrange a visit. *Arrange to visit one's husband in order to conceive a child? Unthinkable!* Well, most non-African South Africans refuse to think about it, shut it out of their minds, forget it by all means, and go right back to their own comfortable routine. Kaiser wants to live with his wife now—he says it is high time. Patience has come to visit him at Nyanga Township and she has done everything the law requires, from getting permission from the local magistrate before leaving the Transkei to appearing at Langa Registration Office with her 'book' within seventy-two hours of arrival. She produced her return train ticket, too, and undertook to leave within three months and not to take any paid work while here, even if the children are a bit hungry. Kaiser has rented a house (lucky man! . . . houses are scarce . . .), but must keep up payments on his temporarily unused *bachelor quarters*. He has been striving to obtain a permanent permit for Patience. His firm have vouched for his excellent character, but their testimonial was handed back unopened by the official. His record, carefully filed at Langa with that of every single African in the area, although flawless, was of no help to him. The permit has been refused . . . Influx control, you know! Let us bow before the great God, Policy![1]

This is one of the 4,500 cases a year—eighteen a day—which are dealt with by the Athlone Advice Centre in Capetown, where women volunteers give help and advice and lend the influence of their white skins to the victims of the Pass

Laws. The fact that these women are able to register a high proportion of successes—about forty per cent of the cases handled—is a measure of the helplessness of Africans on their own when placed at the mercy or the discretion of white officials. 'The worst type of case arises with women who have lived here since 1945 unofficially with their husbands, and now with the cleaning up of places like Windermere, they are found and sent out. But if we can prove that their husbands qualify to remain and that the wives have "normally resided" with them then we can sometimes get permission for them to stay.'[1]

The destruction of normal family life, the humiliation of helplessness, the upheaval of deportation—these are compounded by the fact that Bantustans cannot provide an alternative means of livelihood. 'Endorsement out' involves either starvation in the reserves, or acceptance of the exploitation of farm labour, or recruitment for mining or industrial work on contract.

There can no longer be any doubt that the effect of the Pass Laws, the mass 'removals' and the poverty of the Bantustans, is no more or less than a system of forced migrant labour. There will, in fact, be no real 'removal' of Africans from the Western Cape, for their labour is indispensable to the white economy. What is happening instead is that African labour is being turned into a totally migrant force, disciplined, directed and rootless.

For more than a century the towns have been the melting-pot of the different racial groups. Mutual acculturation has gone further than anywhere south of the Sahara. In these urban societies there are significant numbers of Africans whose aspirations, attitudes and culture patterns bind them closer to the mores of white society than to tribal society. Instead of welcoming this development towards a common nationhood and a 'shared society'—what else was the original objective of the professed 'civilising mission'?—the authorities are dedicated to destroying these points of growth. This, indeed, is the *raison d'être* of apartheid. The application of apartheid involves the complete breaking up of established urban communities.

While it is convenient to lump together the 'urban Africans', it can be misleading for the purpose of analysing social and political forces. We need to distinguish between four groups of urban Africans—excluding, of course, the wholly migrant labour force on the mines who are segregated in bachelor compounds and are in any case peripheral to the urban society.

(i) *The Migrants*

The first group comprises comparative newcomers[1] to the towns, or migrant workers who have never settled there. They are derisively referred to by the townee as 'the blanketed people', or, in Xhosa-speaking areas, as the 'Red people'.* These newcomers generally perform the lowest-paid jobs; they are unsure of town ways, and still have strong roots in the reserves. They tend to clannishness and bind together for security. Although they may be politically conscious, they are not politically articulate. If it comes to strike action they are among the first to defy the political leadership; but if roused by bread and butter issues of immediate importance (police raids, pass laws, endorsement-out procedures, or housing grievances) they often prove the toughest and most reckless of antagonists. It was largely from this group that *Poqo* drew its recruits (see page 179). These are men of two worlds: the need to earn a living has driven them to work in twentieth century industrial society, while their loyalties and their aspirations rest in a rural, tribal past. Today they are a minority. But it is the declared purpose of government policy to convert the entire black proletariat in the 'white' areas into migrants moving thus between two worlds.

(ii) *The Black Proletariat*

Among the urbanised proletariat two elements emerge: the one not yet fully detribalised, still trying to find a permanent place in industry and commerce, but still tied partly to the reserves; the other wholly rejecting tribal authority and rural life—these constitute the backbone of the permanent labour force. These groups also form the rank and file of the African nationalist movements, and contribute in some measure to its leadership. Both these groups share an over-riding anxiety

* 'Blanket' because this is what they mainly wear when they come out of the reserves; 'red' because of the ochre with which Xhosa tribesmen smear their clothes and bodies.

that at any time they might be expelled from the urban areas, and returned to a rejected past and a poverty-stricken future in the reserves.

(iii) *The Tsotsis*

A third group is the *tsotsis*: the anti-social elements in the urban community. *Tsotsi* (meaning a little boy) originally referred to delinquents, but it is now used to decribe all anti-social groups, including adult layabouts and the straightforward criminals who often operate in Chicago-like gangs. They prey on white and black society alike, making life highly insecure. In cities like Johannesburg white women seldom go out on their own at night, and most homes are heavily barred against intruders. A judge has felt it necessary to warn: 'I regard it as inadvisable and most inconsiderate of any woman in South Africa to walk alone across big empty spaces, particularly where there are dongas [gulleys] and bridges, during the day or at night. I should like this opinion to be made known far and wide.'[1]

But the *tsotsis* offer an even greater threat to Africans than to whites. They hold life cheap, and they choose their victims indiscriminately. Out of 594 murders in 1961, 506 were by Africans on Africans, and only 23 by Africans on whites. Many African townships are held in the grip of *tsotsi* terrorism. The violence in Johannesburg's African townships produces casualties every week-end which invite comparison with battle casualties. A surgeon at the Baragwanath hospital—which serves the great complex of black townships around Johannesburg—recently wrote in a medical journal: 'The hospital is often described as being in the vicinity of a continuous war.... It is perhaps difficult to imagine a hospital in which more than 3,000 head injuries and 1,468 penetrating wounds of the chest, more than 2,000 wounds of the stomach and 495 combined chest and stomach wounds, are treated yearly.' Needless to say these casualties are all Africans. Of the background to these appalling casualties, the surgeon wrote: 'The regulations regarding the movements of non-white have, as a by-product, produced bands of outlaws and illegal immigrants who prey on the law-abiding inhabitants of the large townships.'[2]

At the other extreme are the technical offenders against apartheid. In 1960, 251,921 cases were heard in Johannesburg alone under the Pass Laws: one for every four Africans in the city. In 1963 the prison population was 67,636: one out of every 226 inhabitants. These figures tell of a society in a deep inner conflict, with the authorities trying to maintain some semblance of law and order, while yet clamping down fresh restrictions on the non-white majority.

The *tsotsis* are one of the predictable outcomes of this situation. Dangerous though the problem of the hardened criminal class is, it is less alarming than the rapidly rising rate of juvenile delinquency. This is primarily the consequence of the large-scale breakdown of family life among Africans in the urban areas, of economic and social insecurity, and of contempt for authority. Nor is it surprising if one examines the conditions under which Africans live in the towns. Housing standards are generally inadequate for proper family life. For economic reasons it is usual for both parents to go out to work, almost invariably at great distances from their homes. The children are left without parental control. There are not enough schools to take them; and there is a crippling shortage of community centres. Non-working relatives are 'endorsed out' as 'surplus'.

Unemployment among the youth is high, and training for careers negligible. The government's Froneman Commission, which reported in 1962, estimated that over half a million Africans in the Republic were unemployed: 14 per cent of the total African labour force. Such facts belie the impression the government tries to convey that prosperity is the characteristic condition of South Africa's Africans. The fact is that a high proportion of the African population has no visible means of support, and an even higher proportion lives in constant fear of unemployment. Juvenile delinquency is encouraged by the presence in all the towns of large numbers of adult criminals, driven to crime through unemployment and the consequent need to resort to illegal methods to avoid 'endorsement out'. Thus the young delinquent becomes the hardened criminal at a comparatively early age. In these conditions crime and violence take the form of a savagely angry revenge against society, which is characteristically amoral. The *tsotsi* elements are usually too cynical and too busy looking after 'number one' to care much about getting redress through political action. In times of upheaval they show up, but usually only as thugs ready to take advantage of any opportunity that presents itself. They often complicate the task of the political leadership.

(iv) *The Middle Class*

The history of nationalism everywhere has shown that it is a mistake to suppose the middle class is automatically a defender of the existing order. It invariably makes an important contribution to the nationalist leadership. This has been so all over Asia and Africa; and there was never any reason to suppose that it would be different in the Republic. A second mistake commonly made about the African middle class is that its acceptance of Western standards entails severing its links with its own past. As long. ago as 1935 Professor Z. K. Matthews—one of South Africa's leading scholars and a veteran of the African National Congress—wrote: 'It seems altogether unwise to attempt to drive a wedge between the urban group and the so-called purely tribal native by refusing to recognise what they have in common, and the contribution which the former can make and are making to native life and thought by their synthesis of Western and Native conceptions wherever they are complementary and not contradictory.'[1]

The African middle class in South Africa includes professors, ministers, lawyers, doctors, teachers, clerks, shopkeepers, domestic workers and the better paid industrial workers. If still a comparatively small minority, this elite is highly significant. It represents the point of greatest acculturation between the two societies, and therefore acts as a valuable link between them. And it has provided the modern African leadership, which apartheid rejects in favour of the tribal traditionalists.

Some idea of the size of the middle class may be derived from figures like the following. In 1960 there were 25,000 qualified teachers, with 6,000 student-teachers in training. There were 1,700 students in universities.* There were 2,000

* There was a time when South Africa could claim to lead most African countries in the education field, and especially in its higher educa-

Christian ministers and 30,000 lay preachers. There were 7,500 nurses, 14,000 policemen, and 1,265 civil servants in clerical jobs. In the professional classes there were 49 lawyers, 81 doctors, 73 chartered secretaries, 176 laboratory assistants and 61 chemical analysts. There was a total of 1,734 Africans with university degrees, 250,000 with Standard VI certificates (pre-high school), 70,000 with Junior Certificates (intermediate high school) and 15,000 Matriculants (high school graduates).* There are no reliable statistics for the middle class component in industry, commerce and in the trade unions. In 1946 there were only 24 owners of small industrial undertakings; in 1962 there were 1,200 traders, and a small but successful number of transport operators; in 1964 the first small African mining company was launched.

On the other hand, of the 400,000 Africans in the mines, none holds a supervisory or skilled job; their average cash wage is less than £100 a year. Of the 340,000 Africans in industry in 1946 (comprising more than half of all the workers in industrial employment) only 10 per cent held skilled jobs, 40 per cent semi-skilled, and 50 per cent unskilled. Only one per cent of all unskilled workers were white. There were 600,000 African domestic workers in 1946.

The middle class was a specially favoured group in African society in the days before apartheid. Not only was it better off than any other African group; it was also accorded a special status. It enjoyed a measure of security in urban society. It set itself, and maintained, Western standards in housing and material possessions, and it took a special pride in education. But because this group stood to lose so much, it became especially vulnerable to apartheid rule. A single wrong step could destroy all a middle class family had built

tion programme; but this is no longer true. In 1963 there were 1,200 non-white students in university, of whom 540 were students at the new Bantu Universities created in 1959 when the 'Open Universities' were prohibited from taking in non-white students; of the 540 in the Bantu colleges, 175 were non-matriculants. There were another 1,200 students pursuing degree courses privately through correspondence courses. These figures show hardly any increase on 1954. By comparison, there are 1,400 students in the University of East Africa alone, and an estimated additional 1,500 at universities overseas.

* Expressed as percentages of the total African adult population these amount to less than 3 per cent Standard VI certificate; under 0.7 per cent Junior Certificate; just over 0.15 per cent matriculants, and only 0.026 per cent university graduates.

up: the surest wrong step is to participate in political opposition to the government—whether by supporting strike action or defiance campaigns, belonging to political organisations and trade unions, or just acting in a way that draws the attention of the police. For today—as has been described—no matter how long an African has lived in an urban area, he can be ordered to leave it; and with it his home, his employment, and the possibility of future opportunities to earn a living except under much reduced circumstances. It might mean also the break-up of the family. To cross the authorities, therefore, can mean—and often has meant—exchanging a life of middle class comfort for poverty and insecurity. The sword of apartheid hangs over the middle class as a constant threat to all they have built up. Teachers have had to become labourers after refusing to teach under the Bantu Education Act.

Small wonder, then, that the middle class has grown cautious of overt political action. Instead of being the spearhead of struggle, as it once was, this elite now tends to caution. Only the strongest and most politically conscious among them continue to function within the effective leadership. There are still enough of them to provide a tenacious leadership; but the need for more militant methods, and the greater risks involved, are tending to produce younger and more revolutionary leaders —men who have less to lose, and who are less patient than the older leadership. But even if large numbers of the middle class are not politically active, it is a mistake to suppose that their attitudes are passive. They have grown angrier, more bitter, and less tolerant.

POPULATION REMOVALS

> Perhaps the apex of nationalism is reached when it comes to be regarded as an enlightened policy to remove men, women and children forcibly from their homes and transfer them from place to place to create homogeneous national units.
>
>   *E. H. Carr*, Nationalism and After, *1945*

Apartheid requires that people of different races and colour— and even of different tribes—should not dwell together, or even too closely together. One result is that, throughout the Republic, people are being uprooted from their homes and employment, and compelled to live wherever officialdom decides. The Group Areas Act empowers officials to destroy homes and livings in the cause of racial peace. Already over 100,000 people have been moved: the officially declared aim is to move literally millions.

The dimensions of this upheaval are reflected in the figures involved in plans already approved. In seventeen months, 3,000 Chinese, Indian and Coloured families have been moved in Johannesburg, and another 5,694 families are awaiting removal. Nearly 1,600 African families were moved in Boksburg to make room for Coloureds. Altogether about 9,000 Coloured families are to be moved on the Witwatersrand. In Pageview—a suburb of Johannesburg originally given to the Indians by President Paul Kruger—5,000 families are to be moved to make room for whites. One street in Bethal, which provides a living place for 365 Indians, is to be cleared for whites. More than 6,500 Indians are to be moved from South End in Port Elizabeth. Thirty thousand Indians will be moved from Johannesburg to Lenasia twenty miles away; another 20,000 Indians on the East Rand will be resettled. In Johannesburg 60,000 Coloureds in all will be uprooted. Eighty thousand Zulus are to be resettled in one part of Natal alone. Whites, too, are occasionally affected: 235 white families are to leave Nancefield near Johannesburg. A total of half a million removals have already been approved.

But what do these figures mean in terms of human beings and family life? Here are some examples:

The 'Eiselen Line'

The most dangerous saboteurs in South Africa were the people in the streets and offices who made enemies and not friends of the Bantu, said the Commissioner-General of North Sotho [a Bantu area in the Transvaal], Dr W. W. M. Eiselen. ... In post offices, at railway stations and in shops, the Bantu were kept waiting. If they did not understand something they were choked off. 'These things worry us. But who has the courage to do anything about them?' It was the small things that hurt the Bantu and made enemies, he said. A big fuss was made about South Africa's 'ruthless' race laws, but these were the big things that did not hurt the Bantu.
A report in DIE BURGER, *April 11, 1963*

Dr W. W. M. Eiselen shared with Dr Verwoerd the responsibility for planning the 'big things' of apartheid: they were the two theoreticians of the policy of Separate Development. But Dr Eiselen has another special distinction: he is the author of 'the Eiselen line' in the Western Cape Province. One quarter of a million Africans are to be expelled across this line to restore to the Coloureds their 'traditional' preserve in the Western Cape Province. The Africans, mainly from the Transkei, at present comprise about one-eighth of the total population of the Western Cape. About 100,000 work on white farms, and the rest are principally labourers in the towns. By April 1962, 26,000 had been 'endorsed out' in just under three years. This process was reinforced by the application of the Job Reservation Act to an increasing number of categories of employment in favour of Coloureds. But despite this action, the African population in the Western Cape did not diminish. Since the demand for labour did not decline, those 'endorsed out' were often allowed back as migrant labourers. The main effect was to shunt Africans between the reserves—where there were no jobs for them—and the Western Cape. People 'endorsed out' on one train often caught the next one back. For them the choice is to be 'illegally' in the Western Cape or to starve in the reserves. Many become chronically 'illegal'; at best they return on 'conditional employment', which means their right to be there depends on their working for a particular employer in a particular category of work.

But although it was quite plain to the authorities what was happening, they chose to speed up the process of expulsions. Even those legally entitled to be in the Western Cape, by virtue of birth or continuous employment, have come under the threat of 'endorsement out' through the Bantu Laws Amendment Act of 1964. The result is a slow strangulation of the African townships in the Western Cape. Of 26,000 Africans living in Langa, 18,000 are housed in barracks which have only 'bachelor' quarters. It was in these barracks that the *Poqo* terrorist movement took root. African children born in and around Capetown have no hope of being able to use their education or developing their urban skills. 'Every year pupils leave us with either the Junior or the Senior Certificate. Few of them are able to proceed to a university or a teacher training college. The majority are absorbed by the labour market. We do not mean that they get decent or remunerative jobs. They are employed as labourers at the docks, the railway goods sheds, or by building contractors. This fills their hearts with bitterness and frustration because they are told that, because of their colour, they cannot get jobs to suit their educational standard.'[1]

The People of Besterspruit

Mr Peter Brown, chairman of the South African Liberal Party, describes a different type of removal scheme.

Besterspruit was a small community of 3,000 people on the outskirts of the northern Natal town of Vryheid ... there were some 400 families living in freehold, and a number of other families living as tenants. When removal came this February [1963], the freeholders were offered alternative accommodation at Mondhlo. The accommodation consisted of a tent on a 2,000 sq. ft. site. Mondhlo is twenty miles from Vryheid. A person working in Vryheid, who wished to continue to live with his family, would have to travel forty miles to and from work each day. His bus fare would be five shillings a day. If he worked six days a week his travelling expenses would be £6 a month. An average wage for an African worker in Vryheid is £5 a month. A man who decided he could not afford this travelling had two alternatives. He could break up his family, deposit his wife and children at Mondhlo and live in 'bachelor' quarters in Vryheid. His other alternative was to abandon his hard-won freehold rights, and agree to move into a municipal location. The implications of such a decision are enormous. Under existing urban areas legislation, the man could be ejected from the location at any time that he became and remained unemployed. ... There was no accommodation in the Vryheid location for the families which had chosen to move there. There they were in their tents, a quarter of a mile away from, and still in sight of, the bulldozed remains of their once substantial houses. Soon after the people moved into the tents, the rain started. It was wet for weeks. Cooking had to be done in the tents, bedding was soaked and ruined, sanitary arrangements were appalling, and thieving was rife. It is said that at least five sewing-machines disappeared from under the flaps of those tents—each one representing how many years of painful saving? If Besterspruit means anything, it will take a long, long time for any 'black spot' family to re-establish itself at anything like the same level of life to which it had struggled up over the years.[1]

Death of a Township

Alexandra township, lying about ten miles north of Johannesburg, had once been a nasty, boisterous slum where 100,000 Africans lived in the space of one square mile. It was overcrowded, squalid, unlit, unpaved and insanitary; and the crime rate was notorious. But it had its points. Because it lay outside the municipal area, Africans could buy property there, and they could have their families with them. If life was rough and conditions bad, at least there was a measure of unregulated freedom.

In March 1957, the Minister for Bantu Administration and Development said it was 'necessary to reduce the number of inhabitants to reasonable limits', though it was not his intention to 'remove' Alexandra. 'Reduction' in this context did not mean 'rehousing', but 'endorsing out' those people not 'entitled' to be there. Still, amenities were provided. And in 1959 the Minister said that 'owners of property who are lawfully entitled to remain there are not being disturbed'. These fortunates set about improving their properties. Although the population had been reduced by half, the 50,000 who had escaped removal looked forward to some kind of security. But in 1962 the Minister changed his mind. *All* family accommodation was to be 'eliminated': there was to be provision only for single men and women. 'Property owners would have the choice of obtaining property rights in the Bantu homelands.' Old people, wives and young dependants are being 'endorsed out' and expelled to the reserves. Police swoop in at night to discover those staying on 'illegally'. There are cases of parents being removed without their children's knowing about it. Alexandra township is being replaced by neat rows of barracks, each with dormitory accommodation for single adults. Their families have been prised loose and flung into the reserves. This is the way the government seeks to establish racial peace.

Stateless Citizens

> How can one greet with anything but revulsion and a feeling of approaching doom any arrangement which results in a situation such as has now arisen in Paarl where a married couple had to fight in the courts for the right to live together?
>
> *Professor Wouter de Vos*, DIE BURGER,
> *November 21, 1962*

Apartheid laws have turned law-abiding citizens into 'stateless persons'. They can stand directly between a husband and wife to prevent their living together. These two aspects of the kafkaesque legal tangle are illustrated by what happened to Mr and Mrs Jackson Mapheele of Paarl. Although he is legally entitled to live in Paarl, having 'worked continuously for one employer for ten years', his wife was declared to be in the area 'illegally'. Her attempt to prevent separation failed in the courts. Even the Minister of Bantu Affairs and Development was stung. He offered Mr Mapheele work with the Bantu Development Corporation in Herschel, where his wife was entitled to be with him. But if Mr Mapheele took this job and stayed away from Paarl *for more than one year*, he would forfeit permanently his legal right to return there. Furthermore, if he left or lost his job with the Bantu Development Corporation at Herschel, he would then have no legal right to stay anywhere in the Republic for more than seventy-two hours. 'Mr Mapheele is, in point of fact, being asked by the Minister to stay in Paarl without his family, or to live in Herschel with his family as a virtually "stateless person".'[1]

2: POLITICAL MOVEMENTS

You cannot withhold from a people its political rights.
General J. B. M. Hertzog, 1921

It would be the greatest folly to try and assume that
non-white nationalism, which has arisen everywhere in
Africa, would not also extend to the south of the
Limpopo. Indeed, everyone who is familiar with the
facts knows that... non-white nationalism has already
appeared here for a long time. Every white man
should thus adapt himself spiritually to the altered fact
that the Native here is also cultivating his own national
sentiment.   DIE TRANSVALER, *May 11, 1961*

Like Afrikaner nationalism, African nationalism is the product
of the interaction of different races in South Africa. But
unlike Afrikaner nationalism, African nationalism rejects
racial exclusiveness. It has always looked on South Africa
as the home of whites, Indians, Coloureds as well as Africans.

Africans in the Republic have enjoyed a higher average
standard of living than Africans further north, because it is
incomparably the richest country in the continent. At the
same time they have suffered the worst disabilities of a voteless proletariat: bad housing, unemployment, malnutrition,
squalor, frustration. These are the classic conditions of an
industrial revolution in a capitalist society, but here intensely
aggravated by racial discrimination. Africans have also been
able to taste some of the fruits of a materially rich society:
they have had access to education; their elite has absorbed
some of the bourgeois standards of a capitalist society. One
result is a much more sophisticated attitude to politics than in
many other parts of Africa. Both communism and anti-
communism, for example, have taken root in their nationalist
movements.

The nationalist struggle is much more complicated and
difficult than in other parts of Africa where anti-colonialism
offered a simple formula for a charismatic leader. Such a
straightforward approach could not unite the diverse economic
and political elements in the South African population. And
their leaders have not been given the liberty of movement and

action essential to the mobilisation of popular forces. The nature of South Africa's society and its uniquely restrictive legalisation makes the task of organisation infinitely more difficult than elsewhere in Africa: rousing calls to 'positive action' are simply an invitation to police action and firm repression.

There are three problems which increase the complexity of the African nationalist struggle. The role of whites and other non-Africans in the struggle raises crucial issues: can non-Africans, in fact, participate effectively within an African nationalist movement, and what should their relationship be with the leadership? There is the problem of economic survival and self-interest. Africans in the urban areas have much more to lose by conflict with the authorities—and, until recently, have stood to gain far more by keeping in with them —than Africans elsewhere. Finally, the degree of formal education, a strong commitment to Christian values, and industrial experience have produced a sophisticated leadership which is open to fundamental ideological argument. Because South Africa is not faced simply with the familiar anti-colonial situation, the struggle there is not always understood by African leaders elsewhere in the continent. It is a situation more easily understood by American Negroes.

STRANDS OF NATIONALISM

From its birth in 1912 two strands have dominated the thinking of African nationalism in South Africa. The dominant strand favoured moderate, conciliatory and constitutional tactics to persuade whites to allow Africans a fair share in the government and resources of the country. The second, the radical strand, favoured a more assertive challenge. It rejected the approach of 'turning the other cheek', and looked with disfavour on any form of co-operation with the dominant regime. Nevertheless, both schools of thinking have certain common objectives. They agree that the purpose of the struggle is *not* to expel the white man from South Africa but to compel him to accept a shared society; they reject tribalism for themselves in the same way as they reject it for the whites; they repudiate racialism; they select as their enemy the *practice of white supremacy*, not the whites themselves; they deliberately choose the goal of a multiracial or 'non-racial' South Africa.* Also, they steadfastly reject violence as a method of struggle. With only one serious exception, these remain the aims of African nationalism: the exception is that violence has now come to be accepted as a necessary weapon of struggle.

For the better part of half a century the African National Congress—the historical movement of African nationalism— was led by Christian middle class leaders, starting with the Reverend John K. Dube and continuing the tradition through the Reverend Z. R. Mahabane, Dr P. Seme, Dr A. B. Xuma, Dr J. S. Moroka, down the years to the current President-General, Albert Lutuli, the 1961 Nobel Peace Award Winner. Only once was there a communist President-General—Mr J. T. Gumede—but this was not the choice of the rank and file. He was 'converted' on a visit to Russia during his term of office, and when he tried to assert his new-found communist views on his return home he was overwhelmingly rejected.

Through all these years the unswerving African demand was the right—as Chief Lutuli recently repeated—'*to share* in the governing of the whole country'. In marked contrast to Afrikaner nationalism, African nationalism (again in Chief Lutuli's words) is 'broad, progressive and all-embracing'. This non-racialist approach appears in a speech made by one of the younger, more radical elements in Congress, Dr J. Njongwe.

> Our creed has been developed with due regard to the multiracial character of South Africa. We accept and know that the European, Indian and Coloured people are South Africans, no less than the Africans themselves. Their culture and history may be different, but the fundamental point is that they are all South Africans. An understanding and appreciation of this South African outlook is very important at the beginning of our struggle. We shall not be a party to the development of racial arrogance on the part of the African people. If my people developed racial arrogance and *herrenvolkism*, I would fight this menace just as we are now fighting Afrikaner nationalism.

* Multiracialism has become something of a swear word for African nationalists because of the way it was used to justify the now extinct Central African Federation.

The African National Congress

The ANC—now banned like the other congresses—can best be described as a movement with a strong élite leadership, with mass goodwill, considerable prestige and influence, but little effective organisation. It always had many more adherents than actual members. Its main strength lies in the urban areas and rural towns of the Transvaal, Natal and Orange Free State, and in Port Elizabeth and the Eastern Cape. But it has always been comparatively weak in the rest of the Cape Province. In the last few years it has developed strong pockets of influence in the reserves, partly because many politically conscious urban Africans have been expelled to these areas. Its organisational weakness was accentuated by its banning in 1960, and by the fact that its top leadership is either restricted to a particular rural district (like Lutuli), or imprisoned (Nelson Mandela, Walter Sisulu, Govan Mbeki and scores of less well-known personalities), or forced into exile (Oliver Tambo, Duma Nokwe, Moses Kotane). All its new leaders come to be placed, as a matter of course, on the list of banned peoples. This means, *inter alia*, that nothing they say, write or do may be reported in any newspaper in the Republic. This blanket censorship is pierced only when banned people appear in a court whose proceedings may be reported. Thus the dock has become the only platform for free speech by African leaders in the Republic.*

The ANC now operates mainly as an underground organisation. Inside the Republic it has a system of secret branches which exist in most of the large towns and in the reserves. Contact between them is maintained by specially chosen cadres of younger men. So long as the older, well-known leaders were connected with these cells, it was comparatively easy for the police to uncover them. But a new generation of leaders is coming up: these are generally young men—students, trade union leaders, teachers, urban workers with industrial experience. Many of them have been 'endorsed out' into the rural areas. Many are unknown to the police. Their attitudes are in some ways different from the former generation of leaders:

* A number of whites, mainly communists and liberals, have been similarly banned.

they are less compromising; they have had little political contact with whites or Indians; they are not uncritical towards Christian teachings; they are militant, and believe in the necessity for a violent struggle. This new leadership continues to accept the authority of the older leadership: but while they still revere Chief Lutuli, they identify themselves more easily with his younger lieutenants like Nelson Mandela, Walter Sisulu, Oliver Tambo and Duma Nokwe.

Contact between the new leaders and the old continues to exist despite police efforts: a courier service operates right into the prison cells of the detained leaders. But, increasingly, the initiative is passing into the hands of the leaders in exile. They have their headquarters in Dar Es Salaam, Lusaka and London, with branches in other African capitals. This network links the ANC with the independent African states and with sympathetic governments abroad.

But the ANC's most important change of character followed the formation by some of its leaders of *Umkonto We Sizwe* (Spear of the Nation). Its manifesto, published on December 16, 1961, said: 'The time comes in the life of any nation when there remain only two choices—submit or fight. That time has now come in South Africa. We shall not submit, and we have no choice but to hit back by all means in our power in defence of our people, our future and our freedom.' Organisationally, it was deliberately kept separate from the ANC, and it included individuals of all races from other organisations. In his remarkable defence speech at the 'Rivonia' trial, Nelson Mandela described *Umkonto*'s relationship to the ANC: 'It (ANC) was a mass political organisation with a political function to fulfil. Its members had joined on the express policy of non-violence. Because of this it could not and would not undertake violence... One cannot turn such a body into the small, closely knit organisation needed for sabotage... (And) it would result in members ceasing to carry out (its) essential activity: political propaganda and organisation. On the other hand... the ANC was prepared to depart from its 50-year-old policy of non-violence to the extent that it would no longer disapprove of properly controlled violence... I made it clear that I would at all times subject it to the political guidance of the ANC...'

The decision to adapt its policies was forced on the ANC leadership by six factors. First: once it was proscribed it could no longer use overt methods of opposition. Second: it ceased to believe that the whites in South Africa could be persuaded to abandon their traditional ideas by peaceful persuasion. Third: the police apparatus mounted in the Republic made non-violent methods of struggle impossible: the shootings at Sharpeville in 1960, which followed peaceful demonstrations against the Pass Laws, and the military and police measures taken to defeat Nelson Mandela's call for a stay-at-home demonstration in 1962, showed that these methods were no longer appropriate in what had become (for the Africans certainly) a police state. Fourth: the mood and temper of the African people had changed under the pressures of apartheid. Fifth: the Africans have lost faith in the willingness of the Western nations to apply effective pressures on the Republic's regime, to abandon apartheid without a fight. Finally, there was the example of Kenya and Algeria to demonstrate the effectiveness of violence, and there was the offer by the independent African states, as well as by some of the Asian countries and the Soviet bloc, to support a violent struggle.

The Pan-African Congress

In 1958 the African nationalist movement spawned a new party, the Pan-African Congress (PAC). Essentially the quarrel between them concerned tactics, and especially the role of non-African allies in the struggle. The ANC is allied through the Congress Alliance with four other bodies: the South African Indian Congress, the Coloured People's Congress, the (white) Congress of Democrats and the South African Congress of Trade Unions. Each of these bodies is significantly influenced by communists. When PAC broke away from the ANC in 1958 it claimed that the latter was dominated by the non-Africans in the other congresses, and it accused the communists of subjecting the movement to doctrinal and tactical considerations deriving from cold war priorities rather than from local needs. The PAC proposed a strictly 'Africanist' programme. Reacting against the Alliance, it went to the other extreme by rejecting in principle any participation by non-Africans in the nationalist struggle. It is true that the leadership propounded the theory that other races had a part to play *within* their own racial groups. But it is also true that the PAC message was understood by its rank and file as fairly straightforward racism, and that it achieved much of its support for that reason. Mr Robert Mangaliso Sobukwe, the leader of the PAC, has made his movement's position clear both on this tactical question and on its long-term objectives.

> Our contention is that the Africans are the only people who, because of their material position, can be interested in the complete overhaul of the present structure of society. We have admitted that there are Europeans who are intellectual converts to the Africans' cause, but because they benefit materially from the present set-up, they cannot completely identify themselves with that cause.

Of the long-term objectives, he has said:

> Politically, we stand for government of the Africans for the Africans by the Africans with everybody who owes his loyalty to Africa and who accepts the democratic rule of an African majority, being regarded as an African. ...I have said before and I still say so now that I see no reason why, in a free democratic Africa, a predominantly black electorate should not return a white man to parliament, for colour will count for nothing in a free Africa.[1]

The quarrel between the ANC and the PAC is not the first division in the history of African movements in South Africa. And it is essentially about the same two tactical questions which have divided African political opinion before: the role of the communists and the question of co-operation with the authorities or other racial groups. The All-African Convention was the first to reject co-operation both with the communists and with consultative bodies set up by the regime, such as the Native Representative Council. This was the basis of its quarrel with the ANC. The same kind of consideration lay behind the formation of the PAC.

But it is a mistake to regard the ANC and the PAC as irreconcilable rivals. They share the fundamental traditions of African nationalism, forming two currents in the same main-

stream. The PAC reflects what had been an attitude within
the youth wing of the ANC. Even now there are many
prominent ANC members who hold views similar to the PAC,
but who have refused to take part in 'splitting' the African
front. Moreover, events since the split occurred in 1958 have
considerably diminished the differences between them. Today
they agree not only on objectives but largely on tactics as well:
the major remaining conflict is over the entanglement with the
Congress Alliance and the communists.

The Pan-African Congress, like the ANC, has turned itself
into an underground organisation operating through a network
of contact groups in many parts of the country. It is strongest
in the Cape Province and in some of the Transvaal urban
centres. These internal groups are linked to the exile leadership in the High Commission Territories (especially Basutoland
and Bechuanaland), and through them to offices in Dar Es
Salaam, Cairo, Leopoldville and London. The PAC has also
changed its tactics by admitting Mr Patrick Duncan as its
first white member—in this respect going even further than the
ANC. Whatever the truth about racism at the 'grass-roots'
level, the PAC leadership has shown a willingness to
co-operate with South Africans of all races in mobilising its
resources.

In October 1962, Mr Potlako K. Leballo, PAC's Secretary-
General, warned at a press conference in London: 'White
South Africa is irrevocably set on its course to maintain and
perpetuate white domination . . . and the African people are
equally determined to rid themselves of foreign rule at all
costs. Given this situation, an armed clash is inevitable. . . .
The African people recognise that to effect any change in South
Africa, the present position whereby white South Africa holds
the monopoly of military power must be changed. This can
be changed only by our acquisition of the means of challenging
that power.'[1]

This mood of desperation broke surface in 1963 in the
angry explosion of *Poqo*, a new political phenomenon which,
Mr Leballo subsequently claimed, had its origins in the PAC.
Its significance is twofold: it foreshadowed a pattern of terrorism which might be produced in the future when the present
forces of law and order are no longer able to operate effectively

throughout the country; and it revealed the desperation to which Africans are being driven by the Pass Laws.

Poqo caught the headlines in early 1963 when bands of Africans attempted to capture the police station at Paarl, the important centre of the wine industry near Capetown. They failed in the objective, but succeeded instead in terrifying the white inhabitants by killing three civilians. This episode caused alarm among whites throughout the country. Subsequent police investigations showed that there were *Poqo* cells spread widely in the Western Cape and the Transkei. Unlike the traditional congresses, *Poqo* was led and actively supported by the less sophisticated group of urban Africans in the Western Cape; its appeal was particularly strong among the worst casualties of apartheid: the chronically 'illegal' and the unemployed; its breeding place was the 'bachelors' quarters' in the barracks where married men are compelled to live separated from their families. It is not difficult to understand the appeal for these rootless people in the racism and atavism of *Poqo*, with the desperate challenge of its name 'We Stand Alone', and the encouragement to wreak vengeance on those responsible for their plight. To label them 'communist'—as did the Commission of Inquiry into the Paarl Riots—is simply a ludicrous reflex action. The communists were among the first to charge *Poqo* with 'racialism, opportunism and indiscipline'. But although *Poqo* appears to have been ruthlessly crushed, neither the conditions which bred it nor the spirit of desperation which it expressed have been eliminated. On the contrary, both have been fortified by subsequent government measures. Mr Justice Snyman, who headed the commission to inquire into the Paarl riots, felt impelled to issue this warning: 'There must be a change in our attitude to the Bantu and, unless there is a change, this country is doomed.'[1]

The PAC spirit, as reflected in its leader, Robert Mangaliso Sobukwe (now detained on Robben Island, a former leper colony where 'political lepers' are today confined), is unquestionably strong among young people, among the harassed migrants who have secure roots neither in the towns nor in the reserves, and among the more radical or embittered intellectuals. Sobukwe and Mandela have both succeeded in capturing the new spirit of Africans. They worked together in the

ANC youth movement; and now the strands in their respective movements which they represent have begun to draw together to reflect the dominant mood of African nationalism. What separates them still are largely tactical considerations, but these disagreements cannot be dismissed as simply selfish or personal. They affect in a very real manner the choice of methods by which the new phase of the activist struggle is to be fought. At present each mirrors an important aspect of the struggle, and neither has been able to unite the liberation forces behind it.

AFRICAN NATIONALISM AND THE COMMUNISTS

South Africa is one of the few African countries in which the Communist Party has a respectable number of educated, convinced supporters among Africans, and many informed and passionate African opponents, including a cadre of Trotskyites. The reasons should be clear. The industrial aspects of African subservience make a classic class analysis of the situation more plausible in South Africa than in other parts of the continent. European and other non-African communists have thrown themselves selflessly and with great courage and tenacity into the struggle to overthrow white supremacy. Their actions, no less than their teachings, have contributed in some measure to the multiracial attitudes of many of today's African leaders. A third reason, less sophisticated but easy to understand, is that the authorities have characteristically labelled all efforts directed towards establishing equality between the races as communist-inspired. In this way they have helped to contribute towards building up the wholly false picture that the only people who stand for equality are communists: thus the ardent efforts made by socialists, liberals and christians are converted, by the authorities, into grist for the communist mill. This service to the cause of communism by unthinking, reactionary propaganda is not unique to South Africa. But it has been particularly potent in the Republic. Mr Jordan K. Ngubane, Vice-Chairman of the South African Liberal Party, points out that 'apartheid is the best recruiting agent communism has in the Republic'.[1]

But the communists' role in the African nationalist

struggle has always been strongly divisive. Between 1921 (when the Communist Party was founded) and 1950 (when it was made illegal), the Communist Party set itself up as a rival to the African nationalist movement for the leadership of the 'black masses'. Its main antagonism was directed towards the ANC and the All-African Convention. Its tactics, closely resembling those of the American communists, periodically changed to meet the 'objective realities' determined in Moscow. Sometimes they attacked the ANC as 'a bourgeois nationalist movement' and as 'an enemy of the working-class'. At other times they made attempts to capture control from within, or to establish 'a united front alliance'.

In 1950, after its banning, the Communist Party sought to retain support as an illegal movement by sending its African members into the ANC, and by establishing an alliance with it through various front organisations. One of these is the Congress of Democrats. These tactics do not always work to the best advantage of the communists: to assume they do is to under-rate the independent-mindedness, the self-interestedness, and the intelligence of African nationalists. The fear that the Congress Alliance was not working in favour of the communists was strongly hinted at in a report of the *International Bulletin* of the South African Communist Party in December 1962. 'A new unity is growing in practice between the illegal peoples' organisation on which the peoples' hopes of liberation now centre. We must take care, therefore, not to present the legal Congress Alliance* as the sole symbol of leadership of the people's struggle. For it is not, and under present conditions cannot be. Attempts to portray it as such will only result in discouraging the people, leading them to a loss of confidence in the movement, and ultimately alienating them from the movement.'

Because the communists came to realise that the liberation struggle can be led effectively only by the African nationalists, they were obliged to take second place to them. This decision is consistent with the five-point doctrine of the national-liberation struggle formulated by Stalin in 1928. Their task, as they see it, is to project their separate identity through the liberation struggle, clinging firmly to the coat-tails of the ANC.

* Later banned.

In 1963 the Communist Party was resuscitated as an underground movement, but with its leadership mainly in exile.

The communists offer the African nationalists several advantages. They can contribute dedicated revolutionaries committed to working for the overthrow of white supremacy. They can provide a link with non-Africans who share the ANC's immediate aims of working for a change of government. And, perhaps most useful of all, they offer a link with the powerful communist world from which financial and military help might be expected, and which can be counted upon to maintain a vigorous diplomatic assault on the South African Republic. Against these advantages, the African leadership weighs the liabilities of an association with the communists. In its own eyes the worst liability is that many independent African states strongly disapprove of the close association; some even share Western suspicions that the ANC might be actually communist-dominated. Second, the open association with communists makes it easier for the Verwoerd regime and its supporters in the Western countries to label the ANC as communist-led, and makes it harder to lobby for support in the West and in the UN. Third, its own experience of the communists has shown the ANC that the communists' long-term objectives are different from, and often in conflict with, its own. Fourth, communists make it harder for ANC to maintain a policy of non-alignment. Finally, the alliance with the communists is a crucially divisive factor within the African nationalist movement.

Nevertheless, the ANC believes it is wrong at this stage to reject the help of those who share their primary objective. In his 'Rivonia' defence speech, Mandela clarified the relationship between the ANC and the Communist Party: 'Its (ANC's) chief goal was, and is, for the African people to win unity and full political rights. The Communist Party's main aim... was to remove the capitalists and to replace them with a working-class government. The Communist Party sought to emphasise class distinctions, whilst the ANC seeks to harmonise them . . . It is true that there has often been close co-operation between the ANC and the Communist Party. But co-operation is merely proof of a common goal—in this case the removal of white supremacy—and is not proof of a complete community of

interest.   The history of the world is full of similar examples.
Perhaps the most striking is to be found in the co-operation
between Great Britain, the USA and the Soviet Union in the
fight against Hitler . . .   Theoretical differences amongst those
fighting against oppression is a luxury we cannot afford at this
stage . . .   For my own part, I believe it is open to debate
whether the Communist Party has any specific role to play at
this particular stage of our political struggle.   The basic task
. . . is the removal of race discrimination and the attainment
of democratic rights on the basis of the Freedom Charter.
In so far as that Party furthers this task I welcome its
assistance . . .'

As for communists in their ranks, ANC leaders claim that in
their own experience African communists are nationalists first
and marxists second; if there is a conflict between these two
interests, the African communists, with few exceptions, take
the side of the ANC.   Even staunch anti-communists and
devoted Christians like Chief Albert Lutuli and Professor
Z. K. Matthews argue that under present circumstances there
is no sufficient reason for refusing to accept the help of anybody willing to assist.   'Meet them on their own terms', Professor Matthews has said: 'Be tough and determined.   The
only way you can deal with them is by you yourself knowing
where you are going.'[1]   Mr Nelson Mandela's view is that 'in
spite of the criticism of communism as a creed, the record of
those men from the point of view of sacrifice in the interests of
African freedom was very praiseworthy indeed.'[2]   Nevertheless, there is a difference of opinion within the ANC over this
question.

But in the long run the influence of the communists not
only on the ANC but on the future course of events in South
Africa, will be determined as much by the policies of the West
as by the efforts of the Communist Party.   Western equi-
vocations provide a strong justification for the ANC's inclina-
tion not to give up the support of people committed to fighting
apartheid for the hope of attracting support from the
West.

If the ANC leadership should come to the point of wishing
to break its association with the communists, will it be

able to shake them off, or is the ANC already communist-dominated? The last part of this question has been answered by the courts of South Africa. One of the objectives of the Treason Trial which ended in Pretoria in 1961 was to prove that the ANC was a communist-dominated organisation. In acquitting all the accused, Mr Justice Rumpff declared that although the ANC had had communist members before 1950 and that 'a strong left-wing tendency manifested itself' between 1952–60, nevertheless there was no proof that it had become a communist organisation nor that it had been infiltrated by communists.[1] There could hardly be a more clear-cut verdict than this, delivered as it was after a trial lasting several years in which all the ANC's records had been meticulously examined by judges whose record on communism would stand comparison with the late Senator McCarthy's.

A better perspective might be achieved by avoiding the smear-tactics used by the communists themselves, and judging the communists strictly on their own record. Their role, as they have officially defined it, is to 'educate' the liberation movement so that the revolution itself should be controlled and led by 'class-conscious' (meaning 'communist') elements. However loyal their members might be at this stage to the ANC leadership, such tactics must inevitably lead to divisions. They involve the familiar communist use of pressure-groups to impose standards upon the African political leadership which are not only irrelevant to the needs of the struggle, but a severe obstruction to its development. Their role inevitably entails intrigue and manoeuvre against 'non-class-conscious elements', and the introduction of organised factions on issues which are not germane to the struggle in South Africa. It involves deliberate efforts to deflect any real support there might be from the West for fear that this would diminish the relative contribution of the communist countries to the struggle. For the communists' own purposes, the struggle in South Africa must succeed in the teeth of Western opposition. Equally, the struggle must not succeed too quickly, too easily, or with too little disruption. By virtue of their doctrinal interest in revolution and extremism, they would less easily with sympathetic governments abroad. The ANC still suffers survive an early and relatively peaceful ending to the South

African struggle. Is the West assisting them to achieve their purposes?

3: THE AFRICAN MOOD

> The Afrikaans-speaking people would have to pay the highest price for the government's folly. They would have to deal with similar hate and bitterness as was felt against Germany because of Hitler's action, if they did not get rid of the government soon.
>
> *Mr Japie Basson, MP, a former government*
> *supporter, 1961*

More significant than the present effectiveness of African political organisations, or even than the apparent unwillingness of Africans to come out in open revolt, is the mood of the African peoples. This, in the long run, will determine not only how the struggle for power will develop, but also its eventual outcome. The authorities are blinded by what they need to believe. 'The first five years [of the Republic] have passed like a dream,' said Dr Verwoerd in a speech which has been expensively reproduced and widely distributed throughout the Western world. 'We believe that these years were but the beginning of a future upon which we can enter with equanimity, knowing that it is based on firm foundations. . . . Here in the Republic we have greater peace and order [than in the United States]. We have less rude handling or oppression, and far less ill-feeling between Bantu and whites.' One of his leading supporters, 'Piet Politiek', writing on the day South Africa became a republic, exclaimed: 'My old Afrikaner heart sang a melody as it can only come from a heart which feels completely free. Yes, it is pleasant to be a human being in the Republic of South Africa.'[1] What do Africans feel about life in the flush of the Republic's 'golden years'?

The white foreman, supervising the work-gang swinging their picks in rhythmic unison, does he have any idea of the meaning of the refrain of their work-song?[2]

Abalengu ngo-damn
(White people, be damned!
White people, be damned!
be damned!)
Abalengu ngodoti
(White people are dirt!
are dirt!
White people are dirt!
are dirt!)[1]

Strongly as the sophisticated African political leaders still cling to their belief in the importance of creating a non-racial society, the fact is that racism is rapidly corroding previously tolerant attitudes. This is not just an opinion: it emerges strongly from a number of studies made in recent years.[1] J. C. de Ridder concludes from his thematic apperception test study:[2] 'In South Africa, the country in Africa with the largest European minority and possibly the largest urban African population, the position is rapidly being reached where the urban Africans are becoming almost obsessed with feelings of being discriminated against. Feelings which are hardly conducive of racial harmony, let alone to the appreciation of democratic principles....'

D. H. Reader's survey of Xhosas in East London shows: 'The deep feeling of withheld rewards in many cases leads to anti-white sentiment, and was obviously a potent factor in the 1952 riots.'[3] These riots, which grew out of an African National Congress non-violent demonstration against the Pass Laws, ended in a number of atavistic killings, one involving a nun, Sister Aidan. The violence itself was the result of the *tsotsis'* running wild. In a study, covering the background to these riots Philip Mayer observed:

... The notable fact [is] that the murder of Sister Aidan served to sap resistance rather than inflame it. The murder did this because it caused the original issue—that of black versus white—to be suddenly blurred by the internal issue between ordinary black citizens and black 'gangsters'.... The *tsotsi* and the white man have this in common (sociologically speaking) that ordinary location people can regard them both as common enemies.... The rapid collapse of the riots shows that, generally speaking, the anti-white feeling of the ordinary Xhosa in East London—not having reached the untrammelled stage proper to an all-out struggle—could not command a wider moral support than the feelings against *tsotsis*. To many migrants . . . the whole episode simply illustrated the nightmare quality of life in town, as such, where 'nothing is safe' and 'people behave like animals'.[1]

Mayer's study also brings out very clearly the rising resentment against the way whites practise Christianity. Here are some typical reactions: 'I do not think white men accept the word of God as we do, for if a native is Saved he loves everybody—a religious native sympathises with everybody in trouble.' 'One day religious white men, who have been Saved, will come forward and treat native peoples as human beings.' 'Many white people who hate the natives will leave, and we shall stay with those who have love for us. Our living together will be very harmonious.'

The most comprehensive and valuable insight into the attitudes of Africans of the middle class is provided by a recent study conducted by E. A. Brett.[2] His group of interviewees included teachers, professional men, ministers, clerks, students and high school pupils. Their response to a question on what they thought was the state of white-black relations showed that eighty-eight thought they were bad, eight thought they were good, and fifty-four gave responses of an intermediate kind. But even among the favourable responses the most frequent was 'the suggestion that some whites are good, others bad. Generally it was felt that only a minority had escaped the prejudices prevailing in white society.' Despite these feelings of hostility to the white group 'the great majority felt that they would like to see a community developing in South Africa in which all races would be able to live on an equal basis'. Fifty-seven per cent had no reservations about it; only three interviewees stated outright that they did not feel it would be desirable; the rest felt it would be desirable under certain specified conditions. Four felt that 'Africans had now been pushed so far that they would have to take revenge for past injustice'. A further effort to discover revenge feelings was made without result through projective material. What the results did show, however, was 'the existence of a small, but not insignificant group of individuals manifesting a high degree of racial aggression which could, in a period of crisis, lead to anti-white violence'.[1]

The study showed a considerable rejection of the whole apparatus of state. 'The legislation affecting Africans was seen as being designed to maintain Africans in a position of inferiority, the authorities delegated with the task of carrying out these laws were generally regarded with suspicion and dislike, and the courts of law in which disputes arising out of these laws are tried, were generally regarded as partial in their judgements.'[2]

But the most important trend in thinking is revealed in the answers to questions about methods to effect political changes. Forty-three per cent felt that 'force of some kind had now become inevitable'. 'This was a response to the present government's policy of no consultation and no concessions. Since peaceful means had been tried and had failed in the past, it was felt that force would now be the only means of influencing the government.' Eight of the group felt that overseas intervention would be necessary to complete the government's destruction. Only one individual specified the source of this intervention: 'the only method now left is force, civil war or Russian intervention.' A second said: 'I think persuasion has worked itself out, and in the end Africans will have to resort to violence. Seems it is the only time they will listen.' A third commented: 'I think the carnage will be terrible. I would not myself advocate it, but I think the bastards, black and white, think in blood, and we are going to influence the government. There is only one method: have it.' A schoolboy wrote: 'Africans should attempt to V.I.O.L.E.N.C.E. We outnumber Europeans 5–1 and with good weapons at our disposal we can wipe them out in time.'

Predictably, the bitterest racial feelings are expressed by young students. There is growing up a new generation of Africans who have known nothing all their lives other than the regime of apartheid. Segregated entirely from whites, compelled to attend schools and institutions much inferior to those available to whites, frustrated in their capacities and ambitions, their rebelliousness comes out in riots and protests at schools and colleges, and in political activity. A group of students attending the segregated Tribal Colleges of Ngoye, Turfloop, Fort Hare and Bellville, defied the authorities to speak, at a press conference in Capetown early in 1961, of the isolation and consequent hates which were growing up in these centres.

Even the supporters of apartheid are aware of this growing bitterness. A commission of the South African Bureau of Racial Affairs (SABRA), which made a study of the reserves and urban areas in 1961, reported that all the spokesmen for the Africans emphasised that a great deal of bitterness and friction was caused by the application of the pass and liquor laws.* They were struck by the general poverty among the Africans in large areas of the reserves and in urban areas, and found that many problems and grievances were caused by this factor. Everywhere, they said, the Africans felt aggrieved over the lack of prior consultation about legislation and other matters affecting them.[1]

These attitudes cannot be dismissed as representing the feelings of only the black elite, nor can it be argued that they are unrepresentative of the Africans in the rural areas. Three of the surveys referred to included people who were migrants, or recent arrivals, in the towns and therefore still rooted in tribal society. Besides, there is considerable evidence of the presence of similar tendencies among Africans in the Transkei[2] going back a long time.

The African mood is well summed up by Mr Jordan K. Ngubane:

> No attempt is made to deny that some Africans are thinking seriously of, and planning for, vengeance. Others are thinking in the opposite direction. That is how human communities behave. Forces are at work in the African community that move thought in different directions. This is as things should be in a racial group that has been affected in the way we have been by so many conflicting influences. The wise thing to do, then, is to note that there is as yet no collective racial mind on the African side, and to be grateful that this is the case.[3]

* The liquor laws were amended in 1963, but not the pass laws.

WHAT DO AFRICANS WANT?

The political demands of representative African leaders are generally agreed. Chief Lutuli speaks for all of them when he says: 'We all desire to see a prosperous and peaceful South Africa. Let us face the future with a determination to work with others of like mind to make our multiracial South Africa a democracy.'[1] For Africans, the basis of any democratic society rests firmly on the notion of 'one man one vote'. Sobukwe calls for 'government of the Africans for the Africans by the Africans, with everybody who owes his only loyalty to Africa and who accepts the democratic rule of an African majority being regarded as an African'. Of the country's future economy, Sobukwe says: 'We stand for a planned economy and the most equitable distribution of wealth.... Our problem, as we see it, is to make a planned economy work within the framework of a political democracy.'[2]

What African leaders mean by democracy was made explicit by Chief Lutuli in the text of his Nobel Lecture in 1961.

In government we will not be satisfied with anything less than direct individual adult suffrage and the right to stand for and be elected to all organs of government. In economic matters we will be satisfied with nothing less than equality of opportunity in every sphere, and the enjoyment by all of those heritages which form the resources of the country which up to now have been appropriated on a racial 'whites only' basis. In culture, we will be satisfied with nothing less than the opening of all doors of learning to non-segregatory institutions on the sole criterion of ability. In the social sphere we will be satisfied with nothing less than the abolition of all racial bars. We do not demand these things for people of African descent alone. We demand them for all South Africans, white and black. On these principles we are uncompromising.[3]

The official ANC programme is its Freedom Charter. Its main points are: universal franchise; equal rights for all national groups and races; outlawing of national racial or colour discrimination; national wealth to be 'restored to the people'; mineral wealth, banks and monopoly industry to be transferred to the ownership of the people as a whole; termination of restrictions on land ownership on a racial basis; equality before the law; full and equal human rights for all; abolition of colour discrimination in employment and trade unions; education to have the aim of teaching the youth to love their people, their culture, and to honour human brotherhood, liberty and peace.

The immediate objective of African leaders is to achieve a new National Convention on the lines of the 1908-9 Convention which drafted the Act of Union—but this time representative of all the racial communities. 'Our situation may be grim, but it is not hopeless,' says Lutuli.[1] 'There is still enough goodwill and charitableness among South Africans, black and white—if only leaders, black and white, and the government would get together to talk things over.' This demand was conveyed in a letter by Nelson Mandela to Dr Verwoerd on behalf of the All-In African National Action Council in 1961.[2] 'It was the earnest opinion of conference that this dangerous situation (facing the South African people today) could be averted only by the calling of a sovereign national convention representative of all South Africans, to draw up a new non-racial and democratic constitution,' he wrote. 'Such a convention would discuss our national problems in a sane and sober manner, and would work out solutions which sought to preserve and safeguard the interests of all sections of the population.' He never received a reply to this letter.

With the exception of leaders like Chief Kaiser Matanzima, partition in any form is rejected outright. 'White South Africa,' Lutuli wrote in 1961, 'can no more do without us than we without them—and this on a basis of equality.... I do not think of the South African nation as a black nation or as a nation of any particular colour. To me the only proper South African nation is a nation of people—I do not care what colour their skins are.'[3] On another occasion he said: 'No one ever asked if we wanted to be herded into Zulustans or Xhosastans. Some of us do not want a divided South Africa. I certainly do not.... What we want is to share in the governing of the

whole country. We reject the . . . plan of Separate Development, a Divided South Africa.' That it is Lutuli rather than
Matanzima who speaks for Africans on this issue is shown by
the defeat of Mantanzima's programme in the 1963 Transkei
elections.

AFRICANS CHOOSE THEIR WEAPONS

> At the moment we are confident that the West will not
> lend itself to 'direct' action against South Africa by
> economic, political or military intervention. In a
> Sharpeville atmosphere I would not have that confi-
> dence. . . . Not foreign pressure in itself or internal
> difficulties in themselves are our danger. It is the com-
> bination of the two.
>
> DIE BURGER, *November 10, 1962*

The strike is the obvious immediate weapon in the hands of
Africans, since the economy rests on their labour. Strike
action, stay-at-home demonstrations and boycotts have been
tried with varying results. But strikes on a sufficiently massive scale are not likely to succeed unless they arise spontane-
ously from specific grievances and are designed simply to redress these. Africans in employment (and especially those in
the middle class) stand to lose too much by coming into conflict with the existing laws: to strike is not only to lose one's
job, but also the prospect of getting another. It means the
probable loss of one's home, the break-up of the family, the
deprivation of schooling for the children, and expulsion to conditions of rural poverty. The organisation needed to prepare
for strike action is made virtually impossible by laws which
bring political strikes into the category of 'sabotage' liable to
the death penalty; which prevent political movements and
proper trade unions; which prohibit meetings unless approved
by the authorities; and which proscribe 'undesirable' publications. A strike is met by the mobilisation of the police force
and the army: this was the fate of Nelson Mandela's attempt
to organise the last general strike in 1961, for which he was
sent to prison.

Thus the strongest peaceful weapon in African hands cannot
be used for the same reason as makes organised opposition

impossible in any totalitarian state. Non-violent resistance has
ceased to be practical. This was the burden of Nelson Mandela's
defence at his trial in 1962. 'We have been conditioned
by the history of white governments in this country to accept
the fact that Africans, when they make their demands strongly
and powerfully enough to have some chance of success, will be
met by force and terror on the part of the government . . .
government violence can do only one thing and that is to breed
counter-violence . . . ultimately, the dispute between the government and my people, will finish up by being settled in violence
and by force.'[1] The magistrate's answer was that the court was
concerned not with politics but with maintaining law and order.

What does counter-violence mean in the conditions of
South Africa? How do African political leaders envisage success? There is nothing to suggest that either the ANC or the
PAC, or the group of whites who launched the first sabotage
group—the African Liberation Committee—envisages a military struggle on the lines of Mau Mau or Algeria. Nevertheless, the 'Hill Movement' in Pondoland and the *Poqo* out-
breaks show the danger of atavistic terrorist movements which
would reject African political movements as we know them
today. This is no doubt a serious risk if things drag on for
too long.

African nationalist strategy is based on a combination
of violence and non-violence. Violence is intended to achieve
two results: to undermine white confidence in its ability to
maintain its supremacy and to make international opinion take
South Africa's race problems seriously. It is argued that
whites have refused in the past to consider alternatives acceptable to Africans because they are confident of their ability to
maintain their position, if only by naked force. Therefore
(runs the argument) it is necessary to shake white confidence as
an essential prerequisite for possible constitutional talks. As
for international intervention, the African leadership is convinced that this is possible only if the problem becomes sufficiently alarming to Western nations.

Based on these two major premises, the strategy of violence is conceived along the lines of *maquis* activity in the
European underground, rather than as an overt military campaign. For this purpose, the first need is for groups of well-

trained and disciplined saboteurs to operate inside the Republic. To judge by the pattern of sabotage already emerging, it is clear that the main targets will be property and communication systems rather than people, although it is always doubtful whether strictly non-personal violence can be maintained in the kind of situation which mounting violence must produce.

Both the ANC and the PAC (and of course the communists) have men undergoing training in African countries, in communist countries, and in one or two Western countries. The numbers involved are a close secret, but they probably run into hundreds. Although some of these groups have already been trained, large-scale activities must be postponed until the countries closer to the Republic's border offer a better chance to maintain supplies and ensure mobility. The likelihood, therefore, is that the underground will not be ready for sustained activity before 1965 or 1966. But the tempo of sporadic sabotage is certain to increase meanwhile.

It is envisaged that the South African underground will be financed, armed and trained by the independent African states. The Organisation of African Unity has already established its African Liberation Committee (comprising representatives from nine states) to give direct aid to the liberation movements in Southern Africa. It is to these African states that the South African leadership looks primarily for guidance and support, though help from other quarters will not be spurned. Individuals sporting Castro beards and Mao Tsetung tunics may make their appearance, and should cause no surprise. However, the main spur will almost certainly derive from Africa itself.

Thus in the overall strategy of resistance for South Africa, a direct military confrontation is not envisaged. Nor is it believed that there will be an invasion of South Africa by black armies from the north. The recipe is a mixture of internal explosions leading to increasing external pressure—resulting finally in international intervention. This recipe has already begun to work. Year by year pressures for sanctions against South Africa have mounted, and have met with an increasing response as evidence of internal tensions in the Republic become undeniable. The outstanding example of such interaction was the sudden hardening of world opinion following the death of sixty-seven people at Sharpeville in 1960.

World opinion will almost certainly become less 'sympathetic' to the victims of apartheid as they become less passive; people feel more compassion for passive victims than for armed rebels. But serious violence will probably cause the international community to think less in terms of sympathy and more in terms of political realities.

This is what African leaders would prefer.

IV

THE NON-WHITE MINORITIES

1: THE COLOUREDS

> With all the love of which I am capable as a Christian and of whom my fellow Afrikaners should be capable (yes, I say my fellow Afrikaners) I must permit myself to repeat what I emphasised in my recently published book [*Die Eerste Steen*], namely, that the Brown people are not merely concerned about bread and butter affairs, and that note must be taken, because Christ demands it of us, of the diabolical humiliation of the spirit which these people of ours have to endure.
>
> *Mr Adam Small, Coloured author and lecturer*, DIE BURGER, *July 11, 1961*

> 'No, Mr Small,' replied a correspondent. 'Dry your tears; let me and my children weep, for we shall have to pluck the bitter fruit of these things. . . . It is we who supply the fuel that stokes the cauldron of the Coloured peoples' aspirations. And then our government comes along and sits on the lid. You do not have to be an engineer to know this is a recipe for the development of an irresistible and perhaps even a hellish force. . . .'
>
> DIE BURGER, *July 12, 1961*

In terms of political power, neither the Coloured nor the Indian community is a significant force. But their existence presents an embarrassing flaw in the structure of apartheid and troubles the white conscience. In human terms, both communities suffer deeply under the tightening screw of apartheid laws. The predictable result is that after years of equivocation and division, increasing numbers of both communities have come to ally themselves with the African struggle.

The Coloureds—'God's Stepchildren' in the memorable phrase of Sarah Gertrude Millin's novel of that title—number about one and a half million. All but about 180,000 live in the Cape Province, mostly in the farms and towns of the

Western Cape Province. They originate in miscegenation between the settlers and slaves, but their 'race classification' includes Malays, Hottentots and Bushmen. Their average standard of living has been higher than that of the Africans, for they provide not only the labourers, but also the industrial semi-skilled and artisan workers.

Before the enforcement of apartheid legislation in the Cape there was a natural, if slow, process of integration between Coloureds and whites. A Dutch Reformed Church missionary, the Reverend D. P. Botha, expressed the deep uneasiness of many Afrikaners about the treatment of the Coloureds in a book published in 1960. 'The culture of the Afrikaner and Coloured is the same. An Afrikaner would be in much greater danger of losing his culture, especially his language, if he married an English-speaking person . . . than if he married a Coloured. The nation is not threatened by the mixing of white blood and Coloured, but rather by the large-scale mixing of Coloured and Bantu blood.'[1]

But apartheid envisages neither for the Coloureds. They are to have no Bantustan of their own, but a curious form of 'state within a state'. A Coloured Representative Council, with thirty elected and sixteen nominated members will take 'office' in 1966. Its functions will be to give advice on Coloured affairs when asked to do so, to recommend plans for the Coloured community, and to provide a link between the people and the Minister for Coloured Affairs. Specific functions may be delegated to it if the Ministers of Coloured Affairs and Finance approve, and if the 'legislation' they pass does not conflict with the Republic's existing legislation. This Council represents the full extent of the political rights intended for the Coloured community—and, one day, it will be allowed to enter into a 'commonwealth relationship' with the white parliament and the Bantustans.

The removal of the 135,000 African workers from the Western Cape is represented as being to the benefit of the Coloureds. The effect is quite different. The Coloured artisan is hit as hard as the African labourer—and becomes, himself, a labourer. Coloureds are recruited for the lower paid jobs formerly taken by Africans. The proportion of Coloureds employed as dock labourers has risen from 10 per cent to over 40 per cent. Moreover, industrial legislation is being used to replace Coloureds by whites in some of their better paid jobs. Particularly resented is the closure of two traditional fields of employment: artisans in the building industry, and traffic policemen. The removal of Africans from the Western Cape will inevitably result in Coloureds' replacing Africans as the lowest economic class in the caste structure. Nor are they offered even the illusory hope of a geographical area where, 'ultimately', they may hope to rise to the top.

The Coloured elite are the teachers, of whom there are over 10,000. They, together with a small number of lawyers, doctors, businessmen and trade union leaders, provide political leadership in opposition to those who believe that the Coloureds have most to gain by co-operating with the authorities. The Coloured community is divided between two conflicting viewpoints; but the majority is inclined to submit fatalistically to its fate.

The fact of belonging, culturally and socially, to neither black nor white society has produced the quickness, neuroticism, sharp humour and feckless ambition of an unstable and rootless community. The majority has aspired in the past to acceptance in white society; and the politically active, rejecting 'collaboration', have lacked unity and organisation. They have been, in more senses than one, the 'Trotskyites' of South Africa. The Coloureds' Teachers League of South Africa was, until its banning, a militant though small political organisation. Recently its members have been prominent in the new political party, the African People's Democratic Socialist Union—an offshoot of the Non-European Unity Movement. The Coloured People's Congress—never a large group—was allied with the African National Congress. There is growing evidence that the Coloured intellectuals, like the Africans, have abandoned the hope of achieving a peaceful transition to acceptance on equal terms with the other communities, and several underground groups have been formed with the avowed purpose of starting a violent struggle.

2: THE INDIAN COMMUNITY

Setting out the government's Indian policy, the Prime Minister said that attempts at repatriation had failed. The Indians were an alien element who had been brought to the country for selfish economic reasons, and the present problem was an example of how social problems could be created by purely economic action. The Indian community could not be accepted and regarded as part of a multiracial nation. It was realised, however, that this group could not remain here without rights in their own affairs or their own group. 'We are prepared to give the Indian authority over himself, not joint authority with us.'

DIE TRANSVALER, *August 25, 1961*

Relations between Indians and whites left something to be desired.

Mr W. A. Maree, Minister of Indian Affairs,
DIE TRANSVALER, *August 7, 1961*

The Indians are the smallest of the non-white communities, numbering half a million. Until 1961, they were regarded as foreigners, so that no provision was made for them under the scheme of apartheid. Financial inducements were held out to them to return to India, whence their ancestors had been recruited in 1870 as indentured labour for the sugar-cane fields. But this repatriation scheme failed, and in 1961 the government set up a Department of Indian Affairs: the Indians were acknowledged as permanent inhabitants of the Republic. Most of them live in Natal, the home of the sugar industry. The great majority work as unskilled labourers, but there is a substantial class of small traders, and a few wealthy property owners and merchants.

Many of the laws which discriminate against Indians apply to no other community. Thus, Indians may not move from one province to another without a permit, and then only for holiday or study purposes, or under recruitment for specific jobs such as hotel waiters. They may not even pass through the Orange Free State without a special 'in transit' permit.*

* The extreme case was of an Indian who was given a passport valid for a number of countries, but stating 'this passport is not valid for the Orange Free State'.

Having been declared permanent inhabitants for apartheid purposes, the Indians are to be granted much the same machinery for political expression as the Coloureds. However, Dr Verwoerd has said that they will not be permitted to participate in the eventual 'commonwealth'. The official description of the functions of the Indian Council shows the extent of self-government envisaged. It would 'eventually consist of elected representatives with legislative and administrative powers in respect of all matters *directly affecting* the Indian community, such as social services, education, local government, etc. In addition the Council will . . . consult with the government and with Ministers on all matters *of importance to* the Indian community, such as opportunities for employment, industrial development and the development of local government.'[1] (Authors' italics.) Here the semantic niceties of the apartheid rationale are shown at their best: social services are considered a matter 'directly affecting' the Indians, while opportunities for employment become merely a 'matter of importance' to them, and hence a subject for consultation with the government and not for legislation by the Indians themselves. The clear intention is that neither the Indians nor the Coloureds are to be allowed autonomy in any matter, however important to them, wherever it might also affect whites.

But it is the Group Areas Act which falls most cruelly on the Indian community. This is the legislation under which the 'white' cities are ethnically zoned. Ethnic groups are not only socially segregated; they are also not permitted to carry on business in each other's areas. The Indians are compelled to dispose of properties in the 'white areas' and to move to specially constructed townships at some distance outside the cities. There the wealthy few may purchase property, the others must pay the standard rents of government housing, as well as considerably increased transport costs to and from jobs in the cities. In the past, the livelihood of the small shopkeeper or trader has depended upon siting their properties in business areas accessible to the custom of other racial groups. They are now expected to trade only within their own communities, except where special concessions are made in strictly controlled 'multiracial trading areas'.

The appalling effects of the Group Areas Act on Indians in Pretoria were the subject of a warning issued in 1958 by Professor Pistorius:

> In South Africa it is not customary to condemn children and infants to death, nor is death by starvation an accepted form of execution. . . . If any measure by which we intend to preserve our Western way of life and our Christian values should, on examination, prove to be in fact a death sentence on innocent children, it would without a doubt be admitted by us that no Christian value can be preserved by destroying the Christian conscience. Nevertheless, as far as I can see, that is the only logical outcome of the Group Areas Act as applied to the Indian community in Pretoria. . . . Practically the whole Indian community lives on commerce, and it is clear that Indian shops in a township at least twelve miles away from Pretoria will not draw custom from Europeans or Natives, and that the hard fact is that the Indians cannot exist unless they have access to non-Indian buyers. . . . As things are now we are in fact condemning a whole community to ruin and starvation.[1]

Indian leadership is, understandably, divided and confused. On the one side are those who, fatalistically, believe that they have no alternative in the meantime but to agree to co-operate with the government proposal for an Indian Council. In this way they hope they might still be able to save something out of the wreckage brought on their community by the Group Areas Act and other discriminatory laws. On the other side are those who proclaim their belief in Gandhi's philosophy of defiance and a refusal to submit without protest to injustice. The militants in the latter group continue to pin their faith in the banned Indian National Congress which was born out of the long struggle to win recognition as full citizens of South Africa. Its roots lie in Mahatma Gandhi's passive resistance campaign launched in Natal soon after the turn of the century. Originally its leadership was in the hands of the merchant class; but after the introduction of the Indian Pegging Act in 1946—the so-called 'Ghetto Act' introduced by General Smuts under pressure from his supporters in Natal to prevent Indian 'encroachment' into 'white areas'—Congress turned to more militant leadership. Their leader for many years has been Dr Yusef Dadoo, now in exile, who had been a prominent member of the Communist Party. While many of his associates were militantly left-wing, they were by no means all communists.

V

MILITARY POWER

Dr H. F. Verwoerd, the Prime Minister, addressing a meeting in his constituency, declared that South Africans faced a simple choice between survival or downfall, and would defend themselves in all ways, even with the rifle if it could not be otherwise. 'Concession,' he added, 'is surrender.'

SOUTHERN AFRICA, *London 1963*

The armed forces of the Republic of South Africa form the largest and most diversified military establishment in sub-Saharan Africa. It is unchallengeable by any army in Africa: only the Egyptian army begins to compare with its striking capacity. If the military forces of all the African states were to combine, they would not be able to offer a frontal challenge to the Republic for reasons of logistics—provided that there is no simultaneous internal subversion. This is, of course, the great 'if'. In a statement in 1963 the Minister of Defence, Mr J. J. Fouché, said: 'There will always be a fifth column, but I am certain that the day will come when black and white will stand together to defend our freedom.'[1]

On what did he base his confidence? 'Today, we whites are free. The old imperialism has gone. Now, *we are leading our non-whites to freedom* in their territories and we shall never allow agitators to influence us.' (Authors' italics.) Major-General Sir Francis De Guingand made the same forecast in 1962: 'As regards a fifth column, I hope we have sufficient internal forces to deal with that. I do not want to go into politics, but the more understanding we can reach with our various racial groups the less danger of that, provided extremists are controlled.'[2] Non-whites are not allowed to bear arms in defence of the Republic, even if they should wish to do so; they are forbidden, at any time, from carrying arms: a measure, perhaps, of the Defence Minister's confidence in their loyalty.

The South African army is intended to play three roles:

as an ally of the West against the communists in the cold war; as a security force to deal with internal trouble; and as a force to repel military threats against its frontiers. The Republic, no longer sure which is its greatest enemy—world communism, internal rebellion, or threats by African states—deals with this dilemma by rolling the three into one: everybody threatening South Africa is seen to be part of the international communist conspiracy against the West.

Whether or not the West approves, South Africa firmly plants itself in the NATO camp dedicated to the defence of the West against its enemies. In return, the Republic expects the West to come to its defence if necessary. The South African Army chief, Commandant-General D. H. Grobbelaar, told businessmen in 1963: 'It is our defined policy in the case of a conflict between the East and the West that we support the West. We must not forget that because of South Africa's geographical position it is of extreme importance to the West, and is therefore a target for the East.'[1] This is official policy. NATO leaders subscribe to South Africa's importance as an ally in the event of a world war: thus they insist on its being armed with modern weapons to withstand external attack. Their attitude explains Western reluctance to impose an arms embargo against the Republic. Even when the United States agreed to accede to the 1963 UN decision calling for an arms embargo, Britain and France insisted on their right to supply arms which are 'not suitable for dealing with internal troubles'. Where does one draw the line?

Even before the Addis Ababa Conference of African Heads of State decided in 1963 to support the liberation struggle in Southern Africa, the Verwoerd Government took the view that the Republic had to face the threat of 'a black invasion' from the north. This threat was used to justify defence expenditure which was multiplied five-fold between 1960–1 and 1963–4 to a figure of about £130 million (including the police). Although the government insists that the Africans inside the Republic would be loyal to the whites if they were attacked from outside, it simultaneously presents the threat as a racial conflict. The Defence Minister told Parliament that 'the black man in Africa was driving the white man back—step by step. He was no longer making any secret of it.' The government now accepts the fact that they can count on Western support only in the event of attack by the Soviet bloc countries. 'If we become involved in a war tomorrow because of aggression against us by a state not far from our borders,' the Defence Minister told Parliament in March 1962, 'then I accept that no Western Power will step in. Then we will have to take a stand alone.'[1] They have recognised that the Western Powers would not side with South Africa in what would amount to a racial clash. 'But should the country become involved in a war against communism, the West would come to our assistance.'[2]

Nevertheless, though the government makes much of its role as 'a Western bastion against the East', its defence forces are primarily intended to look after internal security. Its role in the event of trouble has been carefully described by the Defence Minister:

> The task of the Army and the Air Force is to take action for internal security as soon as the disturbances have reached a degree where the police are unable to control them.... Greater mobility, armoured protection and increased striking power have been given to twelve of the infantry units at strategic places, in the form of Saracens. These Citizen Force units, together with the two Mobile Watches which are organised as Saracen units for internal security, form a shock element in the Army.... Besides these Watches, the units of the Citizen Force and the commandos have been organised in the past years in order to ensure that they will be able to act more efficiently for internal security. At the moment, there is a Scout Corps of twenty-five men with each Commando, and these will be available immediately in case of internal emergency.[3]

DEFENCE IN OUTLINE

> When you are really in need of a firearm, it is worth more to you than all your other earthly belongings.
> —*Adjutant-Officer Mr Badenhorst, instructing a hundred women at the Paarl Women's Shooting Club,* CAPE TIMES, *February 25, 1963*

By the end of 1964, South Africa plans to have 140,000 trained white people in uniform, serving in permanent or part-time units. The Permanent Force in 1963 consisted of 15,288 officers and men (9,019 in 1960). Armed with modern weapons, it is mobile and decentralised. The First Parachute Battalion has been established with 200 men.

The Permanent Force is backed by the Commandos and the Citizen Force. All white youths over nineteen are compulsorily called up for nine months' training in the Citizen Force in the first year, and three months for the next three years. ('Our aim is to train every young man for military service whether he is flat-footed or not'—the Defence Minister, June 3, 1963). The annual input of the Citizen Force is 10,000.

Every able-bodied white South African, who is not a member of the Permanent Force or the Citizen Force, is required to serve for four years in the Commandos, which are divided into Afrikaans- and English-speaking units. They are trained in weaponry and in combat operations.

The Police Force is co-ordinated with the Army. In 1963 it totalled 29,343 (whites and non-whites in roughly equal numbers). White police units are armed with revolvers, sub-machine guns and Saracen armoured cars. The staff of the Security Staff was tripled in the first six months of 1963; it is still being expanded.

The Police Reserve—a voluntary force of citizens with separate units for Coloureds and Indians (but not Africans)— is about 15,000 strong. The target is 50,000. Together with the Commandos they can be called up for security duties.

Women's Shooting Clubs have been started all over the country; 27,250 women are being trained by police to handle guns.

Aircraft include about 130 first-line combat type and 440 support types many of which, including the mothballed T-6s could be used against insurgents. To these must be added eight Navy aircraft and 21 Army liaison aircraft, making an inventory of 600.

The Navy has 3,000 men with 29 active vessels. These are being reinforced with three Whitby class anti-submarine frigates of 2,577 tons. Armament will include two 4.5-inch twin-mount guns, two 40 mm. Bofor anti-aircraft guns, twelve tubes for homing torpedoes, and two three-barrel depth bomb-mortars.

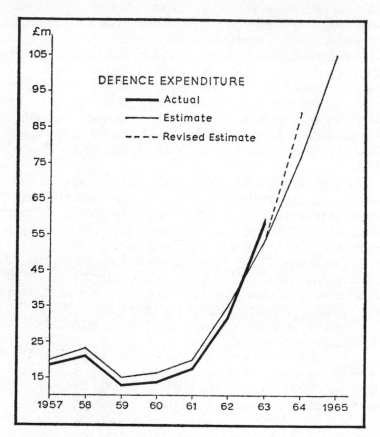

South Africa is virtually self-reliant for its munitions. Three new armament factories have been built at a cost of £10 million in a deal between the government and AECI. Apart from .303 ammunition, local plants are now manufacturing 7.62 mm bullets for automatic rifles, and for the 9 mm. sub-machine guns, as well as .380 revolver ammunition. Armoured cars, radio equipment, and service equipment are built locally. The forces stated needs include 300,000 rifles. The standard weapon is the 7.62 mm. NATO rifle, the 7.62 mm.

light machine gun, and a 9 mm. sub-machine gun. The Saracen, the Ferret Mark I and II, and the Centurion Mark 325 are being replaced by the French Panhard armoured car.

Behind the existing forces and the defence planning stands a steel industry with an annual capacity of 2,350,000 ingot tons, and the scientific and technical skills needed for major defence production.

ORDER OF BATTLE AND MILITARY STANCE

AIR FORCE

Fighters/Interceptors

16 Dassault Mirage 3CZ   40 HS Vampire FB-5
N. Amer. F-51 Mustang   30 Canadair Sabre 6
Philco ASM-9 Sidewinder   Nord AS-20 ASM
Nord AS-30 ASM   2 Squadrons at Waterkloof
        9 Fighter-bomber Squadrons (2 PF and 7 ACF)*

Bombers/Patrollers

7 Avro Shackleton MR-3   6 BAC Canberra B-12
        16 HS Buccaneer S-2 (2 squadrons)
        Shackletons No. 35 Squadron
        4 Maritime Squadrons (3 PF and 1 ACF)

Transports

18 Douglas C-47 Dakota   2 HS Devon
2 HS Heron 2   1 BAC Viscount 781D
2 Dornier Do-27B (VIP)   7 Lock C-130 E (Waterkloof)†
No. 28 and 44 Squadrons
    (Waterkloof)   1 PF and 1 ACF Squadron

Trainers/Support

3 Dassault Mirage 3 BZ   260 N. Amer. T-6 Texan
18 HS Vampire T-55   few Auster AOP-9
        23 Cessna Skywaggon

* PF = Permanent Force.   ACF = Active Citizens Force.
    † This new E version is strategic as well, capable of multi-mission logistics.

Helicopters

5 Sikorsky S-55   3 Sikorsky S-51
6 Sud Alouette 2   few Sud Alouette 3*

1 Training Group   1 OTU
Citizen Forces fly T-6s

Air Bases

Langebaanweg (ASW), Swartkop, Pretoria (MU), SAAF college established in 1951 DE Airport, Cape Town, Rooikop, Dunnottar (AFS) Lyttleton, Ysterplaat, Bloemsprit, Citizen forces at Pretoria, Durban, Cape Town, Germiston, Bloemfontein, Port Elizabeth.

The Air Force is now divided into three groups: the Inland Group, Pretoria, which consists of transport and ground support aircraft; the Maintenance Group, also stationed at Pretoria; and the Maritime Group at Langebaanweg, Cape, for coastal reconnaissance and co-operation with the Navy.

ARMY

The Union Defence Forces are relatively small with elements of only a few battalions, but capable of rapid expansion from extensive reserves in the Active Citizen Force, the Rifle Commandos and the cadet school organisation. The Union is divided into ten territorial commands and a Coastal command, also including the new base at Walvis Bay, in South West Africa.

Commandos 80,000; Citizen Army 70,000; Police 12,200 (whites) Emergency total (whites) 205,000. The hard core is 16,200 men.

Army Ordnance

Ferret 1; Ferret 2.

A new vehicle and a surface-air missile are planned. Centurion Mark 325. Panhard AML armoured car, built locally.

NAVY

The Navy has patrol responsibilities in the Atlantic and Indian Oceans, and is planned to work with the British Royal Navy

* Up to 35 planned.

in defence of the sea-lanes and approaches to Durban and Capetown. It is a minesweeper and frigate force though it is at the moment undermanned, with elements in cadre. The two biggest ships, Van der Stel and Van Riebeeck, are being converted for helicopter deployment.

Ships

Carriers	CV	0	Cruisers	0	Escorts	0
	CVL	0	Destroyers	0	Mine Vessels	4
Battleships		0	Frigates	7	Transports	0
Submarines		0 (4 planned)			Light Misc.	22
Oilers		0			Yards	3

Aircraft
8 Westland WASP

POISON GAS AND MISSILES

Gas is coming back as a low-cost military weapon of destructive power, Professor L. J. Le Roux told a meeting of the [S.A.] Association for the Advancement of Science.

THE TIMES, London, November 8, 1963

The South African government leaves nothing out of its calculations to prepare for the coming struggle. Its plans include research into poison gas, rockets, and nuclear power.

The Defence Research Council is in charge of work into the utilisation of poison gas. Professor L. J. Le Roux, vice-president of the Council for Scientific and Industrial Research stated publicly that the Council realised that chemical bacteriological warfare was no longer impractical. A special group of scientists are learning 'everything there is to know' about virulent poisons like tabun, soman and sarin developed in Nazi Germany and known now to be in Russian hands. 'These poisons are capable of being delivered in vast quantities by aircraft or long-range missile, and they can have a destructive effect similar to that of a nuclear bomb of twenty megatons', Professor Le Roux said. 'These gases are ten times more poisonous than any other substance you can name.

The most dangerous have no smell and can be sprayed like an insecticide as an aerosol.'[1]

The Council for Scientific and Industrial Research established a National Institute for Rocket Research in 1963. Its immediate task is to build non-nuclear guided ground-to-air missiles. Scientists have been sent abroad to study methods of making missiles. The Defence Minister, asking Parliament for large sums of money for defence research in 1963, explained that the Republic needed to be independent of overseas supplies 'in case purchase eventually became impossible'. A French factory in Johannesburg has started manufacturing high density graphite for nozzles, vanes and re-entry cones for rockets.

The directors of the South African Atomic Energy Board has stated that the country has the knowledge, ability and industrial potential to produce nuclear weapons. In 1959 the Board initiated a £4 million research programme to adapt developments in nuclear power to South African conditions. A reactor centre is in operation at Pelindaba near Pretoria, where a 20 mw research reactor is installed. The Government Metallurgical Laboratories in Johannesburg have built a pilot plant to produce nuclear-grade uranium metal and compounds suitable for nuclear fuels.

The director of the French Atomic Energy Commission, after visiting South Africa in 1963, said that a number of nuclear scientists and technicians might soon come to France for nuclear training. South Africa exports over £50 million of uranium a year.

*   *   *

The Republic's main remaining concern is over the danger of undersea attacks. It maintains a continuous air surveillance 'for Russian submarines'; and recently decided to extend its sea-limits from three to six miles. It has plans for buying submarines in addition to its anti-submarine ships; but this part of its defence build-up is carefully hushed up.

VI
SIXTEEN YEARS OF APARTHEID

The period of a white aristocracy above and a non-white
proletariat below will have to disappear.
DIE TRANSVALER, *January 1, 1962*

After sixteen years of apartheid, South Africa is further than
ever from solving its race problems. Apartheid is rejected by
almost one half of the white community and overwhelmingly
by the non-white communities. It remains the ideology of only
a small, but powerful, minority which holds the great majority
in the grip of its political machine, its bureaucracy, and its
police and military forces.

The current economic boom is the result, not of the success of apartheid, but of its failure: expansion has occurred
only because of the continued influx of Africans from the rural
areas and the reserves to the towns. Legislation exists to curb
this influx, but it cannot be effectively used at the same time
as a policy of encouraging economic expansion. Instead it
is used to limit African rights in the centres of economic
growth, and to deny them opportunities to develop and use
their skills. Blanket provisions under this legislation are
circumvented by piecemeal exemptions to prevent damage to
the economy.

There is no real Separate Development, only racial discrimination in an integrated economy. Instead of vertical
separation of the races—as intended by the theory of Separate
Development—the Republic is perpetuating horizontal segregation with the Africans forming the base as a rightless,
migrant, unskilled proletariat. Nor is there any practical intention of changing the pattern. All the government's ambitious plans for continued economic pump-priming—such as the
Orange River project and the expansion of state-owned corporations—are based on migrant African labour. The shortage of skilled labour—the result of Job Reservation and of the

prohibition of the right of Africans to acquire skills in the 'white industries'—is palliated by increased immigration and by granting exemptions to individual employers who cannot recruit enough white skilled workers. The non-white worker knows that his livelihood could be terminated at any moment, but meanwhile he must contribute to the image of a successful economic order. But he also knows that, contrary to what his prospering employer likes to believe, economic expansion cannot fundamentally alter his lot. Expansion can temporarily mitigate the worst effects of Separate Development on his own livelihood, but it can do nothing to change the racial stratification which is the essential characteristic of the apartheid society.

The business man's rationalisation that 'prosperity may yet succeed in vanquishing apartheid, where political pressure, passive resistance and sabotage have failed'[1] has a hollow ring to the African. Denied by law anything like a fair share in the prosperity he helps to create, he knows that the laws will not be changed by prosperity. He knows that economic expansion may increase the size of the nation's cake, but that there will be no change in the relative share allowed to each racial community. Nor can it change by an iota the political and human rights of the African population. On the contrary, economic expansion makes it possible to disguise the worst features of Separate Development, and to finance the expensive forces of coercion to maintain it.

The 1964 budget provides an outstanding example of the effects of prosperity on South Africa's non-white citizens. Discussing the government's priorities in using the 'predictably huge surplus' of £44 million, the Johannesburg *Financial Mail* wrote:

> The Minister has resisted pressure group claims for widespread tax concessions and has applied most of the current surplus to helping finance the bigger spending, mostly on defence, planned for next year.... What does the budget do for the non-white group as a whole? Very little. Yet this group is the poorest and the weakest, politically and socially. One could have expected a substantial grant out of the £44 million surplus towards improving the material lot of non-whites , If anything, the

reverse is true. Take the case of African education in areas other than the Transkei. There the educational subsidy has been severely cut by £1.55 million from £8.8 million in 1963/64 to £7.25 million. In a sense, it is, ironically, the African who is thus partly paying for the further increase in national security expenditure, which has reached a massive £124.5 million, made up of £105 million for defence and £24.5 million for police. Instead of using part of the rich tax harvest to expand educational facilities . . . for the African, and to reinvest in him a small part of the great wealth he is helping South Africa to produce, the concessions and allowances provided for in this Budget will benefit primarily white men, business men, shareholders and property-seekers.[1]

The truth is that the government's political and military power has neutralised both the economic power of English-speaking South Africa, and the labour power of the non-whites. English-speaking South Africa is further inhibited by its own race prejudices and by its reluctance to take steps which might destroy, not only apartheid, but the white aristocracy as well.

Thus, the major internal effects of the years of apartheid rule have been to turn a non-violent situation into one of active violence. The attempt to divide the economy—in defiance of economic laws, and in total disregard for humanitarian considerations—has created only further injustice. To perpetuate unworkable policies, the government fosters a war psychosis. The Africans, in response, have learnt the language of violence; and today they are learning its uses as well.

Externally, apartheid rule has isolated South Africa almost completely within the world community, and strained even the measure of equivocal support which remains to the Republic in some Western countries. In relation to the rest of Africa, the Republic is not only isolated: it has succeeded in uniting the continent against it in active and permanent hostility. It stands branded as a racial autocracy in a world of predominantly coloured nations, and in an international society committed to adjusting itself to the new situation in which European power is no longer dominant.

The Republic's white leadership is aware of the perils of this situation. But because the majority in both white communities fear a sudden change in the status quo more than they fear apartheid, they have drawn closer together. Some choose safety in the idea of a single white laager; others prefer the idea of two linked laagers. Only a brave ten per cent refuse to be drawn into either, recognising the foolhardiness of the 'last stand' mentality.

Despite stupendous efforts to maintain white *baasskap*, the government has admitted intellectually that there is no longer any possibility of maintaining dominance over all the racial communities within the Republic's present frontiers. It has elected to make the totally impractical, if not disingenuous, attempt to divide power by offering the Africans a nebulous independence over the 13 per cent of the country's area earmarked for Bantustans, while retaining for itself power over the wealthiest and largest part of the common estate. The government now stands irrevocably committed to making a success of its Separate Development policy as the only way it knows out of the crisis. But there is no chance that the Bantustans could fulfil their purpose: they are doomed to certain failure.

The government's own lack of confidence about the success of its policies is revealed by its measures to arm itself for a show-down. It is willing, if need be, to maintain itself internally and externally by force. It cannot be dismissed at the polls while the Afrikaner vote remains of such crucial importance. But even if the government were to change under growing pressure, the result could only be another exclusively white government. Such a change would in no way alter the balance of power between whites and non-whites. It might cause a temporary relaxation of Western pressure, but it could not satisfy the minimum requirements of the African leadership.

Although effective political, economic and military power remains concentrated in white hands, the government is unable to convert this massive power into real authority. Despite legislation giving the government powers to create a system of directed labour, the towns and the platteland get blacker all the time. Like Xerxes, Verwoerd can order the waves to be whipped, but he cannot hold them back. His régime can impose its laws, but it cannot make them work. It fills its prisons, but new forces of resistance arise all the time. It creates Bantustans, but the 'Bantu' reject those of their number who appear to collaborate with the government in implementing them. Massive coercion can keep the government in power, but its power can be used only negatively to maintain its position. Lacking political authority, it cannot influence Africans to co-operate in bringing about positive changes. Hence the need to divert more of its resources to increasing its capacity for coercion. The pattern is familiar in all disintegrating authoritarian societies.

The deadlock is clear. Neither side can break it. The white society can rule, but it cannot create the conditions it regards as essential to its own security. The Africans can challenge this rule, but they cannot break it.

Both sides, therefore, have changed their techniques. Both adopt more desperate methods; and each seeks new allies to alter the balance in its favour. The whites appeal with increasing urgency to the West for support, at least to prevent further intervention. The blacks appeal to independent Africa and to world opinion. Only the Africans seem certain to succeed.

Thus the forces of violence escalate, and the Republic remains in pawn to increasingly embittered racial passions. The inescapable conclusion is that deadlock cannot be resolved without the introduction of a catalyst from outside. There is no solution to be found in the internal political forces. In the absence of quick and effective international intervention, South Africa's bitterness can only spread its poison throughout the continent and involve the world in a twentieth-century race war.

Part Two

International Power and South Africa

No system whereby all real power is to be retained, as a matter of law, in the hands of whites alone can succeed or endure... Nor can any system that aims at disguising such retention... We all of us have to face the facts of life in South Africa, one of the most important of which is that we are all so well mixed up that there is no possibility of sorting us out. Partition in any real sense is impossible, and it is most important that our thinking should not be affected by half-beliefs in the back of our minds that there will some day be partition.
The Hon. O. D. Schreiner, Chancellor of the University of Witwatersrand; former Justice of Appeal; January, 1964

Dr Jan Graaff's Partition Plan

I
THE SEARCH FOR SOLUTIONS

On one point everyone concerned with South Africa is agreed: that the present system cannot endure. The question, then, is not whether the present-day Republic can survive, but what should replace it. The search for solutions has produced a number of alternatives which have already been described. But none of these alternatives provides a common meeting-ground for the power forces engaged in the South African struggle. As so often happens when an apparently intractable problem is met, the temptation is to think of partition. This idea may conceivably win support in international circles as a last resort when everything else has failed. Partition, however, can offer no lasting solution to the South African dilemma unless it is freely accepted by whites and blacks: but this essential condition is missing.

The plan around which most current thinking on partition turns is that devised by Dr Jan Graaff, the economist brother of the leader of the United Party, Sir de Villiers Graff. (See map on p. 220.) He calls his plans the 'demotomic line'.* It provides for two states, one controlled by Europeans and the other by Africans. The black state would have 7 million Africans and 1 million whites and Indians; the white state would have 4½ million whites, Coloureds and Indians, and 3½ million Africans. The only areas with sizeable white populations to be ceded to the black state are the province of Natal and a large part of the Northern Transvaal. The 3½ million Africans left in the white state would have no political rights there. The white state would cover about 60 per cent of the land area; while the black state would have about 40 per cent, if the three High Commission Territories were included.

The rationale behind partition is that political integration is unacceptable to the whites; that Bantustans and Separate

* *Demos*, people; *tomos*, cut.

Development are unacceptable to Africans; and that a 'fair division' is the essential prerequisite for Western support. Its attraction is that it provides a reasonable-looking solution: it gives the Africans a state which is politically and economically viable as it stands; and it gives the whites a national homeland of their own. The black state would have coal, water, sugar, pineapples and timber; it would have a strong industrial base around Durban and possibly East London, the future of which is left deliberately undecided. If East London were included, it would have two major ports, the other being Durban, as well as the minor harbour of Port St John.

The white state would contain virtually all the mines (other than coal), the major areas of industrial development (other than Durban and possibly East London), and the wealthiest agricultural areas (other than the sugar-producing areas). Although the whites would still be in a minority—of the order of three to five—this would be offset by denying Africans the right to vote, while allowing this right to the Coloureds. There would be many opportunities for economic co-operation between the two states. The demotomic line would finally cut the Gordian knot of *baasskap* by making each of the racial communities boss in its own state.

The partition line is drawn to involve as little need for population removals as possible. The scheme envisages considerable numbers of all races living in each state, place of residence being left largely to individual choice. But the quarter of a million Africans in the Western Cape would be obvious victims. And unless a large number of whites gave up their farms in the black state, it would have insufficient land for proper agricultural development for Africans themselves.

What are the objections to this neat plan? There is one over-riding obstacle: no section of the population wants it. The majority of the whites are quite unprepared to make the sacrifices it would entail for them: even Dr Verwoerd has officially repudiated territorial partition. The Africans object fundamentally in principle and in practice to any kind of partition. They demand an undivided South Africa shared equally by all its races; and they point out that all the partition plans so far devised allocate the lion's share of the land and resources to the whites, and with it the main sources of the country's wealth. They believe that no partition plan can make a fair division of the soil and its resources.

These objections are powerfully reinforced by big business, by the white vested interests in the areas allocated to a black state, and by liberal white opinion. The Hon. O. D. Schreiner, a former Judge of Appeal, summed up their case in a sentence: 'A system of partition would not necessarily be a sham, but if it were to follow the lines of genuine liquidation and redistribution between the groups, it would be politically and economically impossible.'[1]

It is true that a partition plan like the demotomic line is much more equitable than that achieved in Ireland, Palestine and India. But partition was forced on those countries by rebellion, war and massacre, and was accepted only after external intervention. Partition solutions do not emerge by agreement. Yet this is the essential condition for the success of any partition scheme in South Africa.

If voluntary partition is to be ruled out for lack of local support, what are the circumstances in which it might be forced on the country? The possibility would presumably arise at a time of great trauma, induced possibly by international intervention, the collapse of the Bantustan policy, or internal rebellion. Let us envisage the possible sequence of events. The government persuades parliament to agree to carve a white state out of the Republic; its frontiers are demarcated; the state is proclaimed. A law is passed allowing only Africans and Indians with permits to work to remain, the Coloureds qualifying automatically; the rest are ordered to leave, or are forcibly evicted—what they do in 'their part of the country' is their concern. The army and police are deployed along the demarcated frontiers; the administrative process of sorting out the Africans and Indians surplus to the requirements of the white state is put in hand. Judged purely in physical terms this stage of the operations is feasible. But its success depends on the extent and effectiveness of African resistance.

If African resistance should become open and violent this would mark the start of a race war. The world would have no alternative but to intervene. How it acts would be of decisive importance. If the United Nations agreed to take collective action, it might have to mount a military operation of Korean war dimensions to interpose itself effectively between the two sides. If such intervention succeeded, the next problem would be to pick up the pieces and seek an acceptable, or enforceable, settlement.

If for any reason the United Nations refused to act, intervention would be unilateral: the Africans, the Asians and the Soviet bloc would be likely to come to the aid of the Africans. What would the West do? If it intervened on the white side a race war would become a world war. This is the extreme possibility. If the West decided not to intervene on either side, it would hand the initiative to the Soviet bloc—which in turn might mark a decisive and permanent change in Africa. If, on the other hand, the West decided to help the African resisters of partition, competitive international intervention with all its wastes and dangers would simply take the place of the collective international intervention advocated in this book.

But if we were to assume for the sake of argument that African resistance did not reach the point of rebellion against the attempt to enforce partition, the sequence of events would not be very different. The issue of partition would be brought before the Security Council through an Afro-Asian resolution (backed by the Soviet bloc), calling for intervention by the United Nations to prevent partition. Even if such a resolution were blocked by a Western veto, it could be assured of the necessary support in the General Assembly under the 'uniting for peace' resolution. This process again produces the possibility of a major military operation by world forces operating on South African soil.

There is one other set of circumstances under which an attempt might be made to enforce partition. This would follow rather than precede the beginning of an internal race war, supported from independent Africa. Under pressure, the white military forces might limit the area of its protection to achieve a *de facto* partition. Under threat of internationalisation of the struggle, the United Nations might then be forced to intervene. Its first objective would presumably be to achieve a truce, and to supervise the truce line, as it did in Palestine. But the conflict could not end there. It is inconceivable that the Africans in South Africa would relinquish their right to the rest of the country. They would certainly lay claim to sovereignty over the major natural resources of the country where most whites are now concentrated. They could count on the backing of the rest of Africa, of Asia and of the communist countries—China as well as Russia. Unless the whites were to retreat to a small segment of the country, they would find it very difficult to police the frontiers of their 'white' state against attack from neighbouring Africa; and if they did so retreat, they would lack the resources and man-power to hold out for long. If they still controlled the major industrial and mining areas, they would need African labour: a potentially virulent fifth column. They would have to cope simultaneously with external attack and internal subversion. The Israeli situation is not comparable. Both the external enemy—the Arab states—and the Arabs in their midst were weak and, above all, divided. They were not able to count on international support; and in the end Soviet aid to the Arabs was counterbalanced by Western guarantees for the Israeli frontiers.

These general predictions do not exhaust the possible causes and effects of an enforced partition. But they all lead to the same conclusion: that a white state established by force could not survive. The only doubt is how much wreckage it would leave behind, not only for South Africa, but for the world as well.

Two conclusions must be drawn. Enforced partition can-not be the means to establish a secure white state; and the possibility of voluntary partition without conflict is ruled out by the fact that none of the power groups wants it.

In the absence of agreement between whites and blacks, it is unrealistic to assume that partition might be enforced under international supervision: the United Nations could not muster a majority for a plan opposed by both sides. How-ever, one possibility remains: a negotiated settlement between the two communities (following international intervention) might produce one or two smaller white states within a federal structure. But the creation of these should not be confused with partition. They would remain a part of an integrated and undivided country, providing for those whites who wished

to segregate themselves to do so. But overall political control
would rest with the central government, and the economy
would be essentially integrated. For white South Africans
who cannot bring themselves to live alongside their African
compatriots, this is the most hopeful possible outcome of the
coming South African struggle.

II

FLASH POINTS

1. SOUTH WEST AFRICA

South Africa has been in conflict with the United Nations ever since 1946 on the issue of its mandate over South West Africa. Although three opinions of the International Court of Justice have confirmed the international status of the territory, the United Nations has been unable to agree how to establish its legal rights there. South Africa has refused to respect the Court's opinions or to comply with the resolutions of the General Assembly. The crunch is likely to come in 1965.

The compulsory jurisdiction of the International Court was invoked in 1960 by Ethiopia and Liberia, both former members of the League of Nations. They asked the Court to declare that South Africa's apartheid practices in South West Africa were a violation of its obligations under Article 2 of the Mandate and under Article 22 of the League's Covenant; and to declare that South Africa must cease apartheid practices forthwith. What will the United Nations do if the Court should decide against South Africa, and if the latter refuses to accept its findings? Unlike previous judgements by the Court, the procedure which has now been invoked makes the Court's judgements binding upon both parties and enforceable by the Security Council. The obligation on the Security Council to act would be inescapable. For while it is true that the Charter's Article 94 makes the enforcement of a binding judgement of the Court permissive and not mandatory, it is inconceivable that the Security Council's powers in this matter will be allowed to go by default.

Demands for action in the past have been refused by the Western permanent members of the Security Council on two grounds: that the legal position was not clear and, subsequently, because the matter was before the Court. Neither of these considerations has prevented the General Assembly from passing resolutions demanding a UN presence in the territory. If the Court should declare against South Africa, the grounds for previous Western objections to action would no longer apply.

Action over South West Africa would entail UN measures against South Africa as the mandatory power. There are broadly two types of action the United Nations could take: economic sanctions to induce South Africa to halt and reverse its apartheid measures; or military action to provide cover for the entry of a UN presence in terms of the previous resolutions of the General Assembly. If South Africa were prepared to defend the mandated territory by force, neither of these measures could leave South Africa's 'domestic affairs' unscathed.

How will the West react if this contingency arises? This is a matter which profoundly affects the principle of international accountability. The United Nations cannot allow South Africa in effect to annex South West Africa in defiance not only of international opinion but of international law as well. If it cannot successfully assert its rights in a territory in which apartheid is being illegally applied, then its significance is indeed questionable. It is difficult to imagine a convincing reason for the West's refusal to allow the United Nations to take all measures necessary to restore its authority in the territory.

South Africa's administration as the mandatory power over South West Africa began after the first world war when Germany renounced all rights over its overseas territories in favour of the Principal Allied and Associated Powers. These territories became Mandates under the Covenant of the League of Nations. Article 22 of the Covenant laid down the intention that 'to those colonies which ... are inhabited by peoples not yet able to stand by themselves under the strenuous conditions of the modern world, there should be applied the principle that the well-being and development of such peoples forms a sacred trust of civilisation, and that securities for the performance of this trust should be embodied in this Covenant'.

Simply stated, the mandated territories were to be regarded as the responsibility of the world community whose rights were to be exercised by the League of Nations. Several

South African attempts to get the Mandates Commission's agreement to incorporating the territory were refused. This is not surprising in view of the solemn spirit in which the mandates system was established, reflecting a determination not to allow a repetition of the abuses and atrocities of the German administration. Unlike its predecessor, the South African administration has not been guilty of attempts at genocide. But neither has it corrected the damage inflicted by the German plunder of tribal lands: on the contrary, it has further reduced the land available to the African inhabitants, and has placed Africans in the straitjacket of apartheid legislation. The complainants in the case currently before the Court argue that this is in conflict with South Africa's obligation under Article 2 of the South West Africa Mandate agreement to 'promote to the utmost the material and moral well-being and the social progress of the inhabitants of the territory'.

When the League of Nations died, the mandates system was succeeded by the United Nations' trusteeship system. South West Africa is the only former mandated territory which was not either granted independence or placed under the trusteeship system. South Africa argued that, with the demise of the League, the second party to its original agreement over South West Africa no longer existed; and that its responsibility to the international community had, therefore, lapsed. On this point the International Court has given an advisory opinion and two supplementary opinions (1950, 1955 and 1956). The substance of these was that, although South Africa was not obliged to place South West Africa under the trusteeship system, it was bound by the terms of the original mandate and Article 22 of the Covenant; it was not entitled to alter the international status of the territory except with the agreement of the United Nations; the latter has the right of supervision over the administration of the territory, as long as it does not exceed the supervision formerly exercised by the Mandates Commission.

But these judgements were advisory only. South Africa was within its legal rights to disregard them. Since 1948 South Africa has made only two concessions to the international community, both of which came to nothing. In 1958 it agreed to discuss the territory's future with a Good Offices Committee of the United Nations; but the only proposal South Africa was prepared to consider which involved the United Nations was partition of the territory. This proposal was rejected by the United Nations' Trusteeship Committee as inconsistent with the intentions of the mandates' system. In 1961, South Africa invited two UN emissaries to visit South West Africa; but the visit degenerated into inconclusive conflict over the wording of a final joint communiqué.

Apart from these two gestures, South Africa has not made any concessions to the international community, either in terms of its own administration, or in relation to the United Nations' rights. Early in 1964, the Odendaal Commission, appointed by the government of the Republic, recommended the division of the territory into a white state and ten African 'homelands'. That the South African government should publish and acclaim the report while the International Court is considering the whole issue of apartheid shows a defiant and provocative disregard for international opinion which augurs ill for the future. South West Africa could become the flash-point between the United Nations and South Africa. Is the West ready to face the consequences of an imminent show-down on this issue?

2. THE HIGH COMMISSION TERRITORIES

Embedded in the apartheid complex of southern Africa, the three British High Commission Territories—Basutoland, Bechuanaland and Swaziland—could become the focal point of direct conflict between Britain and South Africa. The expectation that they would one day be incorporated into South Africa was given its quietus in 1961 when South Africa became a Republic outside the Commonwealth; but the long uncertainty about their future has left them weak and under-developed: poor relations in a rich and expanding region.

All the territories are now on the road to political independence as non-racial states. The fact that constitutional development started well after other British dependencies in Africa does not diminish their potential threat to Dr Verwoerd's Republic. The apartheid government sees them as likely springboards for subversion, as potential havens of refuge for revolutionaries and as an infectious source of multiracial ideas. But so long as Britain remains the protecting power, the weight of British influence will be exerted to persuade the three territories not to become openly involved in a clash with their powerful neighbour. In the past, British policy has been characterised by an attempt to maintain a co-operative relationship with the South African government. The British ambassador to Pretoria is also the High Commissioner for the Territories, and responsible to the Colonial Office for their administration. This dual role has made it difficult to maintain an acceptable policy towards the growing divergence of political development and interests between the territories and the Republic.

But their relationships are no longer a matter to be settled between Britain and South Africa. Each territory has its own largely elected government which though not yet fully representative—especially in Swaziland—will soon become so. Full independence may not be long delayed. Already, each territory seeks to establish its own independent relationship towards South Africa. None has very much room for manoeuvre. Bechuanaland and Swaziland are economically largely dependent on South Africa, and Basutoland wholly so. Most of their exports and imports depend upon the Republic, and a substantial part of their revenues derive from customs dues collected by South Africa. In addition, their economies are at least partly sustained by the export of labour to the Republic. Basutoland, a mountain island in the heart of South Africa, is in all respects the most vulnerable: half its adult males work in the Republic; half its revenue is derived from dues under the customs agreement; and much of its food as well as fuel, equipment and manufactured goods come from the Republic.

Thus, even if the territories become independent, their governments are likely to adopt relatively cautious policies towards South Africa. Their sympathies are fully engaged in the anti-apartheid struggle; but they know they are too weak to make an effective contribution at this stage, and that the attempt would invite reprisals. Yet they are neither willing nor able to keep out of the struggle altogether. They accept all political refugees who manage to get past the Republic's border posts; and Bechuanaland provides a pipeline for escaping refugees and political militants passing through to independent Africa.

In a situation of latent hostility between unequal protagonists, a number of things could happen to spark off open conflict. Already the South African government has sent its police into the territories and abducted political opponents, though on each occasion they were compelled under British pressure to return their victims.

Although the South African government is confident that it can deal with purely internal unrest, it is much less certain of its capacity to counter subversion based and equipped outside the Republic. It is not impossible that, even while Britain remains the protector, Dr Verwoerd might decide to risk British antagonism by taking physical or economic retaliatory measures to prevent exile and other opposition activity from becoming effective in the territories. Armed invasion must be considered unlikely since it would create an immediate breach of the peace and invite UN action under Chapter VII of the Charter; but it cannot be ruled out altogether. *Die Burger* has stressed the need to prevent actively hostile frontiers 'by all available diplomatic and economic means, and in the last resort . . . by military action'.[1] Clearly, the Verwoerd Government must weigh the advantages of containing a possible threat by preventive action against the disadvantages of courting open conflict with Britain, which it sees as an ally in the struggle against external intervention.

Economic sanctions against the territories would be less risky, and probably just as effective. The Republic would be technically within its rights to refuse to employ Africans from the territories, to refuse to buy and market their produce, and to end the customs agreement. Spread over a period of time, such a process could mean a slow strangulation which would be extremely difficult to counteract. Another source of possible conflict lies in the Verwoerd Government's current attempts by every means, including financial subventions, to win allies among the traditionalists in the territories. In the familiar pattern of rivalries between African nationalists and traditionalists, the latter are sometimes vulnerable to promises of support on conditions which they are able to justify to themselves. This extrusion of the Republic's Bantustan techniques is already visible in Swaziland; it could conceivably manifest itself also in Basutoland and Bechuanaland. Conflict between the political movements in the three territories, in which a minority group looks to the Republic for support, is obviously charged with explosive possibilities.

Neither economic nor military sanctions against the territories can be allowed to go unchallenged. Britain and the international community must be prepared to act in their defence if the Republic moves against them. It will not be easy. The circumstances under which the Republic might decide to act cannot be controlled by Britain. Basutoland can be reached only by air; and Swaziland only by air or through Mozambique. No one can doubt that failure to act on the part of Britain or the United Nations would produce drastic unilateral intervention by the African states which would ultimately draw in the United Nations. The dangerous possibilities could be minimised by prophylactic action envisaging a role for the United Nations in each territory on conditions acceptable to the government concerned.

There are not only good security reasons for establishing a 'UN presence' in the territories; there are equally valid economic reasons. Because of their long years of neglect, the territories are pathetically undeveloped. A constructive 'UN presence' could take this form:

1. The establishment of sizable UN technical teams providing for about 150 technicians, teachers and administrators in each territory.

2. Creation by the United Nations of a special fund for the High Commission Territories to provide £100 million over seven years for all three. Its main purpose would be development; but its rules should allow for special allocations in case of urgent need, such as might occur if the Republic were to take economic action against any one of the territories.

3. Appointment of a Special Representative of the Secretary-General of the United Nations in each of the territories to supervise these operations.

4. Provision of UN police and military personnel to train local security forces.

5. Plans for the possible establishment of UN 'blue helmet' patrols inside the frontiers of the territories to ensure that territorial sovereignty is respected.

III
WORLD OPINION AND INTERVENTION
TODAY

It is a bitter thing to be forced into the role of the skunk of the world.

DIE BURGER, *March 24, 1960*

World opinion is unanimous in its view of South Africa's race policies. Apartheid has been described as 'abhorrent' by Britain; as 'toxic' by the United States; as 'hateful' by India; as 'thoroughly repugnant' by Belgium; as 'inhuman' by Guinea; as 'slavery' by Nigeria; as 'degrading' by Canada; as 'fundamentally immoral' by Japan; as 'shameful' by the USSR; as 'the negation of all social purpose' by Bolivia; as 'a cancer' by Algeria; as 'a catalyst of violence' by Tanganyika.[1]

But while the world's nations are united in the view that the South African government should be induced to change its racial policies, there is no agreement on the means to be used. The majority of UN members favour collective action beyond expressions of moral disapproval or the piecemeal application of peripheral sanctions, such as a voluntary arms embargo. Their attitude raises three major questions. Has the United Nations the right to condemn a member nation for its domestic policies? Do South Africa's domestic policies constitute a threat to world peace? Is there any effective action which could be taken with the hope of redistributing power in South Africa without racial violence?

Leaving aside for the moment the question of South West Africa—where the issue of domestic jurisdiction is clearly inapplicable—the United Nations has already in practice established its right to interfere in South Africa's racial policies. Nor is this right any longer disputed by a single major nation. Britain has reconciled its doubts over the question of domestic jurisdiction by the consideration that 'the question of apartheid

... is of such an exceptional nature as to warrant treating it as *sui generis*'.[1]

Concern in the United Nations over South Africa's racial policies began at its first session in 1946, when the Indian delegation succeded in getting the matter of the treatment of South Africa's Indian citizens inscribed on the agenda, primarily on the grounds that their treatment was governed by an international agreement between South Africa and India. It is worth remembering that at that time Ethiopia, Liberia and Egypt were the only African members, and that there were only eight Asian members. It is a myth perpetuated by the South African government that UN interference in its racial policies is purely the result of Afro-Asian pressures at the United Nations. The first resolution on the general subject of apartheid was passed in 1952: *eight* years before the rush of new African independent states swelled the Afro-Asian vote in the organisation. By October 1963, no fewer than twenty-seven General Assembly resolutions and two Security Council resolutions had been passed condemning apartheid.

By 1963, impatience over South Africa's failure to respond positively to international moral pressure swelled to a crescendo. It marked the end of seventeen years of verbal condemnation and the beginning of the demand for concerted action. It also marked a new attitude to the Western nations' equivocal policies. For the first time the independent African states embarked on collective action, by making a *démarche* on the Security Council in July 1963, in support of their decisions at the Addis Ababa summit conference the previous May. The result was that the Security Council resolution of August 1963 went beyond ordinary condemnation. It called on member nations to stop selling arms, ammunition and military vehicles to South Africa. And it called on the South African authorities to release all opponents of the apartheid system imprisoned or restricted for their political views. Nine members, including the United States and Norway, voted for the resolution: only Britain and France abstained. Britain argued that its existing defence agreements, including that for the Simonstown base, excluded the possibility of a total arms embargo; but its delegate added that no arms were, or would be, sold to South Africa if they could be used to perpetuate apartheid. The Western nations, including the United States, emphasised that they did not regard the resolution as binding upon them. Since they refused to consider that South Africa's policies represent an actual threat to the peace, the measures proposed were taken to be recommendations under Chapter VI of the Charter.

A few weeks later, on October 11, the General Assembly passed a resolution specifically related to the Johannesburg trial of African and other opposition leaders in South Africa: it asked member states to 'make all necessary efforts' to induce South Africa to end the trial, release all political prisoners and end the 'repression of persons opposing apartheid'. Only South Africa and Portugal voted against; and this time there were no abstentions. Two months later the General Assembly again considered the South African question. It asked all member states to carry out the provisions for sanctions referred to in the Security Council's August resolution and to provide aid, through the United Nations, for the victims of apartheid and their dependents. Again, there were no abstentions, and again only South Africa and Portugal voted against.

Meanwhile, on December 4, the Security Council had passed a unanimous resolution with a dual purpose: to increase international pressure upon South Africa, and to reassure white South Africans that the United Nations was concerned for their security in a future non-racial state. This dual formula, presented by Norway, was inspired by the five Nordic countries. They had embarked in the middle of 1963 on a significant role in international affairs by taking a Western initiative in the South African problem. The resolution widened the existing scope of sanctions recommended, to proposing the banning of exports to the Republic of machinery for the manufacture of arms. It also appointed 'a small group of experts to examine methods of resolving the present situation in South Africa through full, peaceful and orderly application of human rights ... to all inhabitants of the territory as a whole ..., and to consider what part the UN might play in the achievement of that end'. The United States announced it had already extended its ban to include machinery for the manufacture of arms; but Britain and France again drew a distinction between arms (and machinery) for use in enforcing apartheid which they agreed they would not supply—and those needed for external defence, which they proposed to continue selling to South Africa.

Thus the point is long since passed when it is useful to argue whether or not the United Nations has a 'right' to condemn South Africa's domestic policies. The world community has decided that apartheid is part of its business. What is not yet agreed is whether the situation in South Africa constitutes a threat to world peace, such as would justify overriding the provisions of Article 2 (7) of the United Nations Charter:

> *Nothing contained in the present Charter shall authorize the United Nations to intervene in matters which are essentially within the domestic jurisdiction of any State, or shall require the Members to submit such matters to settlement under the present Charter; but this principle shall not prejudice the application of enforcement measures under Chapter VII.*

Chapter VII specifies the kind of collective measures—including economic and military sanctions—which the Security Council may enforce against a member nation whose actions or policies represent a threat to the peace, a breach of the peace, or an act of aggression. If the Security Council rules that such a threat exists, it can then decide what coercive measures to adopt, and these are binding on all member states. But this decision remains subject to the veto of the five permanent members of the Security Council. If an immediate threat is not established by the Security Council, then coercive measures come within the scope of Chapter VI, and become recommendations only.

Britain, the United States, France and most other western countries take the view that all the Security Council decisions to the end of 1963 are governed by Chapter VI and not Chapter VII; and have no binding force on member states. But more than two thirds of UN members take the view that apartheid represents a threat to peace, and that Chapter VII should be invoked. They argue that apartheid is a constant provocation to all coloured peoples, that its outcome must be a race war, and that such a war could not be confined to South Africa. The Asian nations, the Soviet bloc, Yugoslavia, most of the Latin American countries, several Western nations (notably the Scandinavian countries), as well as the African states, see this incipient race war as an active threat to world peace, and one which can only escalate with time. Despite their majority, Chapter VII has not been specifically invoked because the Security Council has not found it expedient to risk a Western veto if it is pressed. It has preferred instead to strike bargains, the West giving a little more each time, and to rely meanwhile on recommendations.

The African states and a number of other countries have refused to wait upon a Security Council judgement, and have begun to intervene directly. The race policies of South Africa arouse more feeling in Africa than any other question: this is a fact, not a value judgement. Concern springs from a feeling of kinship with Africans or people of Negro stock anywhere in the world. Africa's concern at the humiliation and hurt suffered by people of colour in the Republic is comparable to the feelings of world Jewry in the days of Hitler's persecution. Unless this parallel is understood, the West will continue to underestimate the determination of Africa to do everything in its power to destroy the present régime in South Africa. To ascribe Africa's hostility to the Republic simply to the need to find an easy unifying force for Pan-Africanism is a refusal to face reality. The African 'Summit' conference at Addis Ababa in 1963 'informed the allies of the colonial powers that they must choose between their friendship for the African peoples and their support of powers that oppress African peoples'.[1] That sentiment is profoundly sincere.

So also is the determination to act whether or not the United Nations institutes collective measures. The Addis Ababa conference established a National Liberation Committee to give financial, moral *and military* support to the liberation movements in southern Africa. It also began a process of physically isolating South Africa by banning its aircraft and ships from their air-space and harbours; and it resolved to take every measure to exclude South Africa from organisations for international co-operation. Already they have forced South Africa's withdrawal from the Economic Commission for Africa (at considerable and known cost to themselves), from the Commission for Technical Assistance in Africa, from

UNESCO, the International Labour Office, the Food and Agricultural Organisation, the World Health Organisation, and the Olympic Games.

This intervention—including the provision of military assistance for 'freedom fighters'—has the backing of the Soviet bloc, the Asian nations, Yugoslavia and a number of Latin American countries. Thus international intervention is already a powerful ingredient in the South African crisis. Its potential impact, since it cannot be halted, could be decisive. The motives of some of Africa's backers in this enterprise may be considered suspect in the West; but motives are not relevant to a consideration of the extent of a threat to the peace. They may well affect the outcome of the struggle, but they are irrelevant to the question of whether conflict can be averted.

Finally, one should see the trade and consumer boycott movements in their true perspective. These have not so far seriously harmed South Africa's economy: loss of markets in Africa, in the Soviet bloc and in most of the Asian countries has been offset by increased exports either to the West or to new trading partners like Japan. But it cannot be argued that because the Republic's exports have not declined its overall interests have not suffered. Without a boycott, its exports would have been higher still. Moreover, official boycotts in some sixty countries and the consumer boycott movements in Britain and Scandinavia are evidence of an aroused world opinion. The popularity of the boycott movement in Norway, Denmark and Sweden led the Scandinavian governments to take their collective initiative at the United Nations. Denmark's Foreign Minister, Mr Per Hakkerup, stresses the growing sense of a common humanity:

> 'In recent years the peoples of Denmark and the other Nordic countries have watched developments in South Africa with growing concern, anxiety and resentment. This public reaction to a problem which, in view of its remoteness and alien character would hardly have been considered of any concern to us a few decades ago, is the best evidence of the feelings of international solidarity and responsibility that have emerged since the second world war, due not least to the United Nations.'[1]

Sir Alec Douglas-Home has dismissed the suggestion that South Africa's policies constitute a threat to the peace by arguing that the threat derives from the actions taken by the African states, not from South Africa. But the threat itself is not diminished by assigning blame for it. The essence of the international threat consists in the policies of one party provoking a reaction in the other. It is theoretically arguable that the provoked rather than the provoker is at fault; but this contention comes oddly from one who upholds British law which takes full account of the guilt of a person acting in a way that might provoke a breach of the peace. Are the doctrines of British law not a sound enough basis for international law? Sir Alec's indictment of the Africans' reaction is also surprising considering his support for the Eden Government which went to war over the Suez Canal. A crucial difference between the Suez affair and the South African crisis is that patient efforts have been made through the United Nations to get agreement on peaceful methods of redress over South Africa, but no such effort was thought necessary over Suez. Fundamentally, however, the question of blame is not relevant to the question of whether a threat exists. Since neither side is willing to alter course, a collision is inevitable; and the world should be prepared for it.

Apart from its logical flaw, Sir Alec's thinking shows him unable or unwilling to understand why African opinion has become so inflamed over South Africa that it is ready to risk the consequences of intervention. Yet it is certain that no British government of which Sir Alec was a member would be willing to countenance passively a situation in which people of British stock were daily humiliated, dragooned and denied fundamental human rights. It is true that Sir Alec, a prominent and unrepentant 'Munichman', totally failed to understand the outrage of world Jewry at the treatment of Jews by Hitler.* But if he cannot make the effort of imagination required to understand that racial loyalties exist among peoples other than the Anglo-Saxons, he might at least attempt to transfer his own strong feeling about Britain's material

---

* He has subsequently confessed his mistake in failing at the time to comprehend the extent of Hitler's madness. He is in danger of making the same mistake again.

interests, raised by the Suez crisis, to Africa's interests in the peoples and resources of their own continent. He has himself warned that one of the greatest dangers facing the world is the possibility of race conflict. But this concern is useless if he simultaneously fails to understand the precipitating causes of such a conflict.

It should be clear not only that the arguments over domestic jurisdiction have been superseded, but that the effects of apartheid cannot be contained within the Republic. International intervention is already a reality. Unless the West is prepared actively to defend the South African régime—which it clearly is not—there is no way of halting intervention by Africa, supported by over two-thirds of the members of the United Nations. Thus of our questions only the third one is relevant to practical statesmen today: is there any action which could be taken to prevent the South African situation from developing into an international race war? This question is the subject of chapters eight and ten.

IV

THE LOBBY AGAINST INTERVENTION

South Africa and Portugal conduct the two most active foreign lobbies in the West; but South Africa's is by far the more influential and sophisticated. Its friends are to be found everywhere: in the City of London and in the Trades Union Congress; in the House of Commons and in the House of Lords; in the American Republican and Democratic Parties; in the armed services and in NATO..

Like most lobbies, South Africa's operates on two fronts. On the broad front it seeks to create a favourable public opinion towards the Republic, which is represented as being misunderstood, unfairly treated, and the victim of a communist and Afro-Asian conspiracy. Its efforts to win over Western public opinion have been conspicuously, and expensively, unsuccessful—as the South African government has admitted. A Gallup Poll of British opinion, published in 1961, showed that 'those who believe that Britain should oppose South African policies outnumber by four to one those who feel that Britain should be supporting the South African government'.[1] A surprising feature of these results was that more Conservatives than Labour supporters declared themselves against apartheid: 44 per cent to 43 per cent.

The South African lobby's successes have been achieved on its narrower front. There the objective is to mobilise the support of people close to the sources of political power. They have a fertile field among the 800 or so important firms with a direct financial stake in South Africa. More recruits are to be found among business men with trading interests in the Republic. The emphasis on South Africa's value to the Western military alliance attracts soldiers and politicians.

These important sources of influence on western policy-makers are on the whole committed to resisting international intervention in South Africa. But it would be misleading to suggest that everybody with South African business connections is willing to lend themselves to its cause: in Part One we have cited instances to the contrary.* Nor do all those opposed to sanctions approve of South Africa's racial policies: the great majority do not. Nevertheless, they are willing to join the lobby of non-interventionists for their own particularist reasons. It would be hard to over-rate the influence of this lobby which is guided by two organisations: the South African Information Department, and the South Africa Foundation.† The latter concentrates on big business, the soldiers and the diplomatists; the former looks after the rest.

The Information Department has its representatives in all South African embassies in Western countries. They are mostly skilled journalists with the zealotry usually found in communists and MRA supporters. They appear to have almost limitless funds for their expensive advertising campaigns and for massive distribution of their skilful propaganda. They pursue the press, television and radio with terrier-like tenacity. A critical article or programme—whether in Britain, Sweden, West Germany, Holland, Canada, Switzerland or the United States—is immediately pounced upon. Sometimes there are official protests; always there are official denials. Not only the offending critic is pursued, but also the editor, the programme producer and their superiors. Letters are not enough; the technique is personal confrontation, argument and rebuttal. On occasion, the ambassador will himself intervene; often influential lobby supporters will call on the proprietors of an offending newspaper, television or radio network to reinforce the complaint. Sometimes the demand is for an article or programme to 'put the other side'; often the purpose is to persuade newspapers or radio and television networks not to use certain writers and broadcasters. Producers in the BBC for example, know that any programme critical of South Africa will automatically result in an official complaint. Their own correspondents, especially those in South Africa, are continuously under attack; none we know of has so far escaped South Africa's censure. The BBC is put under further pressure by sheaves of letters emanating from all parts of the

---

* See, for example, pp. 114–5, 118–9, 135.
† See pp. 111–16.

country whenever South Africa's policies are adversely discussed; sometimes these letters are spontaneous, but often they
are not. The pressure never lets up; to its credit, the BBC has
not given way to it. The British press comes under similar
surveillance. But the Information Department has long since
given up hope of influencing the major newspapers, with the
solitary exception of Lord Beaverbrook's. One of their
toughest opponents is the *Times* which is reviled in official
South African circles as much as the *Observer*, the *Guardian*,
and the *Economist*. In the United States their *bête noire* is
the *New York Times*, which holds firmly to the view that
South Africa's policies are 'a peril to international peace and
security'.[1] But if the Western press is almost uniformly
critical of apartheid it is also, with a few notable exceptions,
equally opposed to international intervention, which is generally regarded as wrong in principle and unworkable in practice.

The South Africa Foundation's operations inside the
Republic have already been described. Its international
operations are carried on through MM—its 'Man-to-Man
Movement'. It has seventeen national committees of business
and professional men representing the United States, Austria,
Belgium, Canada, Denmark, Finland, France, Germany,
Greece, Israel, Italy, the Netherlands, New Zealand, Norway,
Portugal, Sweden and the United Kingdom. It has offices or
representatives in London, Munich, Copenhagen, Vienna, The
Hague, Paris, New Zealand, Australia, the United States and
Canada. Its international operations are directed by Mr Lief
Egeland, formerly a liberal supporter in parliament of the late
Jan Hofmeyr. He later became South Africa's High Com-
missioner in the United Kingdom, and is now a director of
gold-mining companies. He is a smoothly attractive diplo-
matist of Scandinavian origin.

The MM techniques resemble those of MRA in many respects. The Foundation's crusade is against communism; its
organisers go for the big names—key political figures, influential writers, business leaders, generals. Likely converts are
taken to South Africa at the Foundation's expense: they are
shown around in style, entertained, introduced to members of
the Cabinet and to influential industrialists. If these persuasive methods work, the new recruit is turned over first to

the press in South Africa and then to the press of the visitor's home country: interviews are supplemented by widely distributed Foundation hand-outs. There is of course no way of telling how many of the invited guests are in fact 'converted' or remain so. Among those who have been persuaded by the South Africa Foundation are such diverse guests as the British trade union leader, Mr Jim Matthews, and the French writer Mr Paul Giniewski, now one of South Africa's leading champions in France. The French lobby's activities have been helped by the report of a French Senate Commission which stated after a visit in 1963: 'We believe that it is difficult in Africa to find achievements of a more satisfactory nature favouring the Natives.' The four senators—René Tinant, Louis Jung, Mohamed Kamil and Maurice Verillon—are all members of the French Senate's Commission of Cultural Affairs. They felt France was not only neglecting valuable economic opportunities but that it might have a valuable cultural mission to perform. 'May one think that France, through its liberal tradition and the human qualities of its culture, could play a favourable role?'[1]

1. THE LOBBY IN BRITAIN

The Foundation's real strength lies in its overseas committees of business men. The trustees of the influential London committee are Lord Fraser of Lonsdale (a former Tory MP); Sir Nicholas Cayzer; Mr Harley Drayton; and Mr George M. Mason. The chairman of the committee is Mr William E. Luke, and the President is Major-General Sir Francis de Guingand.* Who are these lobbyists?

Lord Fraser has old and valuable family interests in South Africa and especially in Basutoland. He is chairman of D. and D. H. Fraser and of Thompson Newspapers (S.A.); he is a director of Cyril Lord (S.A.) Pty Ltd†, of K. Nolan Ltd (S.A.), and of Aspro-Nicholas Ltd. He is a leading member

* See Part One, p. 112.
† See Part One, pp. 135–7.

of the South African lobby at Westminster and seldom fails to intervene in any debate affecting policy in southern Africa. The theme of his speeches seldom varies: 'In Britain, instead of deploring everything that is done in the Republic, instead of refusing to see all the good things that are being done, let us rejoice that there is a bastion at the bottom end of that continent, of sound, good government, strong enough to maintain itself in all circumstances, and that law and order will at least prevail in that part of Africa, whatever trouble and difficulties may arise in other parts.'[1]

Sir Nicholas Cayzer, the fifty-two-year-old shipowner, is chairman of the charmed circle of shippers banded together in the *South and South-East African Conference Lines*. 'South Africa should be left alone to work out her own destiny . . . and is quite capable, given time, of finding solutions', he said at a private dinner party attended by South African ministers. He added: 'Your economy is booming and is even beginning to trickle through to my ships. Your prosperity is my prosperity.'[2] No one could say fairer than that. Mr Harley Drayton is—as everybody should know—'the son of a Lincolnshire farmer who started life on 19s. 8d. a week and is today the biggest man in the investment world'. Mr George M. Mason is a director of the Imperial Chemical Industries (Export) Ltd, vice-president of the International Superphosphate Manufacturers' Association, and head of the South African Department of Imperial Chemicals. Mr William Luke is chairman of Lindustries Ltd which is associated with Braitex (Pty) Ltd in the manufacture of fabrics in the Republic.

In 1963 the Foundation brought off an important *coup* by getting the National Association of British Manufacturers to publish an attractive booklet for British businessmen entitled *The British Stake in South Africa*. It is to be found in boardrooms throughout the United Kingdom. It makes no effort to disguise its appeal to narrow business interests: 'Whatever view of South Africa's political and racial problems is held by the individual, one fact he cannot escape: the large industrial stake the people of Britain hold in the Republic. This booklet . . . is also intended to emphasise the damage that could befall the peoples of Great Britain and South Africa if the demand from certain quarters for a trade boycott was satisfied ... In any case, the first to suffer would be those a boycott is supposed to help—the non-Europeans.'[1]

Many British politicians are of course persuaded to oppose intervention in the Republic for other than business reasons. The British tradition of 'trading with the world' is a strong one; many firms with South African connections are at the same time engaged in trading with the Soviet bloc, with China and with Cuba. The deep-seated British view that 'business knows no sentiment' has withstood American pressure against trading with Castro and Peking. These traditions are reinforced by a political instinct that sanctions are wrong in principle as a means of settling disputes, and by a belief that the base at Simonstown is 'somehow' important to the Royal Navy.

All this makes it comparatively easy for the South African lobby to make itself felt—and heard—at Westminster. But in addition there is no foreign country, as far as we know, in which so many British politicians have a business interest as in South Africa. Of these there are perhaps eighty members of the Commons and the Lords combined; but those with strongest financial interests in the Republic sit in the Lords.[2]

Lord Baillieu is the deputy-chairman of the Central Mining and Investment Corporation. Lord Balfour of Inchrye, who is a director of the Consolidated Mines Selection Company Ltd, pleaded in a debate in the Lords in 1961: 'Do not destroy our Commonwealth trade links with South Africa ... I sincerely hope that we shall not speed the process of estrangement in future years in South Africa by hurting her economically.'[3] In the same debate Lord Fraser pleaded: 'Let us be patient with South Africa.' The Earl of Airlie is the father of Mr Angus Ogilvy, who is the director of three important companies in the Republic, Swaziland and Southern Rhodesia.

Earl de la Warr, an influential member of Conservative policy-making groups on Africa, is a director of the Standard Bank Limited of South Africa. So is Viscount Malvern, the former Prime Minister of the former Central African Federation; he is a director of three other large companies as well. The former Minister of Education, Lord Eccles, is a director of Courtaulds Ltd, which has large investments in the Republic. A former president of the Federation of British Industry,

Lord Barnby, is a director of Francis Willey and Company, which has a subsidiary in South Africa; recently he called on the government to caution its representative at the United Nations, Sir Patrick Dean, 'to make references in a language less repugnant to a friendly country which takes such a large volume of imports from us, and in which this country has such massive investments'.[1]

The Earl of Elgin and Kincardine is chairman of the United Dominions Trust which has subsidiaries in Nigeria, Rhodesia and South Africa. Lord Elton is a director of Cape Asbestos Company Ltd, which has extensive freehold asbestos properties in Southern Africa. Lord Ferrier and Lord Rowallan are both directors of Friends Provident and Century Life Office which owns all the shares of Regina House Ltd in Johannesburg, as well as owning subsidiaries in Rhodesia and Nigeria. The Earl of Halsbury is a director of Joseph Lucas (Industries) Ltd, which has a flourishing South African subsidiary. A Lucas of a different complexion is Lord Lucas of Chilworth who told the Lords in 1962 that his visit to South Africa showed him that it 'is a fascist state and three quarters of the population are living in a police state'.[2]

Lord Howard of Glossop is the chairman of Central News Agency Investments Ltd, which controls the Republic's leading publication and distribution firm. Lord Howard de Walden is a director of Parry, Leon and Hayhoe (S.A.), steamship travel and distribution agents. The Marquess of Linlithgow is a director of Eagle Star Insurance Company Ltd, whose subsidiaries in the Republic own a number of important properties. Lord Lyle is a director of Sir J. L. Hulett and Sons Ltd, South Africa's largest producer of cane sugar, which is now controlled by a consortium of seven sugar companies.* Lord Moynihan is a director of Fixed Properties (S.A.) Ltd, a property-owning and township development company. Lord Pender is the managing director of the Eastern and South African Investment Trust. Lord Reith is vice-chairman of British Oxygen Company Ltd, which has important subsidiaries in South Africa, Nigeria and Rhodesia. Lord Nelson is the chairman of the English Electric Company which has a useful stake in the Republic. The Earl of Verulam is chair-

* See Part One, pp. 128–9.

man of the Enfield Rolling Mills Ltd, a comparatively recent arrival on the South African scene. Lord Ridley is chairman of Head, Wrightson and Company Ltd, which has two subsidiaries in Rhodesia and the Republic. The former chairman of British Railways, Lord Robertson of Oakridge, is a director of Dunlop Rubber Company Ltd. He takes a rather different line from many of his colleagues; declaring his dislike of apartheid, he hopes for a return to the principles of the Smuts government.[1] Another Dunlop director is Viscount Weir.

Lord Rockley is the deputy-chairman of Schweppes Ltd, and the Earl of Selborne is deputy-chairman of Boots Pure Drug Company, both with valuable South African interests. Lord Rootes, chairman of Rootes Motors Ltd, and Lord Tedder, president of Standard Triumph International Ltd, both have an interest in the fast-expanding motor-car industry of the Republic through their local assembly plants. Viscount Tenby is a director of Associated Portland Cement Manufacturers Ltd, which has interests in South Africa, Nigeria and Rhodesia. Lord Twining, a former governor of Tanganyika, is a director of the East African Trust and Investment Company, Nairobi, which is a subsidiary of the South African and General Investment and Trust Company Ltd; but he is no friend of the Republic.

Lord Montgomery has no financial interests in South Africa, but he is a close friend of his former wartime colleague, Sir Francis de Guingand. The field marshal's catholic admiration for Mao Tse-tung, Pandit Nehru and Dr Verwoerd are frequently remarked; less well-known, perhaps, is his view that 'the whites must rule and that whites must remain whites'.[2] Lord Colyton is among the score or so peers who have no direct financial interests in the Republic but who usually take the same line as the South Africa Foundation.

In the Commons, Sir Harwood Harrison, MP, a director of Chalwyn Lamps (South Africa) Ltd, was prominent among those who took the view in the debate on the South Africa Bill in 1962 that 'we cannot afford to lose this trade' with the Republic. Mr John Eden, MP, a director of Aberdare Holdings Ltd (which is directly involved in South Africa) attacked

Mr Harold Wilson in Parliament over his campaign for a complete arms embargo on the grounds, *inter alia*, that it 'had already done considerable damage to the British aircraft industry'.[1]   Sir Peter Roberts, MP, chairman of Hadfields Ltd, and of the Wellman Smith Owen Engineering Corporation (both with interests in the Republic) is another active supporter of maintaining close trade relations with South Africa.   After visiting South Africa in 1963 he said: 'There have been political advances in South Africa ...   As to unemployment there is now a system whereby there is no known unemployment in the vast urbanised areas which depend on industry.'[2]   Not even the most ardent defenders of the system of 'endorsing out surplus labour' have been known to advance this preposterous justification for it.

2. THE LOBBY IN THE UNITED STATES

The most influential figure in the South African lobby in the United States is Mr Charles W. Engelhard Jr, of Newark, New Jersey.   Still only in his late forties, he is a thrusting financier and industrialist whose international business interests have expanded rapidly in the last twenty years.   He is the chairman of one of the seven 'Golden Houses'—the Rand Mines—which has a close tie-up with Oppenheimer's holding companies.   The home base of Mr Engelhard's industrial empire is Engelhard Industries.   Besides these two giant enterprises he is chairman of the Minerals and Chemicals Philipp Corporation, holding 18 per cent of its share capital.   It is the largest metal and ore broker in the world; he is also chairman of American-South African Investment Company; Engelhard Industries of Canada; Rand Mines Ltd, Johannesburg; Engelhard Industries Pty Ltd, Melbourne, Australia; Engelhard Industries (*s.a.r.l.*), Paris; Engelhard Industries, Ltd, England; Acme Timber Industries, Ltd, South Africa; South Africa Forest Investments, Ltd, Johannesburg; Industries Engelhard, (SPA) Rome, Italy; Sociedad Suramericana de Metales Preciosos (SA), Bogota, Colombia.

Mr Engelhard is also active in politics: in 1956 and again in 1960 he was a delegate for New Jersey to the Democratic National Convention. He is known for his generous donations to presidential political campaigns. But although he supported the late President Kennedy, he failed to influence the President's policy which was based on the conviction that 'we ought to make very clear our hostility to the concept of racial separation . . . which is inimical, I think, to the future of South Africa as well as repugnant to us'.

Mr Engelhard, too, has had his moments of doubts. In 1960 he told Rand Mines' shareholders that overseas investors had lost confidence in South Africa, and warned that its economic future depended on developing more acceptable racial co-existence policies.[1] Nevertheless, he is prominently identified with the South Africa Foundation which plays an influential role in persuading prominent Americans to defend the Republic's position.

One of South Africa's ardent friends is Mr Clarence B. Randall, former chairman of the board of Inland Steel Company and chairman of the State Department's Advisory Committee on International Business Problems. He undertakes tireless lecture tours around the United States. His utterances are sometimes splendidly naïve: 'South Africa's only problem —the only cloud on the horizon from the economic viewpoint —is its racial problem . . .'[2] However, he is not altogether convinced of the government's policies: 'While I deplore much that has happened in South Africa and would like to see much of it changed, my plea is that we put the picture in proper perspective.'[3] Recently he warned South Africans about South West Africa. 'If the decision of the International Court at The Hague is adverse to South Africa, you will be in serious difficulties. . . . My government would have to comply with any action decided on by the Security Council.'[4]

Another of the Foundation's converts is Mr John W. Snyder, a former Secretary of the Treasury, whose views as broadcast by the Foundation are that 'South Africa is worthy of our closest association in building up a strong world economy, and also in the protection of the world against the encroachment of Communism. South Africa is the only strong viable nation on the African continent. . . .'[1]

The United States offers two fields of recruitment for the South African lobby: the small but influential group of firms with financial interests in the Republic, and the old China lobby which has moved into Africa via the anti-communist lobby and the Katanga lobby. Of the two companies with important mining interests, Newmont Mining Corporation is franker in its support for American-South African friendship than American Metal Climax Inc. Newmont's vice-president, Mr M. D. Banghart, strikes a clear note: 'No matter what government is in power, the principle of private enterprise has been strictly adhered to. There are no unrealistic labour regulations (sic). Labour unions are important organisations but they have no hostility towards free enterprise. Strikes are practically unknown. On the other hand, labour is well treated and wages are in keeping with the lower living cost structure in the country.'[2] American Metal Climax gives the impression of speaking with two voices. In Northern Rhodesia, where the company has large copper interests, it strongly backed Dr Kenneth Kaunda long before he had won his fight against Sir Roy Welensky and the British government. On the other hand, in conferences on American relations with South Africa, its representatives have justified their company's policy of increasing its stake in the Republic. The large oil firms (Standard-Vacuum, Caltex and Esso) and the motor giants (General Motors, Ford and Chrysler) are staunch defenders of South Africa; so is Johnson and Johnson, the pharmaceutical firm.

The old China lobby lives on in what is now called the American Afro-Asian Educational Exchange Inc, of 79 Madison Avenue, New York. It has recently added Southern Africa to its various causes. Its honorary chairman is the Hon. Joseph C. Grew, a former ambassador; its chairman is the Hon. Walter H. Judd, a former Chinese missionary and defeated Congressman who was a leading figure in the heyday of the China lobby. Its vice-chairmen are Senator Thomas J. Dodd, the Hon. Charles Edison and Dr Max Yergan, a former president of the militant National Negro Congress, who has experienced life in South Africa; he was prominent in the Katanga lobby. Senator Dodd—with Senator Ellender

and a Democratic Congressman from Mississippi, Mr John
Williams—is part of a triumvirate of active supporters of
South Africa in Washington.* The treasurer is Dr B. A.
Garside, the secretary Miss Philippa Schuyler, the executive
secretary is Mr Marvin Liebman—all were active in the
Katanga lobby.

The membership includes such well-known figures as James
Burnham, John Dos Passos, Max Eastman and Edgar Ansel
Mowrer. Its publicists include Mr William F. Buckley,
editor of the *National Review*; Mr Ralph de Toledano, the
admiring biographer of Richard M. Nixon; and Mr Anthony
Harrigan, associate editor of the *News and Courier* of Charles-
ton. In 1963, the South African government publication
Bantu carried an article from Mr Harrigan (with strong edit-
orial support) in which he wrote that Americans who realise
South Africa is the most logical ally of the United States can
only wonder what ideological attachments cause the State
Department's policy planners to turn their face against it.[1]

The membership list is crowded with the names of acad-
emics—mainly China experts who were active in the earlier
lobby—such as Professor Kenneth Colegrove, Professor David
N. Rowe and Dr Karl A. Wittfogel. It also lists General
James A. Van Fleet and the tough right wing trade unionist,
Richard L. G. Deverall.

Another crusader, who prefers to play a lone hand, is
Philip K. Crowe, a former American ambassador to South
Africa. He concentrates on two aspects: the value of South
Africa as a bastion against communism, and the importance of
Simonstown to Western military strategy. His advice is the
familiar attempt to neutralise effective action: 'By all means let
us make it crystal clear to the present government of South
Africa that we thoroughly disapprove of her racial policies.
But let us not at the same time weaken a long-time ally and a
potential future one.'[2]

The advertising firms have begun to take an active interest
in South Africa's fortunes. Interpublic Inc, the parent company of McCann, Erickson and McCann-Marschalk, now owns
Afamal, the third largest advertising agency in Africa (with

---

* There has recently been some evidence of weakening on the part of
Senator Dodd.

reputed annual bookings of well over £3 million). Afamal has its headquarters in Johannesburg, where it was formerly owned by the Schlesinger Organisation. Its two main American competitors are the J. Walter Thompson Company (with four offices in South Africa) and Grant Advertising Inc (with two offices in South Africa and another in Southern Rhodesia). The Whaley-Eaton Report has also been taking an interest. In 1962, its editor, Stanley N. Shaw, made a study of the Republic; he gave it a high rating with only one faint fault to report: 'To be sure there is a paternalistic government attitude in the country which is worrisome, notwithstanding its essentially sound purposes.' Risks? 'All factors considered (and this includes the racial question) I should say risks are no greater than in the US.'[1]

CONCLUSION

In assessing the likely strength and influence of the South Africa lobby on Western policies when the chips go down over sanctions, two countervailing forces must be weighed. First, the active lobby working against South Africa in the West: its strength is in the weight of public opinion which regards the Republic's racial tyranny not only as a threat to world peace and a danger to South Africa itself, but also as an offence to the Western ethic. These moral and practical objections will not be easy to over-ride. But strong economic self-interests will compound the effort needed to convert moral opposition into economic sanctions. The second factor is the West's international interests and commitments. However concerned the West might be with protecting its economic and other interests in the Republic, its final choice will almost certainly be even more greatly influenced by wider considerations. How would it fare if it stood out against the rest of the world, divided as it is on the question of sanctions? Where would it stand in Africa at the end of unilateral intervention or a race war, or both?

The South African lobby can be relied upon to do its powerful best to obscure these wider issues and to divert public attention from the realities of the racial crisis in the Republic; but it will not have it all its own way.

V

THE CASE FOR SANCTIONS

Moral judgments must be something about which any twelve men or women drawn at random might after discussion be expected to be unanimous. . . . Every moral judgment, unless it claims a divine source, is simply a feeling that no right-minded man could behave in any other way without admitting that he was doing wrong. It is the power of common sense and not the power of reason that is behind the judgments of society. But, before a society can put a practice beyond the limits of tolerance, there must be a deliberate judgment that the practice is injurious to society.

Lord Devlin: THE ENFORCEMENT OF MORALS, *1959*

The case for collective intervention in South Africa rests on moral and political considerations. The moral case is hardly controvertible. A minority racial community, thinking to protect itself, is subjecting eleven million people to laws and treatment reminiscent of Nazi Germany and Stalinist Russia. The conditions of life imposed on the majority of South Africans would not be tolerated by any community in the world. Their treatment is in flagrant violation of the Declaration of Human Rights and of the Charter of the United Nations. The moral argument for action to end this state of affairs is not met by the political objection that South Africa is not the only offender against moral standards in the international community.

To refuse to act because of the difficulties involved, is to suggest a bankruptcy of human ingenuity, which is wholly unconvincing. One might as well say that the issues involved in the cold war, or in preventing the proliferation of nuclear weapons, are so difficult that there is nothing to be done about them. To refuse to come to grips with problems because they are complex is to condemn the United Nations to impotence. Complex as it is, the challenge offered by South Africa is by no means the most difficult of the problems the United Nations has to face. If the United Nations were to retreat over South Africa it would repeat the rout which followed the League of Nations' abdication over Ethiopia. Appeasement on great moral issues can only weaken the world along all the fronts where the battles for human rights are waged.

Few today doubt the crucial importance of maintaining and strengthening an international body capable of exercising some influence and restraint on our seriously disordered international society. But the United Nations cannot fulfil such a role if its function over South Africa is restricted to moral disapprobation. The leader of the Israeli delegation to the United Nations has put South Africa's moral challenge to the organisation with great force:

> The UN cannot act like the board of directors of a company whose calculated acts are based on cold figures. The UN is the depository of a sacred mandate, and its power is derived from the living fount of the human spirit. There must be faith in the irresistible force of a just idea stated with clarity and daring and defended with courage. The vision of a future of inter-racial co-operation based on equality and full reciprocal respect for the brotherhood of all the peoples of Africa, can scatter the gathering storm-clouds and awaken generous and constructive forces among the sons of different races on which the destiny of the Republic of South Africa rests.[1]

If the United Nations is debarred, for purely technical reasons, from doing its clear moral duty, it will shrivel and decline. And if the world fails to act in time over South Africa, it will face the same moral agony which followed the recognition that it was too late to prevent Hitler's terror from reaching the heights of its horror. There are no extermination camps for non-whites in South Africa, nor is there any intention of practising genocide; but the terror, the torture, the violence, the mass removals, the disregard for human and family rights, the police apparatus—these are comparable to Hitlerism and Stalinism. Unless they are checked they must produce still greater excesses. But in South Africa the master race will suffer more in the end than did the Germans or

Stalin's clique. For those who care for humanity—whether it is black or white—there is little comfort to be derived from this ultimate vengeance. To act on moral principles might seem to favour the non-whites in South Africa; in the end, it will prove the only salvation for the whites.

The political case for intervention rests on the conclusions derived from the analysis of the nature of power in South African society discussed in the first part of this book. These may be briefly restated. The forces engaged cannot resolve their deadlock unaided: both sides are too strong to be defeated, and neither will voluntarily surrender to the other. White leadership is a prisoner in the hands of a frightened and narrow electorate which fears for its own security and privileges. Inevitably, both sides must turn increasingly to violence, and the inescapable result of large-scale violence is a race war. Passions aroused by this encounter have already internationalised the South African question both in the United Nations and through active intervention from outside, especially from the rest of Africa. This situation not only presents South Africa with appalling dangers, but constitutes an active threat to world peace.

Non-intervention is not a feasible reaction to this situation —not even the bogus kind attempted in Spain. Since South Africa is not going to be left alone, only two alternatives are open: international intervention outside the framework of the United Nations, or collective action through the United Nations.

The first alternative holds great dangers for black and white South Africans, for Africa itself, for the United Nations and for the West. Certain probable consequences may be predicted. The non-white underground in the Republic will become stronger and violence will mount. The African states will increase their economic and military support for the underground, while at the same time intensifying their pressures on the West in support of international action. Much of the effective military and financial aid will come from Russia and China, each pursuing its own separate interests. Their practical support will increase the influence of the communists inside the underground—as it did in Spain; and, as in Spain, there will probably be fierce and debilitating internecine struggles between the different groups in the resistance. But unlike the counter-revolutionary forces in Spain, those in South Africa will not have the support of any major powers.

When the situation reaches the point where the black underground can begin to operate effectively, the chances of arranging a truce to discuss a reasonable basis for settlement will have been lost. The African military leadership's demand for 'all or nothing' will be irresistible, as it was in Algeria by the end of the seven-year war there. There would be little chance of a peaceful settlement in which the country's three million whites could rebuild their lives in a non-racial society. The West will have been robbed of its initiative, and its standing in African eyes will have been irretrievably damaged. The struggle in South Africa will have whipped up a new revolutionary spirit throughout the continent. Africa's future is likely to be influenced as deeply by what happens in South Africa as was Asia's by what happened in China. Africa's dry tinder will be set on fire by a race war. It is difficult to say who will be the real victors after the flames have died down; but one can mark down the casualties with accuracy. First, the white community in South Africa; second, the non-revolutionary leaders of African states; third, the West; and fourth, the United Nations.

The prospect may be luridly drawn. But few would deny the fearful potentialities of a race war in the modern world. The day of European dominance is passed; Europe's future standing in the world rests not on its capacity to challenge the non-white world, but on its willingness and ability to come to terms with it. Only thus can the safety of Europeans in any part of Africa be ensured and only then can we hope to avert an international order polarised by colour.

The second alternative open to the world—acceptance of collective action against South Africa through the United Nations—may be the only way to avoid catastrophe. The major Western countries who are alone in obstructing this solution should actively support such a policy. Whatever transitional losses might result, especially for Britain, will be marginal compared with what they stand to lose by fiddling with their cash registers while the faggots of South Africa's pyre are being stacked.

The relevant question is no longer whether collective action is right or wrong, but how it can be made effective. Unhappily, the political leaders in the West have not yet reached that point of decision. They are still paralysed by the forces of their own arguments against collective action.

VI
THE ARGUMENTS AGAINST INTERVENTION

Why should South Africa's particular form of tyranny be singled out for special attention? What makes its policies worse than the tyrannies of the communist countries or some of the African, Asian and Latin American states? The United Nations' failure to intervene in these countries shows that it is not interested in human rights as such but only in those countries against which the Afro-Asians have a particular grudge. It is intolerable that many of the UN *members who claim the right to sit in judgement on South Africa should themselves be guilty of practices which are often worse than those of their selected scapegoat. Look at Russia, at Ethiopia, at Eastern Germany, at Albania, at Ghana, at Haiti . . . what gives them a right to make moral judgements?*

The case against South Africa is not that it is the world's only tyranny, or even necessarily its worst tyranny, but that it is the world's only racial tyranny. Morally, authoritarian rule of a minority over a majority is always unacceptable. When it happens to be that of a white minority over a black majority in Africa, at a time when the worldwide struggle for black emancipation is at its height, then it is not only evil but reckless and a danger to peace. This cannot be said of India's treatment of the Nagas, Ceylon's treatment of the Tamils, or Russia's treatment of the satellite countries, deplorable though all these are.

It is possible to argue that if the United Nations can show itself able to deal effectively with the immediate challenge of South Africa it will be easier in future to tackle other member nations' infringement of the Charter. The precedent can only be morally good, though it may offend the vested interests of some countries. At the same time it is foolish to ignore the weaknesses and imperfections of the United Nations. Because its power structure is what it is, it would be unrealistic to suppose that it could, under present circumstances, impose its will on the United States or on Russia. Must one do nothing to improve situations amenable to the United Nations' influence and power until the organisation is strong enough to deal with the big powers? This is the logical conclusion of the argument that action against the evil of South Africa must wait until the other evils can be halted as well. Neither personal nor national behaviour is governed by the principle that nothing should be put right until everything can be put right: why is this principle then considered paramount in international behaviour?

It is undeniably distasteful that some of the UN members who sit in moral judgement on South Africa should themselves have unclean hands. But this argument seeks to obscure the important fact that only a minority of South African critics are themselves morally reproachable: it is the whole world which has judged South Africa. The Western spearhead, for example, comes from the Scandinavians, who cannot be accused of reproachable conduct under the UN Charter.

★

South Africa's racial policies are its own affair. To interfere in the internal affairs of a member nation offends not only against the Charter of the United Nations but imperils its whole future. There are no legal grounds for intervening in the Republic's domestic affairs.

The suggestion that South Africa's racial policies are no concern of the world community has, as we have shown, been overtaken by events. The United Nations has decided otherwise, with only South Africa and Portugal dissenting. Even Britain, France and the United States—once firm upholders of this argument—now admit UN interest in apartheid. The fact is that the African nations feel themselves unalterably involved in the fate of Africans anywhere on the continent; they have appealed to the United Nations to prevent a breach of the peace, but they are not prepared to alter course if the UN will not help them. The collision course is set. International conflict is inevitable unless the United Nations can prevent it.

The 'domestic jurisdiction' argument is not, therefore, in accord with the facts.

Moreover, South Africa's administration of the mandated territory of South West Africa is not a domestic matter at all. In the past the West has used many different arguments to forestall UN action to restore its authority over the administration of the territory. By the middle of 1965, when the International Court of Justice is due to give a binding judgement in the matter, all these arguments may become totally irrelevant. The truth is that the 'domestic jurisdiction' argument has never applied to UN interest in South West Africa, yet for fear of a clash with South Africa the West has succeeded in preventing UN action for the restitution of its rights there.

★

South Africa's problems are unique, complex and not understood by outsiders. Their settlement requires understanding, time and patience. Given enough time as well as Western support and protection against outside intervention, South Africa will put its own house in order. This approach is the only way to avoid chaos and bloodshed. Any other method will precipitate violence, harden white resistance and bring about the very situation which the interventionists claim they wish to avoid.

Those who hold these views fall into two groups: the first places its faith in Bantustans as providing the way out of the dilemma; the second rejects the Bantustan solution and puts its faith in the capacity of economic forces to undermine the structure of apartheid, and to produce a new government and a fresh situation.

The arguments of both these groups ignore the realities of the situation. One of these is that intervention is already an active factor in South Africa. Even if the West should take the unlikely course of positively defending South Africa, it could not halt intervention. It would simply put itself on the side of the Republic against the rest of the world thus enlarging the conflict and bringing it directly into the front line of the cold war. No sane Western government is likely to walk into such a trap.

The second reality is that neither the Bantustans nor the

forces of economic growth can place South Africa on the road to sanity. Even on the unrealistic assumption that time is available, every effective political force inside South Africa operates against the possibility that the methods of either group can provide a solution. That is the burden of the argument in the first part of this book.

The South African government, however, has its own reason for expecting a 'stay of execution'. It attaches importance to a theory evolved by the former Foreign Minister, Mr Eric Louw, that the pendulum of opinion will begin to swing in South Africa's favour; the cold war will become sharper and the West will need all the reliable allies it can find; the West will become disillusioned with Asia and Africa and will stop trying to 'appease' the non-aligned world; the African states will start warring against each other, or else they will be so busy shoring up their collapsing economies and coping with internal anarchy that they will have neither money nor time for the freedom struggle in South Africa.

But how is the necessary time to be bought? And how much time is necessary for any of the hopes based on delay to be fulfilled? The West cannot provide it, and the rest will do their utmost to reduce even the little that is left. In their more realistic moments the South African leaders themselves understand how little time is left to them. Mr Oppenheimer has spoken clearly about the embittering effects which time will bring to non-whites living under apartheid.[*] Dr Verwoerd's closest lieutenants have shown how little time remains.[†] But even if there were limitless time, they acknowledge that time is no longer an ally of white supremacy: it now serves the ends of its opponents.[‡]

• The facts are inescapable. Violence has mounted steadily both on the white and the black sides since 1948; external intervention has become more direct. Those who hold power are unwilling to share it, even though they might be willing to give up a tiny part of it, under conditions of strict control, in the Bantustans. But the Bantustans are doomed to failure. The conclusion is irresistible: unless the trap can

---

[*] See Part One, pp. 119–20.
[†] See, for example, Part One, pp. 76–7.
[‡] See, for example, Part One, pp. 81–2.

be sprung before it is too late, South Africa will be torn apart by internal and external forces.

Collective action is not without its risks: it is bound to produce some disruption and possibly even some loss of life; but, whatever its price, it will be only a fraction of the damage that will be caused by a violent race war. What is important is to assess which of the alternatives offers fewer risks: uncontrolled conflict and unilateral intervention, or a planned strategy of collective action which will enable the world community to interpose itself between the two sides and induce controlled change.

The choice is not between chaos and anarchy, or peaceful change: it is between violent change and profound disruption, or controlled change and limited disruption. The extent of disruption and control depends on the timing, the effectiveness, and the composition of the international forces operating in the South African arena.

★

The real aim of the Africans is to destroy the security of white society and to drive the white man out of Africa. To surrender power to an enfranchised black majority is to destroy the white man's place in South Africa to which he has as much right as the Africans. Historically his claim to South Africa is as good as the Africans because he arrived there at the same time as the Bantu tribes. People seem to lose sight of the need to ensure justice for the whites as well as for the blacks. There can be no morality or justice in proposals which will simply exchange white supremacy for black supremacy.

This argument contains a number of fallacies. The notion that the whites and blacks arrived in South Africa at roughly the same time is a carefully fostered myth.* The first

* 'The Portuguese records show that from 1554 there were people "very black in colour" south of the Mtata river [in the Transkei] and a little further north "the country was thickly populated and provided with cattle". From 1593 there is evidence that the people *south* of the Mtata spoke a Nguni language (Zulu), and from 1686 we can place the various Xhosa-speaking tribes known today: they occupied the country from the Buffalo River (East London) northwards. Traditions indicate that the Xhosa, Pondomise, and Thembu were living on the tributaries of the Nzimvubu near the mountains, before they came to the coast. They may have been there for many generations: we do not know. There is nothing in the

white settlement which arrived in the south-western Cape in 1652 was met and sustained by native inhabitants—mainly Bushmen and Hottentots. The great Bantu tribes were established a few hundred miles to the west where they existed in large numbers and with great herds of cattle. The earliest European chronicles recording their presence goes back to 1554: more than a century before the white man landed in the Cape. The Bantu tribes were established in different areas throughout the interior of modern South Africa; they had been there since at least 1300, perhaps longer. If primacy of occupation of land were to be the basis on which white rights in South Africa were to be established, the most they could claim is the small area of the south-western Cape—assuming of course that one overlooked the claims of the Bushmen and the Hottentots. On this kind of argument, the Africans could assert their right to most of the rest of the country.

But this argument is a massive red-herring. The only reason for referring to it is that the myth of primacy of occupation is invariably put forward by the Republic's lobbyists overseas. But the Africans have never based their claims to be accorded equal treatment in South Africa on the fact of their earlier occupation, nor do they maintain that the white man is an interloper who should be driven out.

The documented evidence shows that African leadership to this day insists that South Africa is the home of all its present inhabitants irrespective of race;* this is also the view of the leaders of the independent African states; none dissents. The African nationalist movement in South Africa never uses the cry of 'drive the white man out of Africa'.† There is no reason to suppose, therefore, that a proper basis for settlement would not include the right of whites to full citizenship.

The real anxiety underlying these arguments is the fear

---

recorded traditions to indicate any substantial movement of Nguni (Zulu) people from north of the Drakensberg—much less the Limpopo—within the period covered by the genealogies, i.e. since 1300, and it may well have been centuries before that. None of these facts is new; all have been published at one time or another; but their implications appear to have been overlooked by the myth-makers of this generation': Professor Monica Wilson: 'The Early History of Transkei and Ciskei', *African Studies*. Vol. 18, No. 4, 1959.
* See Part One, pp. 173–4.
† See Part One, pp. 178–9.

that when the black man inherits political power he might behave no better towards the whites than the whites behaved
towards him. This is a very real anxiety, and cannot be
brushed aside. But if the future of the white minority is pre-
carious, how much more important it is to seek a settlement
before the bitterness of race hatred puts its future security right
outside the bounds of possibility. The white man's best
chance of justice is to negotiate before he is driven into a hopeless and friendless corner. This is by far a safer and saner
course than to rely upon a mythical past claim to exclusive
control of the country.

★

*South Africa is a strong country with a strong govern-
ment. It is the only African state which has avoided
upheaval. It is pro-Western, anti-communist, and prosperous. Its people are good at business and want to do
business with us. Why do we have to start pushing them
around?*

This is the argument of the average business man and the
average tourist. They see a modern, bustling country, with
fine cities and modern factories. In the streets they see well-
dressed, cheerful-looking Africans. In the factories they see
workers of all races, each doing his job: the whites at the
lathes, the non-whites with the oil rags—not very different from
many factories in the United States or in the Midlands in
Britain. They are entertained by keen, efficient business men
who talk like business men everywhere: running down the
politicians, criticising the inefficiencies of government, dis-
missing outside criticism as ill-informed and communistic.
They see nothing of life in the African townships, in the
reserves, in the prisons. They meet no non-white leaders.
Such white liberals as they question are at once recognisable
as no different from the 'egg-heads' or 'radicals' they know
at home—and who listens to them?

The fundamental flaw in this approach is the failure to
ask any but the most superficial questions. This view is based
upon a lack of interest in the anxious debate that fills the
English and Afrikaans language press. They do not explore
the reasons behind the feverish search for solutions to

restructure the entire basis of the country. They do not want
to know the size of the prison population, or examine the real
reason why the defence forces and the police have been quin-
tupled and sextupled in the last four or five years. The answer
they easily accept is that 'strong' government is needed in
Africa, and that 'strong' governments have a habit of surviving.
They quote Portugal and Spain. But Portugal and Spain are
in Western Europe where none of their neighbours is actively
hostile to them. Their tyranny consists of one group of whites
imposing its will on another group of whites. But South
Africa is in a black continent, and a white minority is engaged
in suppressing a black majority. That kind of government
cannot survive.

★

*South Africa's economy is booming as never before.
Exports are rising despite the boycott movement, overseas
business men are investing with apparent confidence, and
the standard of living for everyone is rising. Surely there
can't be much wrong with a country which is experiencing that kind of economic prosperity—at least nothing
that could not be remedied by letting expansion continue,
and allowing the economic forces to overcome political
ideologies?*

It is true that the South African economy is remarkably
strong and resilient. After two to three years of post-Sharpe-
ville doldrums, all the economic indices show an economy set
fair for expansion and rapid recovery. But there are four
flaws in the conclusions drawn by this argument. First,
economic expansion is a sign of the economic failure of apartheid, not of its success. Economic expansion depends abso-
lutely upon economic integration, and it cannot accompany
'Separate Development'. To the extent that the government
succeeds in separating the present black proletariat from the
'white' centres of industrial activity, economic expansion will
be crippled. But it is not succeeding: the towns, the mining
areas and the white-owned farms are getting blacker all the
time. In practice, therefore, apartheid does not upset the
integrated economy, but it leads to horizontal racial segrega-

tion, with all the lower-paid jobs performed by non-whites; they are integrated into the 'white' economy, but denied all rights and opportunities.

Secondly, even if 'economic forces' can prevent the implementation of 'Separate Development', they cannot solve the country's political problems. Economic expansion cannot liberate people from political tyranny. It can do nothing to alter the laws. It can offer jobs to Africans but it cannot get them votes; it can provide them with a livelihood at unskilled rates of pay, but it cannot give them security or opportunities to develop their skills and abilities. These are circumscribed by the Job Reservation Act, the Bantu Education Act, the Pass Laws, legislation against effective trade union activity, and so on. Economic expansion can alter none of these disabilities. Only a voice in the country's law-making organs can change the basic condition of insecurity and dependence of the non-white worker. And economic expansion cannot give the African these political rights.

Thirdly, the fact of overseas investment in a highly profitable economy (27 per cent for American capital investment) is no criterion either of the way a country treats its citizens or of its inherent stability. Hitler's economy boomed; so did that of the Central African Federation before the inevitable political forces swept it away.

Finally, contrary to popular belief, the South African non-white population is far from prosperous. Their demands for a radical change in political organisation are not simply 'ideological': they are the stuff of bread-and-butter politics. Despite the fact that South Africa is incomparably the richest country in Africa, it has the highest recorded incidence of infant mortality due to malnutrition. Several impartial surveys indicate that about 60 per cent of the non-white population lives *below* the bread-line: a shocking reflection on a country which could provide abundantly for all its citizens. The African's ability to provide adequately for himself and his family is circumscribed at every turn by legislation, which starts on the premise that 'the Bantu stay in the white areas can be justified only by the needs for his services there.'[1] The fact is that the 'white areas' contain almost all the opportunities for employment. But the question whether other means of livelihood exist is not a criterion for employment policy. African employees are bound hand and foot to their employers by their legally created dependence, regardless of conditions of service. These circumstances cannot be remedied by economic expansion—even if the economy is thus enabled to give enormous returns on capital invested.

★

Why should whites be made to submit to black domination? They are a nation like any other, with the same rights to self determination. Why should whites be made to integrate with blacks? If they choose not to do so, that is their right, surely?

This argument invites a counter-question: why should blacks be made to submit to white domination? Not even the most optimisitic interpretation of Separate Development offers the majority of blacks the opportunity of escaping from white domination. At best, Bantustans would offer homelands for half the black population by the year 2000; the other half would live as aliens and as permanent migrants in the part of South Africa, 81 per cent of its area, set aside for whites: this is the official version of the effects of Separate Development.

Whites who live in South Africa cannot escape the consequences of multiracial society. If they feel they cannot live cheek by jowl with Africans, they have no alternative but to move to a continent which will not expose them to such a necessity. This harsh solution might become unnecessary if by agreement a part of the country were set aside for those whites who cannot face the necessities imposed by a multiracial society. But such an arrangement could only follow a negotiated settlement in South Africa; it is inconceivable this opportunity would recur if the whites were defeated in a race conflict.

★

How can the Africans take over the running of an industrialised society with its high level of modern technological and administrative achievements? There are no Africans capable of running a mine, a modern industry or a scientific laboratory. If the whites lose their power,

*modern South Africa will be wrecked; the price of pro-
viding the African with the vote will be to destroy the
whole basis of his economic life.*

This is a pessimistic picture. If there is a proper settlement between the races there is no reason why most of those
now running industries and mines should not remain in South
Africa. The balance of power in the policy-making organs of
the state and industry is bound to change, but the efficient
running of the economy need not be impaired. The danger
of running down the country arises only if the final outcome is
such that there is no future for whites at all.

Besides, there are many Africans at present capable of
high level administration; and many more to whom a short
period of technical training could give a high degree of pro-
ficiency. Existing acculturation in a complex economy, combined with an assisted programme of training, makes possible
a cadre of technical and administrative skills unequalled in
Africa.

★

*The Simonstown Agreement is of great value to the Royal
Navy. Not only does Britain have a strong Common-
wealth interest in maintaining a safe route round the
Cape, but the Western military alliance depends on the
Republic's support in the event of war. Strategically, its
position is vital to Western interests.*

These arguments were undoubtedly valid in the pre-
nuclear age of warfare, but they no longer hold true today.
This is the view of senior British naval officers who question
whether the Cape route is 'vital'. They believe that preoccupations with Simonstown are a relic of outdated thinking.
Convoys would not be sent round the Cape in a major war if
the two sides were using nuclear weapons; and even if nuclear
bombs were not being dropped on densely populated areas,
nuclear-powered submarines and long-distance bombers with
nuclear warheads would be a threat to convoys and to strategic
bases.

British defence planners have already evolved alternatives
to Simonstown. These envisage the establishment of 'island
bases' in the South Atlantic and Indian Oceans. The

favoured sites are St Helena in the South Atlantic, the Falkland Islands off the tip of South America, and the Seychelles and Mauritius off the east coast of Africa.

Suitable anchorages, equal to Simonstown's, are available in St Helena and the Falklands; the former could be used to resite the new naval wireless station now based on Simonstown. The other islands are suitable as refuelling and replenishment stations, and could provide substitutes for storage of the strategic ammunition reserves now kept at Simonstown and Brakpan in the Transvaal. A large part of these reserves have in fact already been removed. Experts in Whitehall admit that the usefulness of Simonstown has already been diminished with the scrapping of troopships, and that existing joint defence arrangements are now almost exclusively to South Africa's advantage. Although it would cost more to establish new 'island bases', naval chiefs believe that recent advances in mobile replenishment make the costs of a changeover less than before; they say they would gladly give up the Simonstown rights in exchange for an increase of 'float support' ships. The main additional costs, therefore, would be the building of installations on the islands themselves. As for the right of the Royal Air Force to fly over South Africa for trooping and air reinforcements, this is important only if Britain should find herself unable to overfly the Middle East; otherwise it would be cheaper to use the Mediterranean routes. But if the Middle East should be blocked—and if a new government in South Africa should prove hostile—modern transport planes like the Belfast, with ranges up to 3,500 miles, make a much safer route possible to the East across Canada to Vancouver, and from there across the Pacific. These ideas were all produced by British military strategists after the former South African Foreign Minister, Mr Eric Louw, had threatened in September 1963 that the Verwoerd Government might cancel the Simonstown Agreement. This reappraisal showed that the Cape route was not vital to British or Western interests.

But there is also a political side to these arguments. How can South Africa strengthen the West's general defence system against the communist bloc while its government pursues a policy which strengthens the communist appeal, and which greatly weakens the West's diplomatic position? To try to maintain in power a government which would ensure British rights in Simonstown—of doubtful value in the event of war— at the price of estranging the West from the rest of Africa, would strike most people as political folly.

No doubt as a result of this latest military thinking, the British government has recently changed the arguments it uses in defending the value of the Simonstown Agreement. 'I have very much in mind that to go to the assistance of Commonwealth countries like India and Malaysia we have to get there', Sir Alec Douglas-Home recently told the House of Commons.[1] This argument, implying that Asian security depends on the Simonstown base, is misleading, if not hypocritical. The fact is that Britain is now 'getting there' through the shorter route of Suez. And as long as Britain, the United States and Canada are in agreement about Far Eastern policies, the route to their Asian allies could be guaranteed, even if the Royal Navy could use neither Simonstown nor Suez.

There are strong arguments—irrespective of the future of Simonstown—for fundamentally reconsidering the old ideas about the value of military bases devised in the context of an outdated imperial defence system.

★

How can we ensure that South Africa won't fall into the hands of the communists? It is clear that the communists already have a foothold in the African nationalist movement, and that the Russians and the Chinese are in deadly earnest in their efforts to get a grip on the valuable material and strategic resources of the country if ever the present anti-communist white government is removed?

There is no chance whatever that the present anti-communist white government can be sustained in power for more than a few years, even if the West were to give it wholehearted support. What is important now is the nature of the government which succeeds it.

If South Africa is plunged into a race war, if the main support for the liberation movement comes from Peking and Moscow, and if the West is seen, or felt, to be equivocal or hostile as the struggle develops, then there is justifiable alarm at the possibility of an authoritarian communist state in South Africa. The only way to reduce this possibility is for the West to gain the respect of Africans and their white supporters, and to make it possible for an independent-minded nationalist leadership to assert its influence and control. The longer the West hesitates and equivocates, the more opportunities there will be for anti-Western influences to do their work.

Those with an interest in denying the communists a foothold in South Africa can make their greatest contribution by setting themselves four targets: first, to reduce the African nationalists' dependence on the communists; second, to recognise the influence and importance of the existing African leadership which is predominantly non-communist, and to help strengthen it in a way sanctioned by these leaders themselves; third, to help produce policies that will avoid chaos in South Africa at the point where power is being transferred; fourth, to arrest immediately the growing disenchantment with Western policies and leadership which is likely to spill over into a trough of entrenched distrust, so deep that it will no longer be accessible to reasonable argument. There are enough recent examples to serve as a warning of the process that has already begun in South Africa. The only way to counteract communist influence is to unite with those black and white forces in South Africa which aspire to build a genuinely independent country.

★

Nobody has the right to try and enforce a gun-point solution on South Africa. It is wrong and it won't work.

Amen to that. The objective of international sanctions should be to compel the South Africans to negotiate a settlement acceptable to all racial groups. The international community cannot and should not itself determine the terms of such a settlement. Its purpose should be to halt the present government's attempts to enforce a gun-point solution— Separate Development—which is unacceptable to all the Africans and to nearly half the whites as well.

Faced with international intervention, the white man will fight and the white man will be right.

Whom will he fight? If international intervention takes the form of collective economic sanctions he can, and probably will, try to resist the effects of sanctions. But South Africa is not economically self-sufficient, despite her advanced industrial economy. The white man cannot win against concerted international sanctions. The country must collapse economically, and such collapse can be secured without firing a shot.

Will the white man be right? Is it right to fight for the privilege of maintaining a racial tyranny? If it is right for the white man to fight to retain his stake in South Africa, why is it wrong for the non-white to fight for an equal claim on his country? Is self-determination proper for the white, but improper for the black? Surely the only right policy is one which allows both whites and blacks a claim on the resources and political life of their common country.

Moreover, the white man's 'right to fight' will be little comfort to him when it ends in the denial of his birthright— for the reason that he persistently denies the African his birthright. To encourage the white man to fight for the maintenance of the present system is to encourage him to march towards his extinction as a community in South Africa. Ulster is not South Africa; to confuse the two is to misunderstand the fundamental realities of the Republic.

★

Experience in Africa shows that a multiracial society will not work. Whites and blacks are two different peoples with their own cultures, levels of development and political methods. To force them into a single political system can lead only to black domination and the end of the white man's way of life. Therefore the answer must be found in some form of apartheid, Separate Development, or perhaps even partition.

What is shown by experience in Africa is that no minority community—whether white as in Kenya, Central Africa and

Algeria; Arab as in Zanzibar; or black as in Rwanda—can establish a satisfactory relationship with the majority if they hold on to power until they are violently overthrown. Nor is this a characteristic of Africa: the same experience was common in Europe. In Africa, the tiny white and brown minorities who were not involved in a power struggle, live harmoniously with black majorities. None of the experiments to achieve multiracial government so far tried out in Africa has been anything but fraudulent, and all have therefore ended in failure. Partnership in Central Africa was a disguised form of entrenching white domination for as long as was thought necessary; multiracialism in Kenya was an avowed attempt to produce a 'moderate' black political movement under white leadership. The right conclusion is that the attempt to secure minority rights by deluding the majority does no service to the minority. Similarly, the attempt to maintain white control by promising Africans an illusory future independence in the Bantustans is doomed to failure. Separate Development offers no solution because it will not work. Partition is supported in South Africa by neither blacks nor whites, for the very good reason that it is politically and economically impossible to implement.

The real experiment in creating a harmonious multiracial society with a non-racial government has yet to be made in Africa. Apart from Algeria and Southern Rhodesia the only country which has enough Europeans to offer a basis for such an experiment is South Africa. The prospects in South Africa are in some respects better than in any other country. Its white community is not an insignificant minority but a substantial community of three million peoples: three times as many as in any other country in Africa. Unlike the French in Algeria or the British in Rhodesia, white South Africans have genuinely lost their roots in Europe. Acculturation between black and white has proceeded further than the whites like to recognise; and the country is rich enough to offer everybody a reasonable standard of living.

But these opportunities can be turned to good account only if individual citizens are protected by constitutional safeguards acceptable to all. The arguments over partition have been examined in chapter one of Part Two.

The insistence on a political system based on 'one man, one vote' can have as its only outcome black tyranny and the growth of a single party state. The United Nations is dominated by countries which would insist on imposing 'one man, one vote' once the UN *became involved in South Africa.*

No formula which does not recognise the principle of majority rule will provide a stable solution in South Africa. Thus the principle of majority rule is a *sine qua non* for any negotiated settlement, whether the United Nations has a hand in it or not. There is no way of erasing the reality of the eleven-to-three preponderance of non-whites over whites. A manipulated constitution which seeks to eradicate this reality cannot survive. But there is no reason why the attempt should not be made to achieve constitutional and legal safeguards which will operate to prevent either the majority or a dictatorial minority from denying the rights and interests of other citizens—white, black or brown.

★

There are no absolutes, such as 'the right of majority rule', 'principles of freedom and justice', 'truth', 'democracy', 'full human rights' which are universally applicable. In South Africa, these 'principles' must be adapted.

To deny the universality of such concepts is to deny the Western ethic, the applicability of the Charter of the United Nations (to which South Africa subscribes), and the Declaration of Human Rights. This argument confuses practice with principle: the principles are capable of absolute definition in universal terms; but the application of these principles may be uneven. That the practice is sometimes in conflict with the principles is no reason to reject the concepts contained within these principles: these must remain the objectives to which democrats stand committed in their efforts to influence the growth of a decent international society. No matter how difficult it might be to get certain societies to observe these principles at different levels of development, one cannot rewrite principles to meet exceptional situations. Democrats cannot criticise the tyrannies of communist and fascist autocracies, or the denial of human rights, or the right to self-determination, if at the same time they accept the argument that there are no absolutes which apply universally. One cannot make up rules as one goes along, using one measurement for South Africa, another for Spain, or Russia or Ghana.

★

The West should not allow itself to be blackmailed into taking action against South Africa by the Africans and the Asians. They are guilty of practising a 'dual morality' and have an exaggerated idea of their own importance.

No nation can be altogether acquitted of the 'dual morality' charge. If the United Nations were to resist taking action because some of those proposing it apply dual standards, there would be no issue on which action could be taken. In asking the West to adopt less equivocal policies towards South Africa in the interests of world peace and on grounds of morality, the Afro-Asians are not guilty of 'blackmail'. None of them has threatened the West with directly injuring its interests if it refuses to comply with their demands. None of them is demanding a special reward for itself as the pay-off for a deal. It is perfectly legitimate for them to point out that the West's refusal to act over South Africa will in fact damage its own interests in Africa: its standing in the eyes of the non-aligned nations will be lowered; and it will play into the hands of the communist world. Nor can the African nations' determination to act alone, if the United Nations will not help them, be described as blackmail. The Western nations should be the last to deny the right of nations to act separately where they conceive their own interests to be involved, and where the United Nations cannot be prevailed upon to act to prevent a breach of the peace.

The African states strongly believe that what is happening in South Africa is of great moral and political importance to the whole of Africa. This is not the view of a few African states; it is the agreed view of all. This view is shared by many in Europe, not least in the West. If it is to be dismissed as the product of immaturity or cupidity, the West should, as Dr Verwoerd suggests, abandon the attempt to seek friendship in Africa. Either the West attempts to understand the political priorities in Africa—a natural enough thing to expect between friendly states—or it rejects any co-operation with Africa, except where there is a coincidence of short-term interests. No sensible statesman will choose the latter.

★

We agree that South Africa's position is morally offensive. We accept that the present political system must be changed or it will be swept away. We also accept that the race war is perhaps the greatest incipient threat to world peace. But we do not see what can be done by the international community. Any concerted action will only drive all the whites into a single camp and precipitate the very conditions which the proponents of collective action seek to avoid.

This is substantially the position of the British government and of many influential organs of Western opinion. It expresses alarm, but it confesses defeat. It also overlooks a number of crucial political factors. The whites are in fact already largely united in their defence of white supremacy. Their unity on this fundamental question has nothing to do with the threat of sanctions; it is a condition of their present society. They disagree only over the methods to maintain white rule: it is on this narrow front that apartheid divides them. It cannot be too strongly stressed that even if the opponents of apartheid were to win office, another white government could do nothing to achieve a significant redistribution of power. The roots of the crisis would remain. Any policy which sets itself the limited objective of securing the defeat of the apartheid régime will simply prolong the agony. A great deal of effort and time will have been wasted only to lead the international community up a blind alley. The proper objective is not simply to bring down the apartheid régime, but to replace the system of white supremacy: this requires a challenge to white supremacy in South Africa. About this there should be no illusions.

In any case, the argument that the gradual process of internal collapse is likely to produce less disruption than would be caused by sanctions, is contradicted by the explicit recognition of the dangers of a race war. These two views are clearly irreconcilable. If the only outcome of South

Africa's internal disintegration is race war, then whatever risks are involved in making positive efforts to arrest it, must be the lesser of two dangers. Whether or not UN action is immediately effective, it would be hard to deny that it would at least have the effect of counteracting the white-black conflict.

The first reaction of South Africa's whites to concerted sanctions would almost certainly be uniformly hostile. But what matters is their second reaction—after their helpless isolation from the West has been borne in on them. This will be the moment of real trauma. The effect of this trauma on white thinking is what matters most. This question is discussed in chapter ten.

★

International economic sanctions have never been made to work. They can all too easily be breached. Moreover they are objectionable in principle as a means of settling disputes between sovereign nations. The only effect of trying to impose them on South Africa would be to destroy the United Nations which could not make them work, and which would be blamed for the chaos of an ineffective operation.

International economic sanctions demand certain prerequisite conditions, and these have not before combined to allow an effective programme of sanctions. First, they must be enforced by an authority determined to allow no breaches. Second, the nation concerned must have no powerful friends who would be prepared to defy the enforcing authority. Third, the offending country must be sufficiently dependent upon the import of at least one strategic commodity, deprivation of which makes it impossible to withstand a siege indefinitely.

In regard to the first point, we argue in chapter eight that a UN blockade of South African ports could be made to fulfil these conditions. The United Nations has the authority required to direct the operation of patrolling the southern coasts of Africa and repelling attempts at clandestine breaches of the blockade. As regards the second point, the only nations which have enough to lose and sufficient naval strength to risk open conflict with the United Nations by defying its blockade are the major Western nations; and the political fool-hardiness of such an attempt, once they had concurred with a UN decision to take action, would surely discourage it. As for the third point, South Africa's economy is dependent upon imports for some ninety per cent of its fuel requirements, and for a significant proportion of its rubber needs and machine tool equipment. Blocking of its oil requirements alone could bring the economy to a standstill in a matter of months.

Thus the effectiveness of possible sanctions against South Africa cannot be judged by reference to the League of Nations' attempts to institute sanctions against Italy over Abyssinia, or indeed to any situation before the authority of the United Nations could be invoked. The only recent attempt at enforced sanctions was the successful American blockade of Cuba, with the object of preventing the build-up of Russian arms on the island. It succeeded because the American fleet was able and prepared to prevent any breaches, and because the Russians were not prepared to go to war over it. America's attempt at general economic sanctions against Cuba has not succeeded precisely because it has not been prepared to enforce them.

So much for the objection that sanctions against South Africa cannot be made to work: given the political will, the techniques are available. But would the attempt destroy the United Nations in the process? The only things which would surely destroy the United Nations is its failure to act in situations which threaten the peace and in which it has the power to act. It cannot be destroyed by an even moderately success-ful bid to prevent an international race conflict; but it can be destroyed by showing itself unwilling to deal with one of the major problems of our time. Obviously it would be better if the problem could be solved without the use of economic pressures, and entirely by negotiation. But we have shown that the political dynamic of South Africa precludes a settle-ment by negotiations without an outside catalyst. The only question is: can the United Nations help? If it decides it cannot, it will have diminished the hope of producing a co-operative world order. The choice is not between collec-tive economic sanctions and non-intervention: it is between collective economic pressures and a shooting war between blacks and whites; not between peace and war, but between two different kinds of war. Only the United Nations is in a position to implement the more humane course.

We are finally left with the fundamental question most frequently asked by radical Western opinion: *What kind of international sanctions offer the hope of producing the desired result?* This question is explored in the following chapters.

VII

THE OBJECTIVES OF SANCTIONS

The programme of sanctions which the United Nations should be invited to apply against South Africa must be devised to achieve a number of specific objectives as quickly as possible. The ultimate objective is easily defined: to produce a situation inside South Africa which will facilitate the transfer of power to a representative form of government under conditions which will ensure a minimum of disruption and provide optimum opportunities for inter-racial co-operation.

The short-term objective is to induce the South African authorities to summon a National Convention of the representative leaders of all the communities for the purpose of drafting a new constitution acceptable to all, and to provide democratic safeguards.

The United Nation's role should be confined to that of a catalyst introduced for the purpose of inducing a process never before tried in South Africa's history: the process of inter-racial negotiation. The only active participants should be the South Africans themselves. The mandate given to the United Nations' Command should explicitly exclude it from interfering in the kind of settlement to be achieved, subject only to certain guiding principles by which it may determine whether the ultimate objectives are being seriously pursued. Four conditions are suggested as the minimum required to satisfy the legitimate interests of all the protagonists.

First, the negotiations must be concluded by the representative leaders of the two white communities, the Africans, the Coloureds and the Indians—their composition to be determined by the communities themselves. Since none of the racial communities is monolithic, negotiations may well involve a large number of interests. Second, the basis of the agreement should be submitted to a referendum. Third, the constitution should provide for a representative and democratic

government.   Fourth, the constitution should contain enforceable safeguards for the rights of all the country's citizens
including the minority communities.

Such questions as whether the constitution should be
unitary, federal or confederal, and whether it should allow for
the establishment of states or provinces for any particular racial
community, would lie outside the UN's prerogative.   If any
durable settlement is to evolve it is essential that South
Africans should themselves decide the constitution under
which they are to live.

Today, neither the long-term nor the short-term objectives
here stated are envisaged by either of the major white political
parties in the Republic.   It is this adamant refusal by the
majority of the white community to admit non-whites to equal
participation in the search for a solution which necessitates
and justifies international intervention.   The duration and
vigour with which sanctions need to be applied depends very
much on how difficult it proves to break down this primary
resistance.

The United Nations cannot expect a change of attitude
simply because it threatens sanctions.   Nor is it likely that
there will be a decisive response until sanctions have begun to
affect the ability of those who now wield power in the Republic
to maintain their position.   But if the UN adopts a sanctions
programme capable of inflicting real economic damage, capitu-
lation could be almost immediate.   Inevitably, those most
likely to suffer first will be the poorest—mainly the non-
whites.   But their representative leaders are unanimous in the
view that temporary hardship is preferred to a continuation of
the *status quo*.   It is ironic to discover that the most ardent
opponents of sanctions, on the grounds of damage to non-
white interests, are generally also the proponents of apartheid.

To reduce the period of hardship to a minimum, and to
secure the maximum advantage from intervention, it is essential that a programme of sanctions should be capable of total
enforcement.   Half-hearted or ineffective measures would not
only discredit the United Nations; it would worsen rather than
improve the situation in South Africa.   Only sanctions
capable of total enforcement by the Security Council under
Articles 41 and 42 in Chapter VII of the Charter could make a

decisive impact. To be fully effective a programme for sanctions needs to be flexible. It should be capable not only of massive pressure, but of being eased or tightened as the situation demands.

In principle, armed intervention is to be avoided. As long as a race war remains incipient, the introduction of armed forces could prove disastrous. Once the United Nations has taken a decision to intervene, it will be in the interests of blacks as well as whites to avoid using violence. The struggle should be conducted on the hard but less bloody field of economic attrition. Nevertheless, the possibility of an eruption of race violence cannot be ruled out entirely. Conditions have already deteriorated to the point where violence is never far below the surface. For this reason it would be advisable for the United Nations to plan to hold an emergency force available for use at short notice. Remote though it now appears, the day might come when the white leadership in South Africa would themselves welcome the presence of UN forces. But UN planning should be limited to the possible need for such a 'Fire Brigade' only in case of emergency.

The next step is to consider a programme of sanctions which could fulfil these broad objectives.

VIII

THE STRATEGY OF SANCTIONS

To achieve its established objectives, a programme of sanctions must fulfil three requirements. It must make it impossible for the South African government to keep its economy moving, and thus compel it to open negotiations. It must minimise the human suffering and economic disruption by producing its impact as soon as possible. It must be capable of enforcement with a minimum risk of armed conflict.

Strong as it is, the South African economy is vulnerable to concerted economic sanctions. Exports constitute about one quarter of the gross national product, imports about a fifth. Nearly a third of capital goods supplies are imported —over and above the import content of capital goods made in the Republic. The engineering and transport equipment industries are particularly dependent on imported components; they buy over forty per cent of the materials they use abroad. But a similar dependence on imports is characteristic of other industries: textile and clothing, forestry products, petroleum and coal products. Gold mining is only marginally dependent on imports. Exports account for about a fifth of total final sales, and gold for nearly half of export earnings. Thus, two forms of sanctions could severely damage the South African economy: an embargo on the sale of industrial supplies and components, and a suspension of gold buying.

But there is a third possibility which could prove both more easily enforceable and of greater immediate effect on South Africa: a world embargo on the sale of oil. The government oil-from-coal industry, SASOL, at present makes only about seven per cent of the country's needs. It could not be expanded at short notice to make a significant contribution. Fuel storage facilities are capable of holding only a few months' supplies—hence the current activity to expand them. It is clear, therefore, that an effective embargo on foreign oil supplies would progressively halt all forms of economic activity. It is, of course, possible that a system of fuel rationing would allow priority industries and defence activities to survive up to eight or ten months. If, therefore, the aim is to achieve maximum impact, a total embargo on all trade with South Africa would be more effective.

How could such an embargo be enforced? A Security Council call for economic measures under Article 41 of the Charter would be binding upon all members, and allow for UN enforcement under Article 42. Considering the widespread international interests in South Africa and the possible profits to be had from covertly defying the United Nations, it would be naive to expect universal voluntary compliance. The United Nations should not therefore rely on member states' goodwill and ability to prevent illegal breaches. Instead, it should invoke Article 42 of the Charter to institute a naval blockade of the relevant ports under United Nations' Command, thus physically preventing breaches of the embargo.

Such a blockade could be mounted only with the help of the great naval powers. The recent American blockade of Cuba to prevent Russian nuclear arms from reaching Castro showed that such a policing operation at sea is feasible; but it also showed the need for a powerful and flexible fleet, such as could be provided only by the major powers. Three naval elements are essential: aircraft carriers, radar ships and swift pursuit craft, including air surveillance planes and possibly submarines. These vessels would not be required to enter South African harbours and risk physical confrontation there.

It is hardly conceivable that South Africa with its existing naval forces would attempt an attack at sea on the world's most powerful navies. At present, in any case, it would not be hard to repel such an attack. The only danger is that South Africa might acquire in the future a fleet of torpedo-armed submarines with which to engage in hit-and-run attacks. At present she has no submarines. It is essential therefore that countries, like Britain, which impose only a limited arms embargo on South Africa should immediately proscribe the sale of submarines and torpedoes to the Republic.

Three major problems can be foreseen for a naval blockade. The first is that the Portuguese-controlled ports of

Lourenço Marques and Beira (in Mozambique) and Lobito and Luanda (in Angola) should be brought within the sphere of interest of the blockading command, since all are linked by rail to South Africa. Portugal should be offered the choice of two alternatives: to allow the United Nations to post observers at these rail links; or to face UN policing of these harbours to prevent their receiving goods destined for South Africa. Portuguese co-operation with the former is greatly to be preferred for reasons which concern the second major problem.

This is the need to minimise the effects of the blockade on South Africa's innocent neighbours who derive much of their trade from, or through, South Africa. These countries are the three High Commission Territories (Bechuanaland, Basutoland and Swaziland), and the three Central African countries (Northern Rhodesia, Southern Rhodesia and Nyasaland). This problem can be met if their trade can be diverted for the period of the blockade through Mozambique, Angola and the Congo. A part of Northern Rhodesia's copper exports and its main imports could be conveyed on the Benguela Railway to Lobito or Kamina in the Congo. Additional exports and supplies could be moved through ports in Mozambique, which already provide an important part of the needs of Southern Rhodesia and Nyasaland. If these ports were kept open they could also supply Swaziland and Bechuanaland. Only Basutoland would be completely isolated. But because it still has a largely subsistence economy, its essential needs are relatively small. The problem could be met partly by stockpiling fuel and food financed by special loans for the purpose. It would also help if the blockade could be timed to coincide with a harvest. An airlift could be made expensive by a government willing to use Basutoland as a hostage. An important element in this situation, however, is the willingness of the Basuto to accept temporary hardships in the interests of a concerted international programme to end the South African régime of white supremacy.

The simplest way of dealing with the other five territories would be to induce the Portuguese authorities to allow UN policing of the railway lines to South Africa. The alternative would be the complicated and costly operation of calculating the combined needs of the Portuguese territories, Central

Africa and the High Commission Territories, and of policing the Portuguese ports to prevent these imports from being exceeded or diverted to South Africa. It is not unreasonable to suppose that, given a choice, Portugal might prefer the first of the alternatives. If she proved obdurate, it might become necessary to start a programme of sanctions by imposing only an oil embargo: this method would hold fewer complications for policing the Portuguese-controlled ports.

The third problem is that of supplying and maintaining the ships engaged in the blockade. The nearest available Atlantic ports are those in the Congo, the Cameroun and Nigeria; the nearest Indian Ocean ports are in Madagascar, Kenya and Tanganyika. The operation would probably require one base on each coast. The distances involved would mean that more ships would be needed to fill the gaps while others turned round for fuel and supplies.

None of these problems can be solved without expert technical examination; but none of them appears to raise insuperable difficulties given the political will and the resources of the world's major navies. It may be that expert examination will prove an oil embargo both easier to operate and sufficiently effective to establish its preference over that of a total embargo. There are arguments against this choice, but the balance of advantage could finally be decided only by expert investigation.

So far we have been discussing the possible strategy for sanctions on the assumption that it will be instituted on the grounds that apartheid represents a threat to world peace. But it is possible that UN intervention might begin over South West Africa. If the International Court rules against South Africa in the case before the Court, and if South Africa refuses to comply with its judgement, the United Nations would presumably seek a way of upholding the judgement by enforcement measures. The quickest and most effective way of doing so, other than direct military intervention, would be to institute a programme such as the one outlined. It might well be that the Verwoerd Government would prefer to abandon its claims to South West Africa rather than face these consequences. If it chose the course of discretion, two consequences would follow. The first is that the weakness of the Republic's international position would be brought forcefully home to the South African electorate. The second is that it would help make clear to the Republic's friends abroad that the threat of sanctions against South Africa could no longer be ignored. The total effect would be to reduce the Verwoerd Government's support at home and abroad. To that extent, a subsequent programme of sanctions on the grounds that apartheid represents a threat to world peace, would be more quickly and effectively accomplished.

IX

THE EFFECTS OF SANCTIONS
OUTSIDE SOUTH AFRICA

A realistic examination of the economic effects of sanctions on South Africa's trading partners should assume a total cessation of trade for the duration of the blockade. Even if South Africa were denied only oil supplies, it is unlikely to be either willing or able to continue to trade in other commodities. We may also assume that the blockade is effectively enforced, so that trade is not merely diverted to new markets and sources of supply.

Nearly three-quarters of South Africa's trade—imports as well as exports—is with Britain, the United States, Western Europe and Japan.[1] If any of these instituted a unilateral programme of sanctions, the effect would be damaging for South Africa, but it would not be irremediable since the others could provide acceptable alternatives. All its major trading partners therefore have an interest in the effective enforcement of sanctions. Among the other trading partners, Iran stands to lose by a blockade, but its government has declared itself ready to suspend its oil shipments in support of a UN programme of sanctions; Southern Rhodesia and Mauritius stand to lose their cheapest source of manufactured imports, while the former and Mozambique would lose an important market for exports. A number of Asian and Soviet bloc countries, including Ceylon, China, Czechoslovakia and East Germany continue to trade with South Africa, although their governments are already committed to participation in sanctions. But clearly, the main burden of sanctions would be borne by the industrialised Western countries. Britain is South Africa's largest customer and largest source of supply; the United States comes second, with Japan a close third.

The economic objection to sanctions which looms largest in most people's minds is the fear that international liquidity would be seriously weakened by a halt in the flow of gold from the South African mines. The Republic's share in the total value of gold production in the non-Soviet world rose in the past decade from about fifty to seventy per cent. If the sale of South African gold stopped, the annual flow would be reduced from £1,300 million to about £400 million. But less than half the annual production of new gold is currently absorbed in national monetary reserves; the rest goes into personal hoards or industrial and decorative uses. Thus it may be assumed that if South African gold exports stopped, nothing would be left to sustain an increase in world trade under the present system of financing trade. On the face of it, therefore, sanctions would have a catastrophic effect on liquidity in the non-Soviet world. But the outcome is less alarming when one considers the remedies which are available.

First, the combined members' gold holdings in the International Monetary Fund amount to some $17 billion. Only a small part of this needs to be released to compensate for a temporary halt in South Africa's supplies. Second, commercial bank reserves in 1962 amounted to $12 billion; these could also be drawn on. Third, the United States' domestic note issue is still backed by a 25 per cent holding of gold. If this outdated requirement were ended—and there is already strong pressure that it should—the United States need only run down its stocks by 5½ per cent a year to offset the total shortfall caused by loss of South African supplies.[1] All these remedies are immediately available, quite apart from several international schemes already being canvassed in monetary circles to increase world liquidity on the current gold base, which is in any case inadequate. But even if none of these long-term remedies proved acceptable, the loss of a year or two's supplies of gold from South Africa could be relatively easily sustained by short-term remedial measures. It is inconceivable that South Africa could hold out for anything like as long as two years, or even one year.

The fact that South African gold is sold through the London market is of no special advantage to Britain's balance of payments, since all British imports from South Africa, whether gold or grapes, are converted into sterling. The only losers would be London's bullion dealers who would relinquish the commissions on their gold dealings for the duration of sanctions.

What of the effects on Britain's economy and balance of payments of a total, but temporary, cessation of economic relations? About 30 per cent of South Africa's trade is with Britain. Exports to South Africa have an annual value of almost £150 million; and these represent 4 to 4.5 per cent of total exports. The largest item is the sale of manufactured goods, valued at between £135 million and £140 million a year. It has been estimated[1] that about 150,000 people are employed in the manufacture of goods destined for South Africa and in their transportation to British ports. Even if one assumed that not all would be rendered unemployed by the temporary ending of trade with South Africa and that, with full employment, the rest would soon be absorbed in other jobs, the numbers and disruption involved is by no means insignificant. The worst affected industries would be railway vehicles (20.2 per cent of whose exports go to South Africa); electrical machinery (12.9 per cent); man-made fibre yarns and woven fabrics (9.8 per cent); wood and cork manufactures (9.7 per cent); cotton yarns and woven fabrics (9.4 per cent); paper and paperboard manufactures (7.4 per cent); and miscellaneous textile manufactures (5.2 per cent). In other industries, exports to South Africa account for less than 5 per cent of their total exports, and hence a tiny proportion of total production. But government assistance would clearly be necessary for firms hardest hit by a sanctions programme. Various proposals have been suggested. They range from simple compensation to the individual firms whose output or exports are severely affected, to the suggestion that the British government might make loans to the developing countries to the value of the losses in production suffered by badly affected firms, 'tying' the loans to their products. Such a programme could—but need not—be part of an international agreement along the lines suggested by Maxwell Stamp to create new purchasing power in the developing countries without damaging the liquidity of the industrialised nations. It need not involve the total figure of £140 million, representing the loss of the South African market; it would provide only for the combined losses of those firms which were substantially affected, and which could not easily find alternative export markets.

The next largest item to be affected by sanctions would be some £60 million[1] of investment income coming to British individuals and firms from capital investments in South Africa. This amount would represent a total loss to Britain's balance of payments for the duration of sanctions. Protection to those liable to losses could be offered by government purchase of stock for its own interest-bearing securities; while the British taxpayer could be compensated once sanctions have ended and South African stock again becomes marketable or productive. The loss of this income would not, however, entail unemployment in Britain.

The third comparatively substantial item in Britain's account with South Africa is freight and shipping, worth £15 to £20 million. It is not possible to assess accurately either the total employment involved or that part of the labour force which would be rendered unemployed by sanctions. It would in any case be a small proportion of those involved in the export of manufactured goods.

Britain's imports from South Africa are of the order of £100 million—about 2.5 per cent of total imports. Alternative sources of supply exist except possibly for gem diamonds. The higher prices which might follow sanctions—mainly of fruit and vegetables at certain seasons—would be borne by the final consumer. Thus the burden would be fairly equitably spread.

On the most pessimistic assumption—that Britain did not manage to find alternative markets for any of the £150 million worth of goods now sold to South Africa—Britain would be faced with a trade gap of £210 million (£150 million plus £60 million of investment income). Normally, a country experiencing a gap of this magnitude would have to resort either to import controls or to deflation of its economy. But if, as we assume, sanctions are internationally initiated and enforced, international mechanisms could be brought into play for dealing with member countries' balance of payments problems. It would also be possible to devise means for sharing the burden by agreement on the part of those countries less affected to take a proportion of Britain's former exports to South Africa.

Essentially the same problems and considerations would

apply to the economies of the United States and Japan and, to a much less extent, to Western Germany, Scandinavia, France, Switzerland and Italy. But even for the larger of these trading partners, the absolute amounts involved are much smaller than for Britain: in the case of the United States, the proportional impact upon exports and production would be negligible.

In showing that the economic problems involved in a programme of sanctions can be solved—and especially that their solution would be simplified by concerted international measures—we do not imply that the burdens can be lightly assumed. Those on whom the transitional burdens will fall will not unnaturally bring considerable pressure to bear on their governments to resist sanctions. When Mr Harold Wilson announced the Labour Party's intention, when in office, to ban the sale of all arms to South Africa, immediate pressures were applied by some trade unions. Though he firmly resisted them he would have much less freedom to manoeuvre once in office. It is hardly likely that even a strong Labour government would voluntarily initiate a unilateral programme of economic sanctions which would cause immediate unemployment and produce a large gap in the trade balance. The effects of such a move—whatever its moral advantages—would carry grave political risks. But the risk would be minimised if a UN decision made sanctions compulsory. A British government would find itself in a much stronger position if it contributed to sanctions in support of an international decision. Indeed, this is probably the only circumstance in which a British government—Labour or Conservative—could support sanctions. Similar considerations would almost certainly apply in the United States: it is hard to see how an American administration could overcome the pressures of the big business lobby for South Africa, unless it acted in concert with Britain and the rest of Western Europe.

So far we have considered only the short-term economic implications of sanctions. But there are bound to be serious anxieties about the longer-term implications. What guarantee is there that the interests of the Republic's present trading partners will be restored after sanctions have achieved their purpose? Might sanctions not cause a permanent change in the pattern of trade and investments? There is, of course, no absolute guarantee that economic relations will be resumed on the same terms as before. But there are good reasons for supposing that, if sanctions proved effective, a new South African government would find it expedient to resume business with its traditional partners. This is what has happened almost without exception in the case of former colonies after they achieved their independence. While their own economic relationships have expanded into a wider field, the share of their traditional trading partners has, on the whole, become larger not smaller. The significant exceptions have been found in situations where the new governments have come to power after a struggle against the business interests. If the established economic forces set themselves deliberately in opposition to the new authority then one must expect to find a weakening, if not a complete breach, of the old trading and economic patterns. Thus if a transfer of power is achieved in South Africa in the teeth of Western business opposition, then one may expect a serious loss to the interests of South Africa's present trading partners and traditional investors. But if the changes were to occur with the benign support—or, at least, without the active antagonism—of the present economic interests, they stand a good chance of survival under the new dispensation.

Naturally, a transfer of power in South Africa will produce a substantially different type of government. But South Africa will still need to import and export; its mines will still produce, and its factories will continue to operate. The possibility of large-scale nationalisation is remote, especially since a substantial sector of its economy—power, communications, steel—is already state-controlled. But a South African economy liberated from political uncertainty and from the artificial economic restraints of an industrial colour bar, will inevitably produce far greater economic opportunities than the country has known in the past. For the first time its human resources could be applied without inhibition to its natural wealth. And once its economy is geared and acceptable to the markets of Africa, South Africa can hope to become not only the most economically powerful nation in the continent, but one of the world's formidable middle powers, at least economically.

X

THE EFFECTS OF SANCTIONS
ON SOUTH AFRICA

There remain two related questions which must be answered to dispel reasonable doubts about the efficacy of sanctions. Could external pressures produce a situation inside South Africa in which negotiations might become possible between representative leaders of all the racial communities? Could sanctions be operated in a manner likely to produce these results without intensifying the inherent dangers of violence?

We have previously discussed the effects of the shocks already administered to white society by internal explosions and external pressures.* Each major shock has met with two responses: angry determination not to be deflected from the attempt to ensure the survival of white rule; and increasing anxiety and doubts about the consequences of rigidly pursuing policies which would isolate the Republic and invite international intervention.

The first reaction is always the more vociferous and emphatic. The anger and bluster of the white electorate are immediately and defiantly echoed in their leaders' speeches. They shake their fists at the world and proclaim their determination to 'fight to the last'. The 'last ditch' threat is common to all privileged groups fighting to retain power: it is a familiar feature of the verbal defiance of white communities in Africa. The second reaction—the more thoughtful mood which reflects the doubts and anxieties of many of the leaders and the intellectuals—is more tentatively expressed. It seldom comes through to the outside world, and when it does it is usually conveyed through private conversations.

But there are times when government leaders and influential Afrikaner newspapers reflect these doubts—usually mixed with protestations of defiance to soften the impact at home.

* See Part One, pp. 74–87 *passim*.

After the UN resolutions of September 1962, the toughest member of Dr Verwoerd's cabinet, Mr John Vorster, Minister of Justice, said: 'South Africa has a small population (*sic*) and it would be irresponsible of the government to ignore world opinion, but the government would neglect its duty if it did not carry out the mandate of the people. South Africa must make it clear that it is not the world's doormat.'[1]

Evidence of the private thoughts of the leaders of Afrikanerdom is given by Dr D. G. Scholtz, who edits Dr Verwoerd's paper, *Die Transvaler*, and who enjoys his close confidence: 'Many Afrikaners say the outside world has no say over us and that we are boss here. This sounds all very well. Everyone likes to be boss in his own country, but we cannot be boss over the non-whites. We have not yet come to realise what is happening in the world.'[2] A month later *Die Transvaler* repeated the warning: 'It would be foolish in the extreme to surrender to the pressure and the demands of the outside world but it would be equally foolish to expect that the present position can remain as it is to the end of time.'[3] And a year later—after a further Security Council debate—the same paper went a step further:

> The solution which must be found for this burning [race] problem must be such that it will satisfy thinking men elsewhere. It would naturally be futile to imagine that everyone would be prepared to endorse everything that is done in the Republic.... Still, the fact remains that the government will have to find a solution which a considerable section of public opinion in the rest of the world could accept as fair and right.... The position thus comes down to this: that on the one hand the government is obliged to take note of what is happening in the rest of the world and that, on the other hand, it has to do its best to try and protect white civilisation....[4]

Thus external pressure does not, as is commonly believed, have the single, exclusive effect of reinforcing stubborn resistance on the part of the white community. Notwithstanding the predominantly defiant reflex, natural to all human behaviour, external pressure has already had the effect of shaking the confidence of the white leadership. We have shown how the combination of internal explosion and external pressures

led the Afrikaner leaders to abandon their hope of maintaining
baasskap; unfortunately they became sidetracked into Separate
Development in the mistaken belief that the Bantustan policy
might restore Western confidence.* The rationale behind this
change in policy is that 'in so far as South Africa's race problems are being made more difficult by pressure from outside
(*sic*), and in so far as there would have to be any concessions
to this pressure, the policy of one-man one-vote for the black
man in his own homeland is infinitely more realistic and more
practical.'[1] Thus, although the response was inadequate, the
intentions reflect an awareness of the need to make concessions
in response to world pressures.

For all Dr Verwoerd's protestations that concessions are
a sign of weakness, his closest colleagues argue otherwise.
But whatever doubts they might have about defying international opinion, the thoughtful white leadership (especially
within Afrikanerdom) is still a prisoner of the electorate. We
have shown that while past pressures have produced significant
changes in the attitudes of Afrikaner leadership, they have
done little to alter the convictions of the electors.† Past
shocks have not been sufficient to shake fundamentally the
belief of the ordinary voters that the white man is still able to
maintain exclusive power. Only a profound trauma could
make them face up to the immediate dangers created by their
race policies. The force of reasoned argument will not alter
the experience and prejudices of centuries. Only power
greater than their own could induce them to accept the essential weakness of their position. But a show of force would
not suffice. They would have to experience a direct attack on
their well-being—not necessarily one of physical violence—
before there can be any hope of basic changes in attitudes.
Until that point is reached we cannot expect the political initiative to move from the obdurate to the more flexible white
leaders.

What sequence of events might be expected once a firm
decision is taken to embark on a programme of sanctions?
Clearly, the answers must be speculative; but informed predic-
tion is a necessary ingredient of success. One assessment

---

* See Part One, p. 52 *et seq.*
† See, for example, Part One, pp. 83–5.

allows for the possibility that the Verwoerd Government would resign or engage in diversionary tactics such as offering to open negotiations, at least with certain Western governments, as soon as it became apparent that sanctions could not be evaded. But it would be safer to assume that the government and the white community would determine first to exploit to the utmost their capacity for defiance. In that case there are likely to be four stages in the struggle to make sanctions fully effective.

The first stage would open with the UN commitment to mount sanctions. There is bound to be a period of ultimatum between a UN call for a National Convention and the implementation of sanctions, and there may be a further period of perhaps a month after sanctions have been imposed when the ordinary lives of whites will remain relatively untouched economically. During this first stage the conservative 90 per cent of the two white communities will draw closer together. At worst, a national government might be formed to provide a single laager. Alternatively, the opposition United Party will maintain its independence hoping to inherit power when the electorate loses faith in the National Party's ability to meet the situation. The radical 10 per cent (the Progressives, the liberals and the socialists) will stand out to prevent a wholly unified white front, and may even enlarge their numbers by absorbing some of the more thoughtful or anxious members of the major parties. They will become more important as a possible bridge between the polarised white and black forces.

The second stage—when sanctions begin to cause economic trouble—is likely to see approaches made by the South African government to Western nations. It is likely to suggest alternatives to the negotiations demanded by the United Nations, putting forward its own ideas about a new constitution, and possibly offering to explore a phased programme of real partition. Meanwhile, the government will be engaged in mobilising the country's economic and military resources, ready to deal ruthlessly with any premature tendency on the part of the African population to show its own strength. If its approaches are resisted—as they certainly should be if sanctions are to be effective—the third stage will begin.

This is likely to produce a change of government under the pressures of growing unemployment among whites as well as non-whites, and increasing disillusionment, insecurity and anxiety. There is bound to be a profound reaction when the white electorate realises that the power of the white aristocracy has ended. The new government might be a coalition between the United Party and the 'moderates' in the National Party. Its first action will probably be to reopen negotiations through Western contacts to try to achieve a *modus vivendi* with the United Nations. The temptations to 'give the new government a chance' would be strong, particularly since the overthrow of the Verwoerd régime would immediately create a sense of release inside South Africa. This may well prove the moment of greatest danger to UN unity: there are likely to be strong pressures to allow the new government the opportunities it will request to abandon apartheid and produce its own new constitution.

The temptation must be resisted. No white government can undertake the effective transfer of power which is the essential prerequisite for the creation of political stability. The *sine qua non* for the suspension of sanctions is agreement to hold a fully representative National Convention to prepare a new constitution. If the United Nations were to relent at the moment one minority white government replaced another, it would not only undermine the purpose of the operation; it would create an even more explosive situation in South Africa —the result of frustrated hopes, exploded expectations and a doubly frightened white population.

The success of a UN programme of sanctions depends on the acceptance of its objectives by all member states. If the West reneged before the basic objectives were achieved, the South African situation would be left wide open for an international struggle with cold war politics as well as racial rivalries competing for influence and power. South Africa would be the sure loser in such a struggle; and the West might see itself permanently damaged not only in South Africa but in the rest of the continent as well. These considerations impose the need for maintaining genuine collective action within an agreed UN mandate.

If the temptation to suspend sanctions at this stage were resisted, the fourth and final stage would be entered with the South African government having no alternative but to negotiate the composition and terms of a representative National Convention. Provided the blockade had not been breached, this final stage can be expected within six months of the onset of sanctions, but could be very much sooner. The state of the economy at this stage would naturally depend upon the speed of the preceding events. Having achieved the primary objective of a National Convention, the United Nations would suspend sanctions; it might be necessary also to introduce measures to relieve cases of severe hardship. But the machinery for sanctions should be kept intact. The process of settling conflicting claims to representation at the Convention could involve delay: it will be necessary for a sense of urgency to be preserved. The white government—whatever its composition—will certainly prefer to lay emphasis on the traditional and middle-class African leadership, which will be disputed by the African nationalists. Algeria provides a useful lesson. In its search for a favourable negotiated settlement, France wasted several years in achieving agreement first with the 'moderates', the apolitical traditionalists and the middle-class, and later with the discredited militant, Messali Hadj; finally it had to come to terms with the FLN. It is essential to recognise that, just as the FLN had established its authority over Muslim Algeria, the African nationalists are today the politically dominant force among black South Africans. No durable settlement can be achieved without their agreement, whatever other interests are also represented. Nor should it be supposed that the conflicts within the nationalist movement are profound enough seriously to delay agreement between them.

The opening of negotiations should not be considered the end of the road: it could mark the point of the greatest danger of an outbreak of violence. With sanctions suspended, the white leaders might lose their earlier sense of urgency and seek once again to establish their authority by playing for time, by seeking to separate the Western countries from the United Nations, and by trying to divide the Africans. If such a situation were allowed to develop unchecked the predictable outcome would be black violence. Delaying tactics such as those used by Mr Tshombe in the Congo could be disastrous in South Africa.

The possibilty of violence from the white side is no less threatening. The militants within Afrikanerdom have a habit of repudiating a formerly trusted leadership which compromises. They regard their former leaders as *hensoppers* (handsuppers), and themselves as glorious *bittereinders* (bitter-enders). Such a group may be formed at the moment of agreement to negotiate with representative non-whites. They could be compared to the Algerian OAS. A violent conflict between the whites might well produce intervention by the Africans, and the result could be chaotic.

It would be irresponsible for protagonists of sanctions to bilk these dangers. But by anticipating them steadily it is possible to avert them altogether, or to minimise their effects. Certain conditions are essential to a successful outcome at stage four. The first is that sanctions be concerted, enforced, and not seriously breachable. A programme of sanctions which goes off at half-cock, or which is subsequently defied by a major trading nation, would be disastrous. Second, the objectives of sanctions must be agreed and accepted by all member nations before they are introduced, and no South African group must be led to expect that it can rely on introducing direct foreign support for its own objectives. Third, sanctions' machinery should remain intact until an agreement has been reached.

Although the United Nations should not attempt to dictate the detailed terms of a settlement, common sense demands that both sides accept two fundamental principles: unless they do, they cannot be regarded as negotiating seriously. The first is that representative government must mean majority rule, and that there can be no evading the political predominance of the Africans. The second is that the rights of all citizens should be effectively safeguarded under the constitution. To suppose that a stable South Africa could emerge from its trauma with a flexible, unitary constitution based on the simple formula of unfettered majority rule is gravely to under-estimate the bitter fruits of the past. While the minority cannot be permitted—as in Cyprus—to hold the majority to ransom, they must nevertheless be protected against arbitrary or vengeful discrimination. No responsible African leader in South Africa today denies this proposition.

Provided both sides accept these principles and are seriously engaged in translating them into an agreed constitution, the United Nations and its member states need apply no further pressure. The details of the settlement must be left to the South Africans themselves. The United Nations should play the role of the midwife who limits her function to seeing that the contractions are kept going.

Although these precautions would diminish the risk that violence or delay might be used inside South Africa to influence the course of negotiations, the possibility cannot be discounted altogether. The United Nations should be prepared, if the necessity arises, to provide a 'Fire Brigade'. Such a limited operation would be useful only if violence were restricted to a minority of either community; large-scale fighting could be halted only by negotiations, possibly accompanied by massive military intervention. The surest discouragement of large-scale violence would be if both sides felt that fruitful negotiations were under way. But if violence were used by either side to influence the negotiations, or if minority elements could not be contained locally, the 'Fire Brigade' should be available at short notice.

What kind of agreement might reasonably be expected to emerge from the negotiations? It is unrealistic to expect that the situation any longer allows for a solution which would satisfy everyone. The best hope would be a settlement providing the framework for a non-racial society to evolve as old wounds healed. It may be that the only way to get negotiations started would be to agree to explore the establishment of one or two largely white areas within a federal state. These could not lie within the country's richest areas, which are today predominantly non-white, and which in any case form the economic heart of the state of South Africa. Despite African and white liberal reluctance to accept white segregated areas within a state striving towards an integrated society, a willingness at least to explore such a proposal might prove to be a not impossibly high price to pay for a peaceful transfer of power.

It is possible that international guarantees might be requested for the constitutional safeguards for a transition period. International help might also be necessary to replace the present security and police forces until a new integrated local force could be trained. It is inconceivable that the police and army, as presently constituted, could offer an effective instrument for security for a different kind of government. Yet a vital requirement during the difficult and dangerous years of the transfer of power is the loyalty of large, well-trained disciplined security forces. These could not be created overnight. A United Nations' police force, responsible to the new government, might be considered to undertake immediate security duties and the training of a fully integrated police and security force. Such a force could provide protection both for the new government and for the white minority.

These suggestions are not intended to prejudge the outcome of negotiations. They are meant to show that a transfer of power need not be followed by a situation in which the non-African communities would find it impossible to rebuild their lives in the land of their birth. And they help to pinpoint a few of the more urgent requirements which might be needed to buttress the new state until its own social and political forces have had a chance to coalesce.

It may broadly be concluded that the possibility of inducing a non-violent transition exists, but that it is accompanied by risks. These are predictable and can therefore be minimised. Not all the risks enumerated are certain to arise. In any event, they are minimal compared to the dangers of allowing the situation to deteriorate to the predictable point where international intervention would have to take the form of a rescue operation for the whites.

Four guiding principles are suggested for the achievement of optimum security. First, collective action must be devised in pursuit of the defined objectives of securing negotiations between representative South Africans to produce a new representative government under a constitution which effectively safeguards human rights. Second, these objectives should not be reduced, enlarged, or suspended before they have been achieved. Third, cold war elements should be neutralised by a United Nations' Supervisory Committee (including the major powers and a number of small nations) keeping a close watch on developments and reporting unilateral intervention to the Security Council for appropriate action. This would discourage

attempts to exploit the situation either by the major powers
or by neighbouring states.   Fourth, military intervention
should be avoided as a form of sanctions; but the United
Nations should have in readiness a 'Fire Brigade' to deal with
any South African appeal for assistance to limit or prevent an
outbreak of violence.

XI

CONCLUSIONS

If civic peace is to endure, the law must rest upon the consent of all men of goodwill; while the majority is entitled to govern, the minority must be safeguarded in its rights: and the order established by law must be just and must be seen and felt to be so.

Sir Alec Douglas-Home, 1964

We share the general distaste for economic sanctions as a means of settling international disputes. It is a blunt weapon, the consequences of which cannot be easily foreseen or controlled. Nor do we disagree with those critics who believe that sanctions carry considerable risks. If there were a reasonable, non-violent alternative to sanctions as a means of effectively dealing with the South African crisis, we would be the first to welcome it.

But is it not enough to reject sanctions on these grounds? Those who do should suggest an alternative course of action. So far, no serious alternative has been put forward. The arguments for doing nothing, and hoping that time and economic forces will provide a solution, do not amount to an alternative policy. They can only lead to a race war, in which the international community must become involved.

The choice before us, therefore, seems to lie between a race war and international economic sanctions. The question is: which of these alternatives offers the greatest risks to the whites and the non-whites in South Africa, to the international community, and to the West? Those who argue that this is not a fair statement of the alternatives must show how the corroding influences inside the Republic can be counteracted before racial bitterness and mounting violence become unmanageable. The evidence of the last sixteen years of apartheid is not easily controverted.

Nor can we choose between international intervention and non-intervention. Intervention is already a fact of international life, and an active ingredient in the affairs of South Africa. There is no way of halting it. The question is whether it can be enlarged and controlled by collective action through the United Nations, or whether South Africa will become the scene of diffuse unilateral intervention. These are the only real alternatives.

Unilateral intervention means a free-for-all; collective action offers a reasonable chance of producing controlled change. It is not difficult to decide which of these would better serve the interests of all the races in South Africa, and of the international community as well.

The proposals we have outlined for a UN programme of sanctions are designed to minimise the dangers of violence and chaos. We have not ignored the serious problems which might have to be faced. Sanctions might achieve unexpectedly swift results—especially if used first over South West Africa. But we believe it is wiser to anticipate all the difficulties which might be encountered. Certainly, sanctions should not be lightly entered into: all the difficulties must be considered and action carefully planned to ensure effectiveness. If the problem were approached in this way, the difficulties would not be insuperable—provided there is full accord within the United Nations.

If, on the other hand, sanctions were finally rejected then we believe the UN must lose no time in planning for massive military intervention to bale out the white community in the not too distant future.

The South African crisis is by no means the most difficult one the UN is likely to have to face; but it is the most urgent. Fortunately, it is also the first major crisis on the principles of which the UN is virtually unanimous. If the UN should fail to muster the political will and the courage to intervene effectively—without resort to military force—the consequences for its future will be no less serious than the fate of the League of Nations when it failed to respond to successive challenges to its authority.

If the UN should fail to meet the challenge, the West will be seen to carry the major responsibility. It is difficult to imagine how the race conflagration, which must follow, can be dealt with by the UN, with its own prestige and significance diminished, and with the authority of the West deservedly undermined.

It is misleading to press the analogy between Hitler's Germany and Verwoerd's Republic; but in their threat to world order they have one feature in common: both represent a situation in which human beings can become victims of violence purely on the grounds of their race. In an age dominated by the fact of the universal urge to liberation of the world's coloured races, the threat of black-white conflict is no less serious than the racial animosities which Hitler provoked. In the 1930s the powerful pro-German lobbies, and the combination of timid statesmen and short-term national interests, rendered prophylactic action impossible. These forces could succeed again. If they do, the cause of world order and racial harmony will have been dealt another disastrous blow. South Africa's sufferings will be many times magnified on the world scene.

A BRIEF GUIDE TO REFERENCES

Frequent references are made to the following South African newspapers and publications:

Burger: Capetown daily; pro-government; reflects views of its least extremist wing.

Britain and South Africa: newsletter of South Africa Foundation, London.

Cape Times: Capetown daily, supports the United Party; sometimes takes a radical line, especially over civil liberties.

Cape Argus: Capetown daily; supports United Party.

Contact: Capetown monthly; organ of the Liberal Party.

Dagbreek en Sondagnuus: Johannesburg Sunday paper; supports apartheid, but adopts independent line towards government.

Evening Post: Port Elizabeth daily; supports Progressive Party policies; trenchant defender of English language rights.

Forward: Johannesburg monthly; journal of Labour and trade union opinion.

Financial Mail: Johannesburg weekly; independent, well-informed, critical.

Journal of Racial Affairs: Stellenbosch quarterly; organ of the South African Bureau of Racial Affairs (SABRA).

Nataller: pro-government; organ of the Natal Afrikaner nationalists.

Natal Mercury: Durban daily; conservative; anti-government; pro-United Party.

Oosterlig: Port Elizabeth daily; pro-government.

Perspective: London monthly produced by South Africa Foundation.

Pretoria News: anti-government, pro-United Party.

Race Relations News: Johannesburg monthly; organ of the South African Institute of Race Relations.

Rand Daily Mail: Johannesburg daily; adopts radical anti-government position; sympathetic to Progressive Party.

Sunday Times: Johannesburg Sunday paper; vehemently anti-government, uncritically pro-United Party.

Sunday Express: Johannesburg Sunday; anti-government.

Star: Johannesburg daily; anti-government and pro-United Party.

Southern Africa: London weekly; anti-government, but patriotically defends it against overseas critics.

Transvaler: Johannesburg daily; usually regarded as the personal organ of Dr Verwoerd.

Vaderland: Johannesburg daily; strongly pro-government.

Volksblad: Bloemfontein daily; voice of Afrikaner nationalists in Orange Free State. Uncritically pro-government.

REFERENCES

Page 7
[1] M. K. Jeffreys, *Kaapse Plakkate*, 1, Capetown, 1944.

Page 8
[1] Theal, *Belangrijke Historische Dokumenten*, 1.
[2] Commissioner-General Van Imdhoff, quoted by Scholtz in *The Origins and Essence of the Race Pattern in South Africa* (SABRA, Stellenbosch, 1958).
[3] de Jong, *Reizen Naar de Kaap de Goede Hoop*, 1, Haarlem, 1802.
[4] The Rev. D. Van der Hoff, State Archives, Pretoria, Lauts Collection.

Page 9
[1] *The Star*, Johannesburg, January 8, 1903.

Page 10
[1] Albert Lutuli, 'The Effect of Minority Rule on Non-Whites', *The Road Ahead*, Capetown, 1960.

Page 11
[1] *Hansard*, South African House of Assembly Debates, 1913.
[2] *Ibid.*
[3] *Gedenkschriften van Paul Kruger*, Amsterdam, 1902.

Page 25
[1] From a private document presented to Gen. Smuts.

Page 28
[1] *The Friend*, Bloemfontein, November 8, 1935.

Page 29
[1] Prof. A. Morrees, *Die Nederduits Gereformeerde Lerk in Suid Afrika 1652-1873* (Capetown, 1937).

Page 30
[1] Quoted in *South Africa*, London, September 26, 1959.
[2] Quoted in *Evening Post*, Port Elizabeth, March 30, 1963.

Page 31
[1] *Cape Times*, November 4, 1963.

Page 32
[1] *Sunday Times*, Johannesburg, October 6, 1963.

Page 33
[1] Quoted by Bernard Sachs, *The Road from Sharpeville*, London, 1961.
[2] *Woord en Daad*, March 1960.

Page 35
[1] G. R. von Wielligh, *Persoonlike Herinneringe van die Patriot-manne: Gedenkboek Genootskap van Regte Africaners 1875-1918* (Potcheftstroom, 1925-6).

Page 38
[1] *No Further Trek*, Johannesburg, 1957.
[2] *Cape Times*, May 4, 1959.

Page 44
[1] *Financial Mail*, Johannesburg, December 27, 1963.
[2] *Financial Mail*, Johannesburg, November 15, 1963.

Page 45
[1] *Journal of Racial Affairs*, SABRA, Stellenbosch, April, 1961.

Page 46
[1] *Volkshandel*, December, 1961.

Page 47
[1] An interesting account of this struggle is to be found in E. S. Sachs, *Rebel Daughters*, London, 1957.

Page 50
[1] D. W. Krüger, *South African Parties and Policies*, London, 1960.

Page 51
[1] *Hansard*, South African House of Assembly Debates, No. 11, Cols. 4141-2.
[2] Quoted by Stanley Uys, *Sunday Times*, Johannesburg, January 27, 1963.

Page 52
[1] *Hansard*, South African House of Assembly Debates, September 15, 1958, Col. 3805.

Page 53
[1] D. V. Cowen, 'Constitution-making for a Democracy', supplement to *Optima*, Anglo-American Corporation, Johannesburg, 1960.

Page 54
[1] *South Africa and the Rule of Law*, International Commission of Jurists, Geneva, 1960.

Page 55
[1] In a personal conversation with one of the authors.
[2] Dr Verwoerd, *Die Burger*, October 9, 1961.
[3] Dr Verwoerd, *The Star*, Johannesburg, September 21, 1963.

Page 56
[1] Dr Verwoerd, *Dagbreek*, August 26, 1962.
[2] Dr Verwoerd, *The Star*, Johannesburg, June 4, 1960.

Page 57
[1] October 3, 1961.

Page 58
1 Mr de Wet Nel, Minister of Bantu Affairs and Development, in *South Africa Today*, October 1960.

Page 59
1 SABRA'S *Journal of Racial Affairs*, March 1962.
2 *Southern Africa*, London, April 27, 1962.
3 *The Transkei and the Case for Separate Development*, Department of Information, South African Embassy, London, December, 1963.
4 *Die Transvaler*, March 16, 1963.

Page 60
1 In an official statement, January 1963.
2 Presidential Address to the South African Institute of Race Relations, 1964.

Page 61
1 *Cape Times*, November 18, 1963.

Page 62
1 *Die Transvaler*, November 13, 1963.
2 Proceedings of the 1962 Session of Transkei Territorial Assembly, p. 33.
3 December 2, 1963.

Page 63
1 Johannesburg, December 6, 1963.
2 *Cape Times*, February 6, 1963.
3 *The Transkei and the Case for Separate Development*, *op. cit.*, p. 8.

Page 64
1 Professor J. L. Sadie, SABRA'S *Journal of Racial Affairs*, January 1960.
2 P. S. Toerien, *ibid.*, March 1962.
3 A report on the initial reactions was given by Mr Walter Stanford, then MP for Transkei, to Parliament in 1959. A summary of his report was published in *Race Relations News*, Johannesburg, May 1959.
4 *The Star*, Johannesburg, April 29, 1961.

Page 65
1 *Survey of Race Relations*, 1962, Institute of Race Relations, Johannesburg.
2 Quoted in *The Star*, Johannesburg, August 10, 1963.

Page 66
1 i.e. Mr M. C. de Wet Nel, Minister of Bantu Affairs and Development.
2 February 4, 1963.
3 Statement made by the Minister of Justice in Parliament, *Hansard*, January 24, 1964.

314

⁴ *Die Transvaler*, May 3, 1963.
⁵ Quoted by Stanley Uys, *Sunday Times*, Johannesburg, January 27, 1963.

Page 67
¹ *Hansard*, South African House of Assembly Debates, September 15, 1958, Col. 3805.
² *South Africa*, London, March 29, 1959.
³ *Hansard*, May 17, 1963.
⁴ *The Star*, Johannesburg, January 25, 1964.
⁵ *The Transkei and the Case for Separate Development*, op. cit.
⁶ *Die Transvaler*, May 4, 1963.

Page 68
¹ May 6, 1962.
² Mr J. H. Abraham, Commissioner-General of the Transkei, *Die Burger*, September 26, 1962.
³ Dr P. S. Rauterbach, SABRA'S *Journal of Racial Affairs*, October 1960.

Page 69
¹ Report of the Commission on the Socio-Economic Development of the Bantu Areas ('Tomlinson Report'), Pretoria, 1955.
² South African Institute of Race Relations, Council Meeting, January 1962.
³ SABRA'S *Journal of Racial Affairs*, March 1962.

Page 70
¹ January 10, 1963.

Page 71
¹ *Optima*, Johannesburg, March 1962.
² 'Economic Future of the Homelands', *Cape Times*, November 19, 1963.
³ *Forward*, Johannesburg, January 1964.

Page 72
¹ Mr W. A. Maree, Minister for Bantu Education and Indian Affairs, *Die Burger*, November 17, 1962.

Page 73
¹ Mr de Wet Nel, *Die Transvaler*, May 7, 1960.
² *Ibid.*, *The Star*, Johannesburg, October 19, 1963.

Page 74
¹ Presidential Address to South African Institute of Race Relations, January 1964.
² *Die Transvaler*, December 8, 1961.

Page 75
¹ G. D. Scholtz, *Het Die Afrikaanse Volk 'n Toekoms?*, Johannesburg, 1954.
² *Ibid.*, 'The Origins and Essence of the Race Pattern in South

Africa', *Fact Paper 61*, South African Information Department, Pretoria, 1958.
3 *Die Transvaler*, September 15, 1958.

Page 76
1 *Die Oosterlig*, December 8, 1961.

Page 77
1 *Die Burger*, April 7, 1961.
2 *Die Transvaler*, November 7, 1960.
3 *Die Burger*, April 17, 1961.
4 *Ibid.*, May 17, 1961.
5 *Die Transvaler*, May 16, 1961.
6 *Ibid.*, April 18, 1961.

Page 78
1 *Die Transvaler*, November 22, 1961.
2 *Ibid.*, June 1, 1963.
3 Mr J. J. Fouché, the Minister of Defence, *The Star*, Johannesburg, April 6, 1963.
4 *Die Transvaler*, May 31, 1963; and *The Star*, Johannesburg, May 30, 1963.
5 *Southern Africa*, London, September 13, 1963.
6 *Cape Times*, February 23, 1963.
7 Statement in The Senate, 1963.

Page 79
1 *Die Vaderland*, March 13, 1962.
2 Quoted in *The Star*, Johannesburg, October 26, 1963.
3 *Die Transvaler*, December 6, 1963.
4 *The Star*, Johannesburg, April 6, 1963.
5 *South Africa*, London, July 19, 1963.
6 'Crisis in World Conscience', *Fact Paper 107*, South African Information Department, 1963.

Page 80
1 *Die Burger*, July 16, 1963.
2 *Die Transvaler*, May 3, 1963.
3 Mr W. A. Maree, Minister of Bantu Education and Indian Affairs, December 18, 1962.
4 Senator J. F. Naude, President of the Senate, *Die Burger*, April 7, 1962.
5 *Die Kerkblad*, quoted in *Die Burger*, May 2, 1963.
6 Mr J. N. Malan, Administrator of the Cape Province, *Die Burger*, October 20, 1962.
7 Mr J. P. Bruwer of Stellenbosch University and a leading figure in SABRA.
8 *Die Nataller*, September 29, 1961.
9 Mr J. H. Schoeman, lecturer at the South African Police College, *Die Transvaler*, August 18, 1961.
10 *Die Burger*, May 24, 1960.

316

Page 81
1 *Die Burger*, July 10, 1963.
2 Dr W. M. Eiselen, Commissioner-General of the North Sotho, *The Star*, Johannesburg, April 13, 1963.
3 *Die Transvaler*, December 3, 1963.
4 *Die Burger*, March 30, 1962.
5 *Die Transvaler*, February 11, 1963.

Page 82
1 Willem van Heerden, *Dagbreek*, September 9, 1962.
2 *Die Burger*, May 17, 1963.
3 M. C. Botha, deputy Minister of Bantu Administration and Development, *Die Transvaler*, September 24, 1962.
4 *Die Transvaler*, October 2, 1961.
5 *Ibid.*, October 6, 1961.

Page 83
1 *Die Burger*, September 25, 1962.
2 *Dagbreek*, November 13, 1960.
3 *The Star*, Johannesburg, May 20, 1961.

Page 84
1 *Cape Argus*, February 19, 1963.

Page 85
1 *Die Volksblad*, August 19, 1963.
2 Mr D. F. Potgieter, MP, *Natal Mercury*, August 22, 1962.
3 *Die Transvaler*, December 19, 1962.
4 *Dagbreek*, September 9, 1962.

Page 86
1 *The Star*, Johannesburg, December 16, 1960.
2 *Die Transvaler*, December 17, 1960.
3 *Die Burger*, March 13, 1962.
4 *The Star*, Johannesburg, May 9, 1959.

Page 87
1 *The Times*, January 21, 1964.
2 *Ibid.*, January 22, 1964.
3 *Die Transvaler*, July 19, 1963.
4 *Ibid.*, April 27, 1963.
5 Dr Verwoerd, *The Times*, January 22, 1964.
6 *Die Transvaler*, October 14, 1963.
7 Dr N. J. Diederichs, Minister of Economic Affairs, *Cape Times*, March 25, 1963.

Page 88
1 Willem van Heerden, *Die Dagbreek*, August 17, 1963.
2 *Die Volksblad*, July 18, 1963.
3 *Die Vaderland*, October 29, 1963.
4 *Die Burger*, December 14, 1962.
5 *Ibid.*, January 1, 1964.

Page 89
[1] *The Star*, Johannesburg, May 9, 1959.
[2] *Southern Africa*, London, July 5, 1963.
[3] *Die Transvaler*, October 11, 1962.
[4] Quoted in *The Times*, March 10, 1960.
[5] *Die Burger*, March 13, 1962.

Page 90
[1] *Die Transvaler*, May 25, 1963.
[2] *Rand Daily Mail*, January 1, 1963.
[3] *Die Vaderland*, October 29, 1963.

Page 91
[1] *Die Transvaler*, August 9, 1963.
[2] *Dagbreek*, November 18, 1962.
[3] *Die Transvaler*, November 9, 1962.

Page 93
[1] Dr Verwoerd, *The Times*, January 22, 1964.
[2] *Die Vaderland*, January 17, 1964.
[3] Chairman of the commission of enquiry into *Poqo*; *Southern Africa*, London, July 19, 1963.
[4] *Die Transvaler*, April 27, 1963.

Page 94
[1] *Dagbreek*, December 1, 1963.
[2] *Ibid.*, August 12, 1962.
[3] *New York Times*, September 5, 1963.
[4] *Die Volksblad*, August 13, 1962.

Page 95
[1] *Dagbreek*, November 18, 1962.

Page 101
[1] *Contact*, Capetown, August 9, 1962.
[2] *Sunday Times*, Johannesburg, September 29, 1963.

Page 103
[1] Christian Molefe, *The Church and the Race Problem*, published by the *Rand Daily Mail*, 1963.
[2] *The Star*, Johannesburg, October 26, 1963.

Page 106
[1] *Safeguarding your Future: The Principles and Policies of the Progressive Party of South Africa*, Durban, n.d.

Page 107
[1] November 17, 1962.
[2] *Non-Racial Democracy: The Policies of the Liberal Party of South Africa*, Pietermaritzburg, n.d.

Page 110
[1] *Britain and South Africa*, South African Foundation, London, June 6, 1962.
[2] *Ibid.*, May 7, 1962.
[3] *Cape Times*, March 2, 1963.

Page 113
[1] *The Story of the South African Foundation*, Johannesburg, 1962.
[2] *Ibid.*
[3] *Ibid.*
[4] *Ibid.*
[5] Quoted from a cyclostyled letter to a business firm, Johannesburg, July 18, 1962.

Page 114
[1] *Cape Times*, April 13, 1963.
[2] *The Star*, Johannesburg, November 26, 1960.

Page 116
[1] Quoted in *The Star*, Johannesburg, June 16, 1962.
[2] *Southern Africa*, London, June 1, 1962.

Page 118
[1] *Cape Times*, October 18, 1961.
[2] *Ibid.*
[3] *Ibid.*

Page 119
[1] *Southern Africa*, London, November 2, 1962.
[2] Cf. his address to the Royal Commonwealth Society, London. November 3, 1960.
[3] *Southern Africa*, London, November 2, 1962.

Page 120
[1] *The Times*, London, June 9, 1961.
[2] *Cape Times*, October 18, 1961.
[3] *Daily Telegraph*, London, May 29, 1962.
[4] Chairman's statement to Anglo-American Corporation, *The Times*, London, June 9, 1961.
[5] *Ibid.*

Page 121
[1] *Rand Daily Mail*, September 17, 1963.

Page 122
[1] *Daily Telegraph*, September 26, 1961.
[2] *The Times*, London, June 9, 1961.
[3] *The Times*, June 9, 1961.

Page 123
[1] *The Star*, Johannesburg, October 7, 1961.

Page 124
[1] *An Expanding Economy*, Department of Information, South African Embassy, London, 1962.

Page 126
[1] *The Guardian*, London, June 2, 1961.

Page 127
[1] *Britain and South Africa*, London, April 3, 1962.

Page 128
1 *Southern Africa*, London, February 7, 1964.
2 *Perspective*, London, October, 1963.

Page 129
1 Quoted in *Daily Mail*, May 15, 1963.
2 *Perspective*, London, October 1963.
3 Press Release, Booth's Distilleries Ltd., London, November 6, 1962.

Page 130
1 *Britain and South Africa*, London, July 5, 1962.
2 *Ibid.*, May 7, 1962.

Page 131
1 *Britain and South Africa*, London, April 16, 1964.

Page 132
1 *Britain and South Africa*, London, May 7, 1962.
2 *Ibid.*, August 13, 1963.

Page 133
1 *Britain and South Africa*, London, April 4, 1963.

Page 134
1 *Britain and South Africa*, London, June 6, 1962.
2 *Ibid.*, May 7, 1962.

Page 135
1 Mr Peter Runge, President of the Federation of British Industries, *Financial Mail*, Johannesburg, November 5, 1963.
2 *Cape Times*, December 1963.

Page 137
1 *Financial Mail*, October 11, 1963.
2 *Ibid.*, October 11, 1963.

Page 139
1 South African Information Services Release, March 1962.

Page 143
1 *Sunday Times*, Johannesburg, January 26, 1964.
2 *Natal Mercury*, July 23, 1963.
3 Personal statement to one of the authors.

Page 144
1 Natal *Daily News*, April 25, 1963.
2 In a statement made in London in 1960.
3 *Pretoria Daily News*, December 16, 1961.

Page 147
1 This epigram is reported by Monica Hunter in her classic study of the Xhosas, *Reaction to Conquest*, Oxford University Press, 1936.

320

Page 151
[1] *Die Transvaler*, January 23, 1963.
Page 152
[1] *Die Transvaler*, March 21, 1962.
Page 154
[1] *Die Burger*, May 3, 1960.
[2] *Die Volksblad*, May 7, 1960.
[3] Margaret Roberts, *Labour in the Farm Economy*, South African Institute of Race Relations, 1958.
Page 155
[1] S. J. du Toit, Address given at the 1959 Council meeting of the South African Institute of Race Relations.
Page 159
[1] *The Black Sash*, October/November, 1963.
Page 160
[1] Mrs R. N. Robb, director of the Athlone Advice Centre *Cape Times*, November 30, 1962.
Page 161
[1] For studies of these groups see P. Mayer, *Townsmen or Tribesmen?*, Oxford University Press, London, 1961; and D. H. Reader, *The Black Man's Portion*, Oxford University Press, London, 1961.
Page 162
[1] *Southern Africa*, London, November 8, 1963.
[2] *Medical Proceedings*, Johannesburg, 1960.
Page 164
[1] Z. K. Matthews, 'The Tribal Spirit Among Educated Africans', *Man*, February 1935.
Page 169
[1] Mr J. D. Zeka, Principal of the Langa High School, *Cape Times*, December 6, 1962.
Page 170
[1] *Contact*, Capetown.
Page 171
[1] Dr O. D. Wollheim, chairman of the Western Cape Region of the South African Institute of Race Relations, *Cape Times*, November 11, 1963.
Page 178
[1] *Contact*, May 30, 1960.
Page 179
[1] Pan Africanist Congress Press Release, October 15, 1962.
Page 180
[1] *Southern Africa*, London, July 19, 1963.

Page 181
[1] Jordan K. Ngubane, *An African Explains Apartheid*, Praeger, New York; Pall Mall, London, 1963.

Page 184
[1] Quoted in Mary Benson, *The African Patriots*, Faber, London, 1963.
[2] *Ibid.*

Page 185
[1] For full statement see Record of Supreme Court (Special Criminal Court), Pretoria, Regina versus Farid Adams and Others, March 29, 1961. A brief report appears in *The Times*, March 30, 1961.

Page 186
[1] South African Information Department *Fact Paper*, *107*, Pretoria, 1963.
[2] *Die Oosterlig*, May 1961.

Page 187
[1] Lewis Nkosi, 'Propaganda and the Non-Violent Struggle in South Africa', Paper read to the American Society for African Culture, Washington, 1962.
[2] J. C. de Ridder, *The Personality of the Urban African in South Africa*, Routledge and Kegan Paul, London, 1962.
[3] D. H. Reader, *The Black Man's Portion*, Oxford University Press, London, 1961.

Page 188
[1] Philip Mayer, *Townsmen or Tribesmen?*, Oxford University Press, London, 1961.
[2] A. E. Brett, *African Attitudes: A Study of the Social, Racial and Political Attitudes of Some Middle Class Africans*, South African Institute of Race Relations, Johannesburg, 1963.

Page 189
[1] Brett, *op. cit.*
[2] *Ibid.*

Page 190
[1] *Southern Africa*, London, November 10, 1961.
[2] Monica Hunter, *Reaction to Conquest*, *op. cit.*
[3] Ngubane, *An African Explains Apartheid*, *op. cit.*

Page 191
[1] Albert Lutuli, 'The Effect of Minority Rule on Non-Whites', *The Road Ahead*, Capetown, 1960.
[2] *Contact*, Capetown, May 30, 1960.
[3] For a summary of Chief Lutuli's Nobel Peace Prize speech see *I Will Still Be Moved* (ed. Marion Friedmann), London, 1963.

Page 192
   [1] Lutuli, *op. cit.*
   [2] For a text of Mandela's 1962 defence speech see *I Will Still Be Moved, op. cit.*
   [3] Lutuli, *op. cit.*

Page 194
   [1] See *I Will Still Be Moved, op. cit.*

Page 198
   [1] D. P. Botha, *Die Opkooms van ons Derde Stand*, Capetown, 1960.

Page 201
   [1] W. A. Maree, Minister of Indian Affairs, quoted in *African Express News Service.*

Page 202
   [1] *Contact*, July 12, 1958.

Page 204
   [1] *Sunday Times*, Johannesburg, June 2, 1963.
   [2] *The Star*, Johannesburg, March 17, 1962.

Page 205
   [1] *Southern Africa*, London, March 29, 1963.

Page 206
   [1] *The Star*, Johannesburg, March 17, 1962.
   [2] *Ibid.*
   [3] J. H. Fouché, debate in Senate, April 26, 1961.

Page 212
   [1] *The Times*, November 8, 1963.

Page 214
   [1] *Economist*, March 7, 1964.

Page 215
   [1] *Financial Mail*, Johannesburg, March 20, 1964.

Page 223
   [1] Presidential Address to the South African Institute of Race Relations, January 1964.

Page 232
   [1] *Die Burger*, April 4, 1963.

Page 235
   [1] General Assembly debate, October 1963.

Page 236
   [1] Mr Peter Thomas, MP, leader of the UK delegation to the United Nations Assembly, 1963; statement to the Special Political Committee, October 21, 1963.

Page 239
[1] Resolution 6, Conference of Independent African States, Addis Ababa, May 1963.

Page 240
[1] From his paper presented to the International Conference on Sanctions, London, April 1964.

Page 243
[1] *Daily Telegraph*, April 14, 1961.

Page 245
[1] *New York Times*, December 6, 1963.

Page 246
[1] *African Express*, Amsterdam, April 22, 1963.

Page 247
[1] *The Times*, November 25, 1963.
[2] *Southern Africa*, London, March 6, 1964.

Page 248
[1] *The British Stake in South Africa*, published by the National Union of Manufacturers, London, 1963.
[2] Andrew Roth, *Lord on the Board* (Parliamentary Profiles), London, 1964, *passim*.
[3] *Daily Express*, London, May 12, 1961.

Page 249
[1] *Perspective*, London, January 1964.
[2] *The Times*, April 13, 1962.

Page 250
[1] *The Times*, April 13, 1962.
[2] Quoted in *The Collaborators*, Anti-Apartheid Movement, London, 1964.

Page 251
[1] Quoted in *The Collaborators*, *op. cit.*
[2] *Ibid.*

Page 252
[1] *Guardian*, May 22, 1960.
[2] Address to *Town Hall*, Los Angeles, April 23, 1963.
[3] *Ibid.*
[4] *Cape Times,* March 16, 1964.

Page 253
[1] *Cape Times*, April 13, 1963.
[2] Reported in *Britain and South Africa*, a press hand-out of the London Committee of the South Africa Foundation.

Page 254
[1] *The Times*, May 14, 1963.
[2] *New York Times*, August 23, 1963.

Page 255
   [1] *Southern Africa*, London, November 9, 1962.

Page 257
   [1] Mr Barromi in an address to the United Nations Special Political Committee, October 18, 1963.

Page 269
   [1] The Hon. M. C. Botha, Deputy Minister of Bantu Administration and Development, August 30, 1960.

Page 273
   [1] *The Times*, March 13, 1964.

Page 291
   [1] We are indebted for some of the material in this chapter to the papers read to the London Conference on Sanctions in April 1964, notably those by Roger Opie of New College, Oxford, and S. D. N. Worswick of Magdalen College, Oxford.

Page 292
   [1] Opie, *loc. cit.*

Page 293
   [1] Worswick, *loc. cit.*

Page 294
   [1] This amount to which Worswick refers, is taken from IMF balance of payments figures: it is considerably higher than that quoted by the South African Information Department (cf. p. 124, n. 1).

Page 298
   [1] *Die Transvaler*, September 17, 1962.
   [2] *Ibid.*, October 11, 1961.
   [3] *Ibid.*, November 15, 1961.
   [4] *Ibid.*, September 18, 1962.

Page 299
   [1] *Die Transvaler*, March 29, 1962.

INDEX

DATE DUE

MAR 2 3 1991 *Late*			
(5-8-89)			
APR 1 4 1990			
	261-2500		Printed in USA